www.lannoo.com

Please register on our website if you would like to receive our regular newsletter and other information about our new books, with interesting and exclusive offers.

Text	Ellen Schouppe & Tara Kuklis
Photography	property of athletes, except Sheryagen evgenij (Achab p 26, 99), Luc Dequick (Devos p 100), International Judo Federation (Verstraeten p 101), Keepthemagica (Swings p 98), Melvin Szerman (Ballenghien p 100), Jonathan Vanooteghem (Doku p 83, p 98), Topvolley Belgium (Herbots p 99), sysm3dia (Vervoort p 99, 169) Caroline Vandercruyssen (photo author), Belga (Gérard p 100; Darcis p 99; Ouédraogo p 83, 100; Kompany p 99, 103; Nikiforov p 101, 153; Benoot p 99, 169; Buys p 98; Vidts p 98; Dirickx p 99; Rakels p 99; Lecluyse p 169; D'Hooghe p 40, 98; Vanasch p 17).
Illustrations	flaticon.com
Cover and layout	Tom Suykens
Graphic design	Keppie & Keppie
Translation	Ian Connerty

If you have any comments or questions, please contact our editorial team: redactielifestyle@lannoo.com

© Uitgeverij Lannoo nv, Tielt, 2024
D/2024/45/216 – NUR 480, 770
ISBN: 978-94-014-9904-0

THE
ULTIMATE
VICTORY

HOW MINDSET & ATTITUDES
DEVELOP TALENT

Ellen Schouppe
& Tara Kuklis

Lannoo

'Follow your dreams, they know the way'

1992, Corsica.

As a sport-minded twelve-year-old girl, I watched that year's Olympic Games in Barcelona from a beach hut on the shores of the Mediterranean Sea. On the screen I saw athletes achieve the most remarkable performances. Their experiences, their emotions and the emotions they aroused in spectators worldwide touched me deeply and made a huge impression.

In other words, I remember exactly where my dream first took shape. It was there, in Corsica, that I decided that I would one day take part in the Olympic Games myself.

At first, I believed that I would do this as an elite athlete, but after a few years I realised that I did not have enough 'talent' to make that possible. But I didn't let this setback discourage me. 'My dream is still my dream,' I told myself.

So I decided to find a different way to get to the Olympics. I tried to find out all I could about who, in addition to the athletes, is necessary to make this gigantic sporting event happen. Coaches, physiotherapists, doctors? The answer to this question came to me when I watched a documentary about a sport psychologist in Australia. That was it! Supporting people to achieve their dream while at the same time realising my own. It sounded like the best job in the world. And that is what it turned out to be.

Following my graduation, as an occupational and organisational psychologist, I attempted to convince several sport federations of the potential value of sport psychology, but this was far from simple – or successful. As a result, I started work a few months later as an HR specialist in recruitment, before later moving on to a more general role as an HR manager. It soon became clear to me that I had a real talent for coaching people in the workplace and this role as 'coach' was also a good fit for both my identity and my dream.

This encouraged me to have a second try at breaking into the sporting world. I believed that my ten years of experience in the commercial world could be a major added value. Fortunately, Koen Umans, the current general manager of our women's national basketball team, the Belgian Cats, believed it as well. Just as importantly, he believed in me. It was Koen who gave me the chance to take my first step as a sport psychologist. But it was by no means the last. I went on to practice as a sport psychologist in a number of different sports and I have had the pleasure of coaching many athletes. And this is how, in 2021 in Tokyo, I realised my dream to take part at the Olympics Games, helping Team Belgium to perform.

In this way, my talent was confirmed – a talent that has formed the basis for my entire career: the guidance and support of the personal development of individuals and teams, irrespective of whether they wish to evolve in the sporting world or the business world. I eventually combined my experience in both these worlds in my own company: Smart Mind.

It was during a Smart Mind training trajectory that I first got to know Tara Kuklis, the co-author of this book. Her openness, her coachability and the speed with which she mastered the Smart Mind coaching method immediately made a powerful positive impression on me. Her desire to learn and her ambition meant that our paths were destined to cross again before she graduated as an occupational and organisational psychologist. Following her completion of a successful internship at Smart Mind, we embarked together on a new adventure: the writing of this book, **The Ultimate Victory**.

Table of contents

Introduction

In this book you will not only read about how world records are broken and gold medals are won, but will also be given fascinating insights into a wider story in which **personal development** is central and where improved performance is a logical consequence of this development.

This story will be told using the testimonies of top performers, offering a unique glimpse into their lives 'behind the scenes'. You will learn how winners think, what attitudes they adopt and how they succeed in achieving their **ultimate victory**.

In the following pages reference will often be made to 'top performers'. In our experience, a top performer is someone who repeatedly performs above the expected norm and thereby continues to constantly develop themselves. Based on the vision that top performers can either be men or women, the appropriate personal pronouns will be used alternately throughout the book.

If you do not yet regard yourself as a top performer, we hope that this book will inspire you and guide you in the direction you want to follow.

The ultimate victory means something different for everyone. For a top athlete, **the ultimate victory** might mean breaking a world record or making a successful comeback after her pregnancy.

Or it might 'just' be finding a turning point on the road that has previously led them in the direction of top performance. For you, **the ultimate victory** could be finding the correct work-life balance, or working in your dream job, or making your own business flourish.

Whatever you want to achieve, the road to **the ultimate victory** always starts with overcoming your own challenges. This involves many different elements, such as your personality, your age, your living and working environments, your experiences, your achievements and your dreams. As a result, your **ultimate victory** will constantly change and evolve.

For this reason, we regard the word 'ultimate' as a flexible concept. Consequently, your **ultimate victory** at the start of your career will probably seem quite modest in comparison with the victories you achieve later on. Consider, for example, a young elite sports talent, who leaves home at the age of twelve to attend a special elite sport school. During this difficult period, overcoming homesickness could be **the ultimate victory**, while this achievement might seem like nothing later on, when the girl in question needs to move to the other side of the world to continue her pursuit of her dream.

——— 'A career is not built on talent alone'

As spectators, we see top athletes excelling on the international stage. They are so good that they make elite sport seem easy and their performances self-evident. Such is their talent that they only need to display it in order to be successful.

As an elite sport psychologist, I am much closer to elite athletes than spectators. I know how much their performances demand of them each day. I see the effort that is required to develop their talent and hone it to perfection. I have been fortunate enough to guide elite athletes right from the start of their career until their eventual departure from the international arena. The way in which they evolve physically, technically, tactically, mentally and relationally is phenomenal, even though this evolution always involves setbacks and difficulties.

You are not born as a top performer; you develop yourself to become one.

In both elite sport and the business world, the identification of talent is a necessary condition for remaining successful in the long term. Nowadays, detecting people with talent has become a specialised skill. Think, for example, of consultancy firms that now focus exclusively on recruitment or of the important role that scouting plays in many elite sports, like football. As well as searching for outside talent, many organisations now also set up internal talent detection programmes to evaluate the potential of their own employees and athletes.

Once talent has been identified in someone, that person is quickly labelled as a ***high potential***. According to the organisation, this high potential has the necessary talent to ensure that her chances of future success are greater than the chances of others.

That being said, both as an HR manager and as a sport psychologist I have seen many people who were regarded as high potentials but who were not able to realise that potential in the way that was expected. The hoped-for performance and the anticipated evolution simply did not materialise. When this happens, both parties tend to ask themselves the same question: where and/or when did things go wrong? Why was the high potential not able to develop her talents?

I, however, preferred to reverse this question. I did not analyse what was 'missing'. Instead, I looked at the things that top performers have in common, in addition to talent for their chosen sport or profession. I came to the conclusion that this has nothing to do with gender, race, origin, age, training or income. What top performers share is a set of behavioural traits that influence their performance positively. In this book, we will refer to these traits as ***attitudes***.

When we are talking about talent development, it is important to emphasise that attitudes can be taught and enhanced! The difference between a high potential and a ***high performer*** is therefore to be found in the attitudes that the latter uses to convert their talents into great performance. This is something that we will explain and demonstrate in our high performance attitudes model.

———— Smart Mind: the high performance attitude model

Based on scientific articles, more than forty structured in-depth interviews with elite athletes, and our own many years of experience in the sporting world, we at Smart Mind have identified seven attitudes that top performers share with each other and allow them to achieve exceptional performance. According to Smart Mind, a person will not have a single 'bad' attitude that hinders their performance. Instead, they will display one or more attitudes either too much or too little. The good news is that the displaying of attitudes can be developed. And the earlier you start, the better! Consistently displaying the right attitudes will help you to realise your full potential.

Here is a list of all seven attitudes, together with a brief definition. In the first part of our book, we will discuss these attitudes at length, illustrating them with testimonies from Belgian elite sport.

	Absolute top performers display intrinsic motivation and a winner's mentality. They work towards their dream and goals in an efficient manner.
	Top performers regard themselves as the owners of their own career. By exercising self-leadership, they can build up a team around them in which everyone influences everyone else in a positive way to strengthen both the top performer and the team.
	Top performers make it a goal to grow continually. As a result, they are open to the learning of new skills that will contribute to their performance. They make themselves coachable by listening to the advice of the experts around them and by responding positively to the feedback of team members.
	Top performers need to push their boundaries and step out of their comfort zone every day. Having the courage to think, train and perform innovatively is essential for achieving the very best performance. Daring to be different by being yourself is an important attitude for consistent success.
	No matter how good they are, top performers will inevitably be confronted by setbacks and disappointments. They will need to overcome physical and mental challenges if they wish to perform at the highest level.
	Energy is the fuel that allows top performers to achieve remarkable things and to set new records. Using this energy wisely and stopping in good time to recharge their batteries, when necessary, is the basis for consistent performance.
	Top performers derive pleasure from the performance process. They celebrate each small step forwards and understand that they have the privilege of being able to do what they love most each day.

All these attitudes are observable. You can see them in yourself and others can see them in you. Optimally displaying just one of these attitudes will not be enough to achieve your **ultimate victory** or to perform at the highest level. The seven attitudes work together and form the links of a chain. The engine will only run smoothly if all the links are well oiled and act in unison. If one of the links is missing, the engine will splutter and stop. To make full use of your potential you need all seven attitudes.

It is not just sport psychologists and top coaches who underline the importance of attitude. Simon Sinek, the author of several books on business leadership, has also recommended: 'Don't hire for skills; hire for attitude'. He, too, understands that your talent, competency or experience can only find their fullest expression if they are applied with the right attitude(s).

The nine box grid model is a classic talent management model from the business world. Employees are classified on the basis of their talent and performance.

Nowadays, this model is being increasingly challenged, a point of view shared by us at Smart Mind. The model takes too little account of the attitudes displayed by people in the daily execution of their work. By being overly fixated on potential and performance, organisations sometimes position employees in the wrong box. As a result, the development trajectory set for them by the organisation is not always the right one. By giving individuals more opportunity to develop the attitudes described by our Smart Mind model, the organisation can help these individuals to develop their potential in the best possible and most appropriate manner. In other words, we argue strongly for more **investment in attitude development within organisations**.

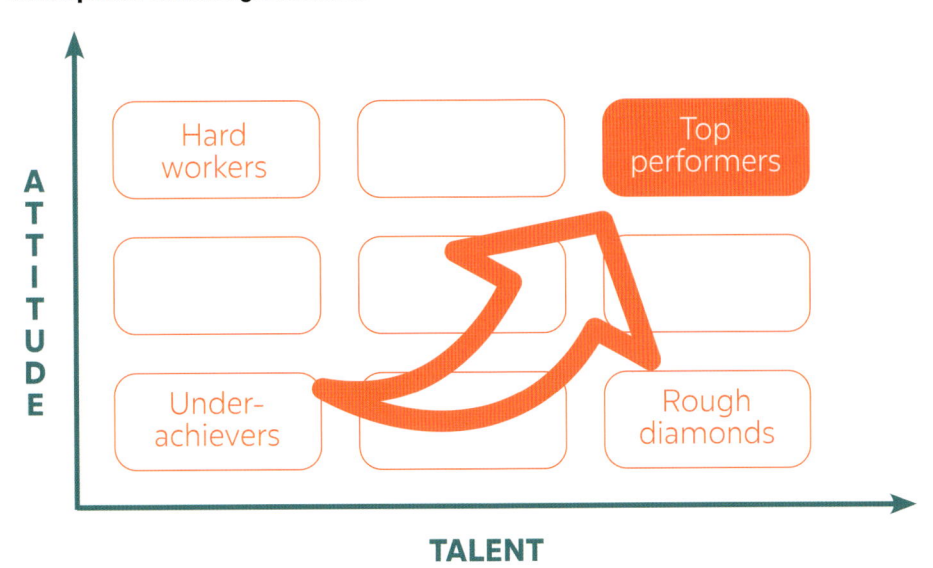

Traditionally, organisations invest in the group of '**top performers**'. The organisations can readily see the potential in this group and, understandably, wish to develop it further. These are the employees and athletes who are channelled into a high potential trajectory. For them, organisations are willing to release the necessary budget to give them extra guidance and stimulation. As a result of this support, it is only logical that their development increases and that they are able to take even bigger steps forward. In other words, their development is largely proactive. In this way, they can develop the skills that they will use in the future. You can compare it with crossing a river: the group of top performers already knows that you will need a raft and has learnt how to build one. They will arrive quickly – and dry – on the other side.

Working with athletes and employees from the '**rough diamond**' group raises other questions. Organisations and coaches are sometimes at a loss to know how they can develop appropriate solutions for this group. These are people with plenty of talent, but who lack the ability and/or the dynamic approach to consistently display certain attitudes. Organisations will also invest in this group, but in a more reactive way. To return to our river example, this group will first attempt to make the crossing on foot or by swimming. It is only when they discover that this will not work that they will be offered a crash course in raft building.

They, too, will eventually reach the other side, but with wet clothes and much slower than the high potentials.

For this group, the development of the right attitudes will be the lever for unlocking their talent. In time, this will result in the rough diamonds performing higher than the standard norm, so that they can make the step **from high potential to high performer**. In this way, the talent pool from which organisations can recruit personnel or top athletes will expand. In today's world, this must be music to the ears of companies and sporting organisations. Or that, at least, is what we coaches and (sport) psychologists think.

Given the dynamic environment in which we currently live, it is better not to wait for things to happen. Proactively supporting the development of talent will teach future top performers how to better deal with the challenges that they will face. And within this process, the development of attitudes is essential.

Because attitudes are translated into observable behaviour, they cannot only be used for self-development, but also form a good basis for coaching sessions with team members or leaders. Taking account of more than performance or a single good attitude alone can open up profitable new avenues to explore. Displaying the right attitudes consistently and in the best possible manner has become hugely important and therefore needs to be discussed more in (sporting) organisations and companies.

In other words, **attitudes can be a lever for talent**!

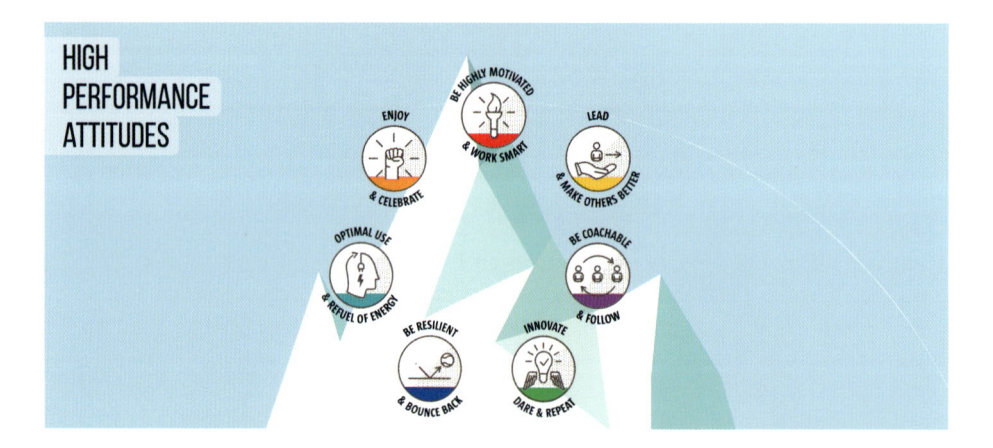

 Let's take **Victor Campenaerts** as an example. Victor began his sporting career as a swimmer, before moving on to triathlons and eventually, at the age of nineteen, switching to cycling. He told us about his path to the top: *'I wanted to be the best swimmer in the world. But at 1.73 metres tall, I was unable to compete with my bigger rivals. It was frustrating. That's why I started triathlons, which went well, right from the very beginning. Until I started to get injuries from too much running. That is why I decided to stick to just cycling – and with success!'*

Victor was certainly not a bad swimmer, but he would never have achieved his current level of success if he had persisted with swimming. In other words, as a swimmer he would not occupy the same position in the nine box grid that he now occupies as a cyclist. By using attitudes as a lever, he was finally able to give full expression to his talent. In large part, Victor owed his ability to display those attitudes to his past experiences. The fact that he was not able to achieve his **ultimate victory** as a swimmer helped to stimulate his intrinsic motivation and focused his thoughts on a different direction. This combination of a high level of intrinsic motivation and smart learning led him to cycling and brought him the spectacular results of which we are all now aware.

——— Feeling competent to deal with challenges

In her own local team, a talented volleyball player feels confident to smash the ball over the net. But as soon as she starts to play for the national team, she starts to hesitate at the net. It is clearly observable that she has less confidence to do the things that she is good at. She says that in her own team she feels competent to deal with the external pressure, but finds this much harder at the national level. The international nature of the context and the increased media attention means that the level of pressure she feels is significantly increased.

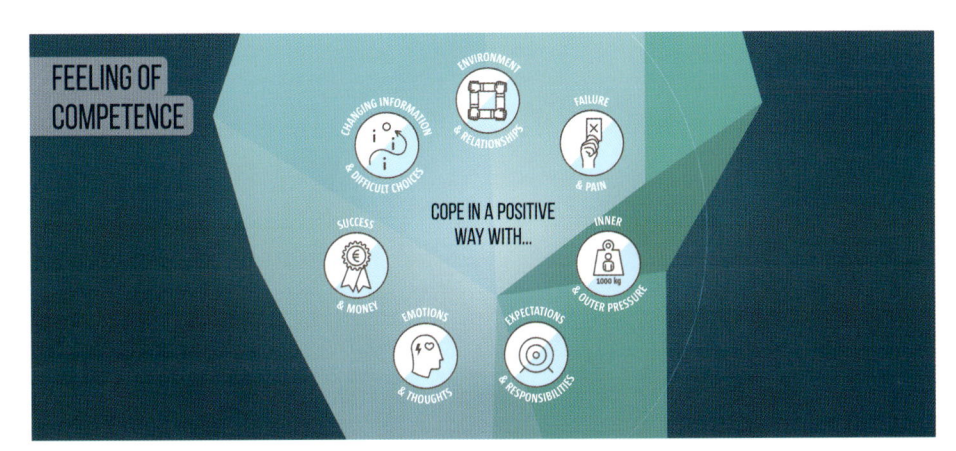

Our coaching model is based on the following premise: the more competent a person feels to deal with the challenges generated by their context, the greater the likelihood that they will be able to optimally display the attitudes that lead to exceptional performance.

As a result, our coaching method is designed to stimulate self-insight in the person concerned. Gaining insight into the challenges they face and the levers needed to deal with them is something that individuals must discover within themselves. **With this book, we hope to help not only professional athletes but also other readers to experience this 'aha' moment.** If you are not able to correctly identify the reasons for the display or non-display of certain behaviour, you will never be able to search for the right solutions.

In our experience, it is only when the challenges are crystal-clear that you can develop the intrinsic motivation – whether as an athlete or just as an ordinary reader of this book – to work at improving yourself.

Returning to our example, it is only the behaviour (attitude) of the volleyball player that is initially observable at certain moments. By talking with her about the challenges she is currently facing, it should become clear why she can be bold and effective when playing in one context (local) and not in another (national). This has nothing to do with her qualities as a player or her game intelligence. It is all connected with the pressure she feels. After she has indicated which challenges she feels least competent to deal with, we can move on to the next step and discuss with her a plan of approach to correct this.

Of course, it is not only top athletes who face challenges during their careers. In the business world and in our private sphere we are also confronted daily with such challenges. On the way to our **ultimate victory** it is therefore important to learn how to deal positively with challenges in all the different areas of life.

Discovering mental skills and using them effectively

After identifying the challenge(s), we look together with our coachee to assess which mental skills can potentially offer a solution for dealing with the challenge(s) in a more appropriate way. Depending on how familiar the coachee is with the relevant mental skills, these are then explained (where necessary) and learnt, so that they can be properly applied.

The development and application of mental skills makes it possible to better deal with the challenges that cross your path. This will result in an enhanced feeling of competence and will ensure that the right attitudes are optimally and consistently displayed.

If you do not yet regard yourself as a top performer, the development of mental skills can be one key step that brings you closer to the **ultimate victory** you desire.

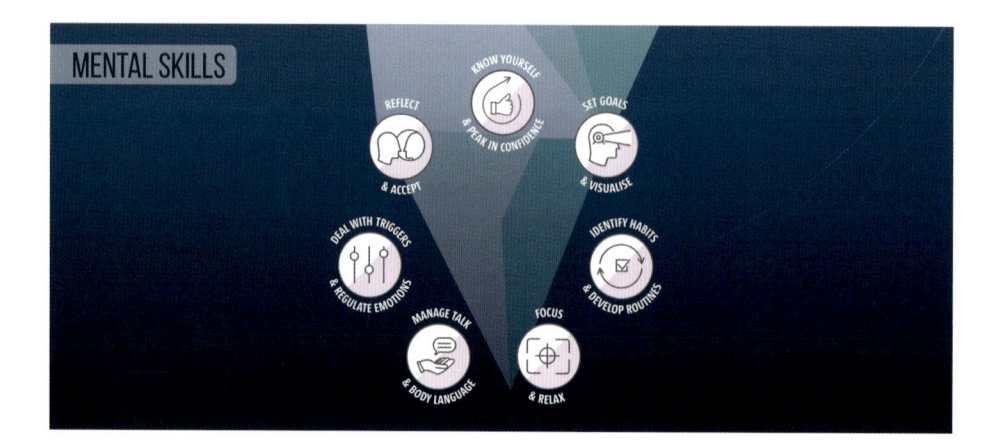

The development of these mental skills can be compared with putting together a survival kit before you start on a long trek. If you only take a torch and a rope, you will still be able to make progress, but you will reach your destination faster and more efficiently if you also take a tent, food, water and firelighters. And you don't want to set off through the forest only to discover half way that you should have brought your climbing gear as well. In other words, you will get where you want to go more quickly when you have all the right equipment – plenty of mental skills – which you can use when the need arises.

How does all this apply to our talented volleyball player? If she wants to play with greater daring, she needs to feel more competent to deal with the pressure she is under. For this reason, she decides to invest time and energy in the development and application of new mental tools, such as positive self-talk and relaxation techniques. As a result, she will feel more competent to keep the pressure of playing at national level under control and will therefore once again be able to smash the ball over the net with her previous level of confidence.

In this way, the three levels – attitudes, challenges and mental skills – work together and also influence each other. Your **ultimate victory** will probably be related to elements that are situated at the second level. The development of mental skills to deal with these challenges will form a turning point in your wider personal development.

——— Become the best version of yourself

The mental aspect is also increasingly regarded as a game-changer in elite sport as well. There comes a point when the differences at the physical-tactical level are so small that you need to look at other areas if you want to make the difference for your athletes or team.

 Emmanuel Stockbroekx has been a stalwart of the Belgian national hockey team for years: '*As an athlete, you enter an arena where you compete with other athletes who are also very good at what they do. In many respects, you are each other's equal. If you want to come out on top, the psychological aspect is key. Having the right mental equipment allows you to take huge strides forwards. It can really set you apart from the others.*'

Experience has shown that in the business world as well – for example, during selection procedures – attitudes can be decisive in deciding who gets the job or promotion and who doesn't. Nowadays, the vast majority of candidates have the necessary qualifications and/or experience. But they can stand out from the crowd by showing that they are, for example, good leaders, coachable or innovative in their thinking.

> **The ultimate victory consists of developing yourself to become the best version of yourself that you can possibly be.**
> This book can be a starting point or an additional push in the back that can boost this developmental process into overdrive. After each chapter, you will have the opportunity to coach yourself and apply the insights from that chapter. Hopefully, the accompanying stories of top performers will inspire you to bigger and better things. You will discover that most of the elite athletes mentioned in the book first achieved one or more major victories in their personal sphere before achieving top performance in their sporting discipline.

HIGH PERFORMANCE ATTITUDES MODEL

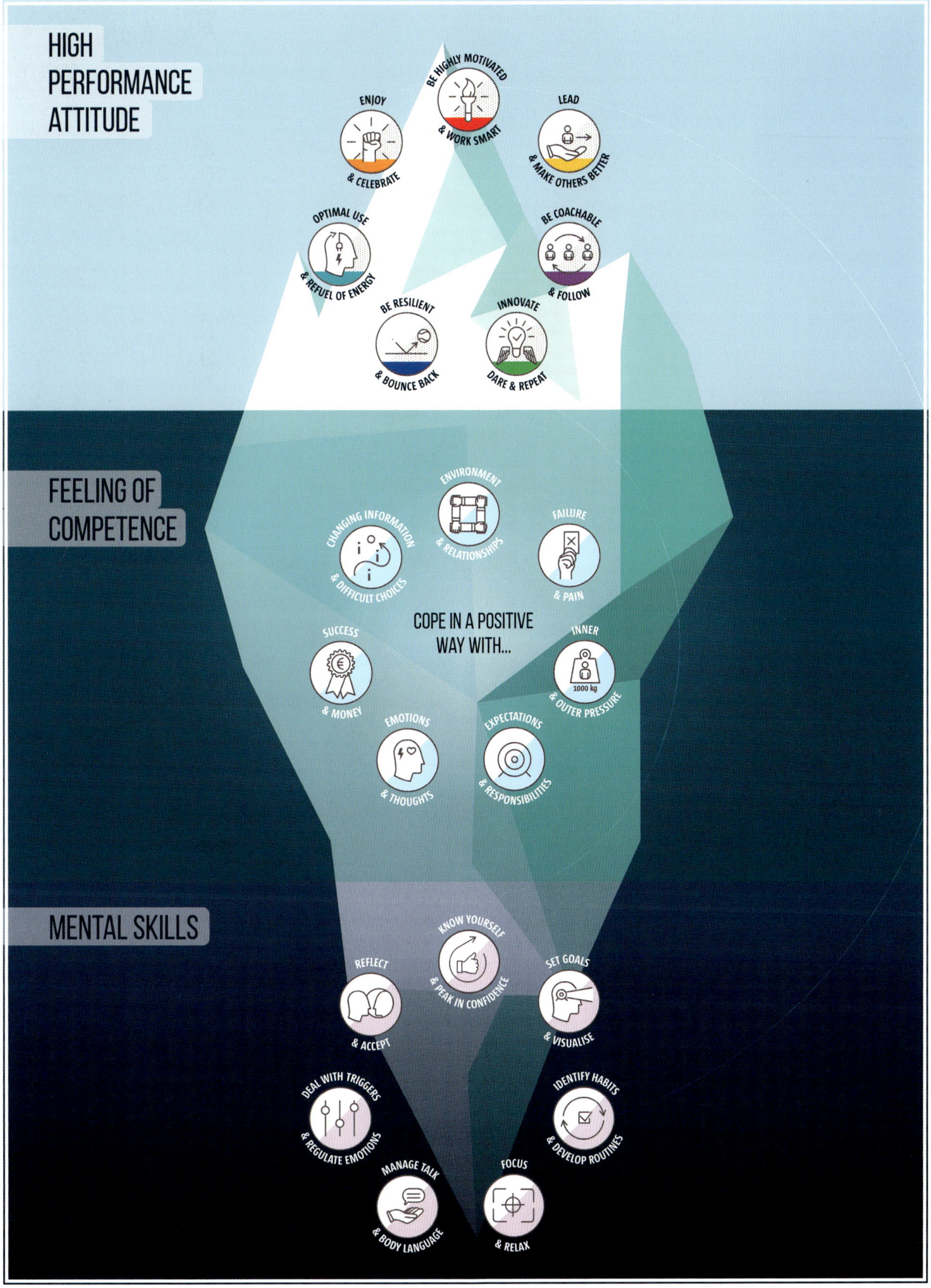

HIGH PERFORMANCE ATTITUDE

ENJOY
& CELEBRATE

BE HIGHLY MOTIVATED
& WORK SMART

LEAD
& MAKE OTHERS BETTER

OPTIMAL USE
& REFUEL OF ENERGY

BE COACHABLE
& FOLLOW

BE RESILIENT
& BOUNCE BACK

INNOVATE
DARE & REPEAT

FEELING OF COMPETENCE

CHANGING INFORMATION
& DIFFICULT CHOICES

ENVIRONMENT
& RELATIONSHIPS

FAILURE
& PAIN

COPE IN A POSITIVE WAY WITH...

SUCCESS
& MONEY

INNER
& OUTER PRESSURE

EMOTIONS
& THOUGHTS

EXPECTATIONS
& RESPONSIBILITIES

MENTAL SKILLS

KNOW YOURSELF
& PEAK IN CONFIDENCE

REFLECT
& ACCEPT

SET GOALS
& VISUALISE

DEAL WITH TRIGGERS
& REGULATE EMOTIONS

IDENTIFY HABITS
& DEVELOP ROUTINES

MANAGE TALK
& BODY LANGUAGE

FOCUS
& RELAX

ATTITUDE I

BE HIGHLY MOTIVATED TO PERFORM AND WORK SMART

'Every time I do something, I want to win, to exceed my own expectations, to perform at the very highest level, and to bring home medals and cups. That feeling is fantastic.'

—— **Vincent Vanasch**, hockey player

Definition

'Be highly motivated
to perform'
is an attitude that is characterised by an inner
drive to perform and an intense desire to take
on challenges.

'Work smart'
is an attitude that is characterised by efficiency,
discipline and focus, taking due account
of priorities and with sufficient attention
for process and performance goals.

Characteristics of top performers with this attitude

— They believe in their own dreams, but have concrete
  plans.
— They believe in an efficient and goal-based approach.
— They demonstrate impressive drive, determination
  and intrinsic motivation.
— They are highly competitive by nature.
— They are prepared to make choices aligned with
  their goals.
— They know why they are doing what they are doing!

Top performers are dreamers with concrete plans

—— Believe in your own dream

The story of most top performers begins with a **dream**. They dream of an achievement inspired by others or dream of doing something that no one else has ever done before. In the first instance, this dream serves as a powerful source of inspiration. It can spur them into action, as a result of which they take their first steps towards that dream.

 Former tennis star **Justine Henin** explains it like this: *'My earliest memory as a child is that as a five year old I locked myself in my room and threw myself on the ground, with my arms in the air: I had just won Roland Garros again! I have always been the driving force behind my own story.'*

The key question is how top performers turn that dream into a reality. How do they achieve the **ultimate victory**?

By **regularly visualising your goal**, your own imagination gives a positive connotation to your dream, drawing you closer and closer to it. Without immediately noticing it, and dependent on the nature of your dream, you will start to make choices in a more conscious manner and take your first small actions. It is only later that you will recognise these actions for what they are: the first concrete steps towards the realisation of your goal. The **attitudes** displayed by the dreamer as he works towards his goal will be decisive for his chances of success: **dare to follow** your dreams, they know the way.

His intrinsic motivation and the extent to which he not only works hard but also cleverly in pursuit of his dream; the ownership that he takes for the dream; his courage and mental flexibility to adapt to different situations; his resilience when faced with setbacks; the energy and pleasure he derives from his achievements: these are the things that will determine whether he succeeds – or not.

—— Limiting and empowering beliefs

As Justine's story shows, dreams can lead to **deep-rooted beliefs**.

Ken Ravizza, one of the most prominent figures in American sport psychology, has expressed this tellingly: *'Beliefs have the power to create and the power to destroy.'* Conscious and unconscious processes influence our way of thinking and our behaviour. With the conscious part of your brain, you plan, solve problems, and experience emotions. Your unconscious brain is a kind of undercurrent, where your beliefs are hidden. These beliefs originate gradually and are often given to us as part of our upbringing or develop out of our own experiences. However, not all of our beliefs help to move us forwards or bring us closer to realising our dreams. For this reason, it is very important for us to be fully aware of all our beliefs.

Without realising it, sprinter **Hanne Claes** had also developed a number of limiting beliefs, like: *'When I have my period I run slower'* or *'I can only achieve personal best times if the weather conditions are ideal'.*

If they want to make progress, top performers must learn how to recognise these limiting beliefs and leave them behind. As part of this learning process, in my role as a psychologist in both the sporting and business worlds, I always ask the following question: 'Imagine that you had a magic wand: how would you want to behave differently in this situation?' The idea of a magic wand helps people to think outside the normal boundaries and beyond their usual possibilities. Elite athletes dare to think with no limits, so that they are able to put their dream into words: 'I would like to see myself running faster in cold weather'. Next, this sentence is translated from the conditional tense to the present tense, on which we can now build further to turn it into a strong, positive and empowering belief.

In this way, Hanne was able to identify her limiting beliefs and transform them into powerful affirmations, so that she was able to run record times even in the conditions that she used to believe limited her performance. What's more, these new positive beliefs pushed her further and further forward, allowing her to qualify for the Olympic Games in Tokyo and Paris, almost a full year before the official deadline!

In other words, it is important to bring the unconscious part of your brain to the surface by identifying your beliefs. This will help you to use them in a positive way that will move you closer and closer to your **ultimate victory**.

—— Motivation as a driving force

Top performers link their dream to strong and stable motivation. They never doubt their dream goal simply because of a single bad performance and do not allow themselves to be influenced by the mood of the day.

 Basketball player **Thibaut Vervoort***: 'As a young professional sportsman, you are constantly faced with new challenges, both physically and mentally. When I don't feel 100 percent – for example, because I slept badly the night before, or the last training session did not go well, or we lost the last match – I get my motivation from the goals I set for myself. These goals can be both short term and long term. My dream goal of qualifying for the Olympic Games has helped me time after time to push beyond my boundaries and deal with the challenges that cross my path.'*

Everyone occasionally has a bad day, week or even month. Elite performers have them too, but they draw new strength from their dream goal, finding the additional motivation that is necessary to get them through difficult moments.

—— The sky is the limit

What's more, most top performers are convinced that there are **no limits** to their possibilities. Thanks to their talent in combination with their effort, focus and determination, they believe that there is almost nothing they cannot achieve. This way of thinking drives them forward, helping them to realise their dream goals and overcome the challenges that stand in their way.

In 2004, Justine Henin went to the Olympic Games in Athens without specific preparation and with no specific expectations in mind. In fact, she was making a comeback after a period out of the game due to a viral infection. On the first day of the Games, another Belgian – Axel Merckx – won a bronze medal in the cycling road race.

Motivated by the performance of her fellow countryman, Justine won her opening matches relatively easily, until she found herself facing Anastasia Myskina in the semi-final. At 5-1 in the third set, Myskina served for the match – and a place in the final.

 Justine Henin: *'I can remember thinking to myself: "What is the worst that can happen to you? In ten minutes you will be under the shower, having lost the match. Tomorrow you will be playing for bronze, but that is also a great achievement. But I don't want to play for bronze…"*
After a remarkable fightback, Justine won the match. 'The next day I was very calm before the final. I knew that I wasn't going to lose against Mauresmo. After what had happened during the semi-final, I felt that nothing could touch me. I was unbeatable, totally convinced that I would win.'
And so it was that Justine won a gold medal at the 2004 Olympics. 'For me, it was a magical story. But it was a story in which many others also played a part. Not least the other Belgian athletes, whose support gave me a huge amount of energy. I was alone out there on the court, but I knew the entire Belgian delegation was behind me. That is what made the big difference. It really was a team victory.'

Justine's story shows just how powerful dreams can be and how deep-rooted beliefs can help you to fulfil those dreams, not only in elite sport, but also in your own professional and private lives. The key factor for success is the ability to **convert your beliefs into concrete objectives** and a set of actions necessary to achieve them.

Top performers work in an efficient and targeted manner

—— Begin with the end in mind

Of course, dreams don't just happen. In other words, you will never achieve your **ultimate victory** by chance. It will always be the result of a positive belief and powerful intrinsic motivation, based on a forward-looking plan that you always keep in focus and link to a series of concrete goals in the short, medium and long term. A successful entrepreneur will only found a company when he is clear about the direction in which it needs to go.

The Belgian Cats, the Belgian national women's basketball team, are an excellent example of this philosophy. In ten years' time, they have grown into a very strong and coherent unit. As the current European champions, they are one of the best teams in the world.

My own story as a sport psychologist with the Belgian Cats began in the summer of 2013 in Slovenia, during their annual training camp. The team had not been able to qualify for a major international tournament since 2007, the year in which they last took part in the European championships. In spite of the recent setbacks, I found a group of passionate players, blessed with a healthy dose of youthful enthusiasm, a strong team spirit and a clearly defined goal: to successfully perform once again at the European level. Secretly, this young and talented generation also dreamed of one day taking part in the Olympic Games.

 At that time, **Sofie Hendrickx** was the team captain: '*Following a period of disappointing results, a new and more hopeful period began in 2013. I regard this as a turning point in the story of the Belgian Cats. That is when the foundations were laid for the current national team. The support structure around the team became much more professional, both on and off the court. As a player, you noticed that steps were being taken in the right direction. People began thinking about the need to create a shared vision between the coaching staff and the squad. This vision was then translated into a set of common values and concrete goals. That gave us confidence!*

When Philip Mestdagh became head coach and Emma Meesseman and Ann Wauters joined the team, success soon followed. For the first time in ten years, the team qualified for the following European championship in 2017 in Prague, where they won a bronze medal. This all demonstrates that creating the right framework and the right group mentality can help you to achieve wonderful results.

The bronze medal meant automatic qualification for the 2018 world championship in Tenerife. This time the goal was to be among the top eight teams in the world. In other words, a place in the quarter finals. The Cats started the competition with conviction, won all their games and suddenly found themselves not in the quarter final, but in the semi-final against the reigning Olympic champions: the United States. For many of the players, this was a childhood dream come true. They stood on the court alongside their heroines and gave an excellent performance, even though they eventually lost. The Cats finished the championship in fourth place.

For the Belgian Cats, the Olympic Games were no longer a dream, but a realistic target. Once again, they made a clear plan. First qualify again for the next European championship, aiming to finish in the top six, and then focus everything on the qualification tournament for the Olympic Games in Tokyo, scheduled for 2020. And that is what happened!

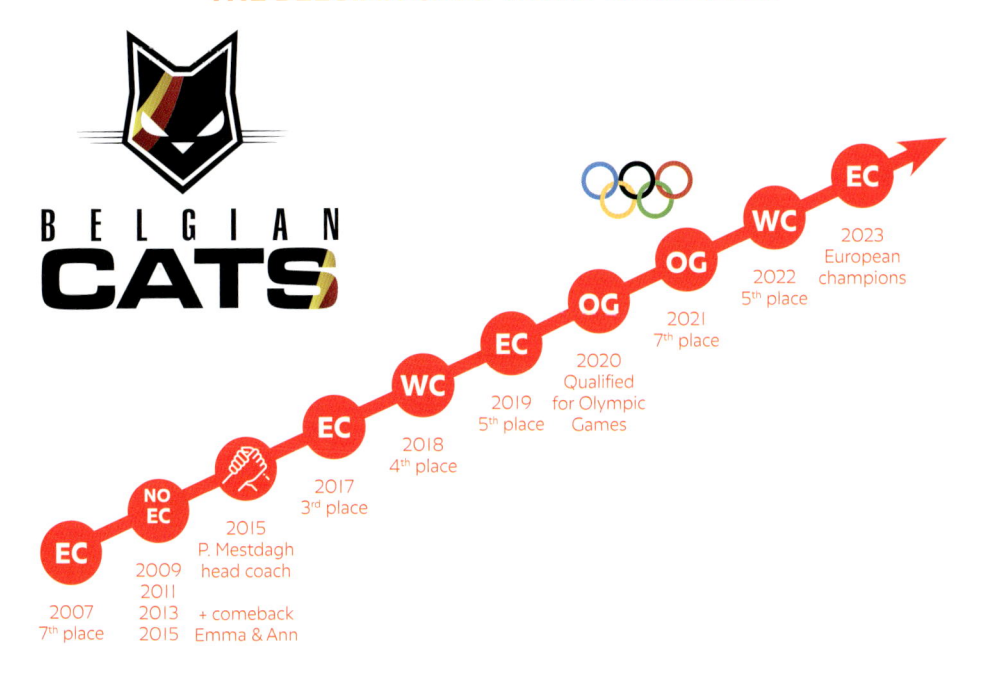

The mindset of the Belgian Cats clearly changed during this series of different tournaments. After a ten-year absence from major championships, the players used the hashtag **#DareToBelieve**. Following their fourth place in the world championship and their qualification for the Olympic Games, they now use the hashtag **#FocusNext**. This shows how mindsets can change over time in response to successes.

—— Personal goals with the right intention

Whether or not you want to perform in the sporting arena, the business world or your private life, the true top performers always convert their dream into a **concrete plan**. This plan takes shape through the identification of challenging performance goals. Top performers gradually move towards these goals by focusing first on smaller process objectives or intermediary goals. You can compare these goals with hurdles that you need to jump over before you can reach the finishing line. Between each hurdle your running technique improves and you systematically jump higher, faster, further and more correctly. You come to see these hurdles as learning opportunities, providing you with success experiences and the satisfaction of continual positive progress. In this way, you gain confidence and your chances of success are enhanced. The emotional release associated with the realisation of intermediary goals is less than with your main goal, but this makes it possible to focus more quickly on the next hurdle.

As an example, let's look – appropriately enough – at the Belgian hurdler Hanne Claes. In 2015, when our collaboration first started, it seemed like things had been going against her for quite some time. She had been troubled by repeated injuries, had a difficult relationship with her then coach and, because of her poor results, had lost her contract of employment with her federation Sport Vlaanderen (Flanders Sport). Even so, her dream goal remained fixed as firmly as ever in her mind.

Hanne managed to achieve the minimum Olympic qualifying standard for the 2012 Games in London, but failed to meet the Belgian minimum standard. Consequently, she was not selected for the Belgian team. Again, she qualified for the 2016 Games in Rio, but this time her persistent injuries meant that this was never a realistic option. Hanne was not in the right shape to meet such a challenge, neither physically or mentally.

It was at this point that we decided to redefine Hanne's goal and describe it more clearly. Qualification for the 2020 Olympic Games in Tokyo was just the 'first hurdle' she would jump. Her real goal was to run in the final of the 400 metres hurdles at the Games, to do so in her best possible physical and mental state and – why not? – perhaps win a medal. Once the goal had been established, Hanne developed a detailed plan to make it happen. She devoted more effort and care to her rehabilitation and trained with greater focus and the right intensity. More importantly, she trained with the right intention. **The athlete who trains with the expectation of winning a medal has a huge advantage over her rivals**. Not only on the day of the competition, but every day and in every training session. As a result, Hanne, along with heptathlete Nafi Thiam, was one of the first Belgian athletes to qualify for the 2020 Games.

Similarly, research has shown that the phenomenon of home advantage in football has a comparable scientific basis. The study showed that coaches expect to win more games when their team is playing at home. As a result, they place greater emphasis on an attacking approach and set their players more difficult tasks. This supports the conclusion that setting challenging goals has a positive effect on the performance of athletes and on the results they achieve (Staufenbiel, Lobinger & Strauss, 2015).

 Footballer **Jeremy Doku** has a clear opinion on this matter: '*I don't like it when people ask: "Was it your dream to be selected for the Red Devils or to play for Manchester City?". Then I reply: "No, it was not my dream; it was my goal". When you know what you can do, you need to set your dream high enough. Make your dream your ambition.*'

—— Work hard, but also work smart!

Working hard is good; working smart is better. Working hard does not necessarily mean that you are working on the right things at the right time. The staircase to success is long, but with a few minor adjustments there are moments when you can take the lift. Of course, this does not mean that getting to the top is easy. But working smart can make it easier. For example, it can sometimes be smart to have the courage to take a step back, to maintain a proper overview of the situation, and to ask yourself some critical questions. The key is to make sure that you work efficiently, that your energy is used wisely.

 According to table tennis legend **Jean-Michel Saive**, a combination of motivation and smart working is crucial: '*If I hear that some players train six or seven hours a day, I am astounded. I don't believe in that. I preferred quality to quantity. I did this by*

integrating hard physical training sessions into my sport-specific training. I preferred to focus 100 percent for four hours. In that way, my training was both efficient and effective. This helped me to concentrate on quality instead of quantity.'

In the business world, efficient working is not always easy to achieve. Promotions often go to the employees who work extra hours and are still answering their mails late into the evening. In other words, they do a lot of work. So surely this means that their output must also be super-high, doesn't it? Well, not necessarily. Someone who leaves the office promptly at five o'clock can have an output that is every bit as high, because they work more efficiently. This allows them to leave on time. But that is often not the way that managers and colleagues look at it...

To produce consistent performance over a long period, we advise you to try and make efficiency gains in the way you work. This will allow you to increase your output without the need to increase your input.

—— Pick your battles: one at a time

Consider the sport of cycling, for example. In the course of a season, there are more races than a cyclist can ride. If he tried to take part in all of them, he would soon be running – or rather riding – on empty. The same is true of employees and the self-employed in the business world: there are countless projects in which your manager might like to involve you. The important thing is to maintain an overview of the total picture, so that you can still see the wood for the trees – and can select wisely. In this way, you can invest your talent in activities and projects where you want to (and are able to) perform to the highest standards, but in the most efficient manner.

Swimmer **Fanny Lecluyse** explains how important it is to identify specific events and then target all your effort on them: *'I focus on working towards the major events like the European championship, the world championship and the Olympic Games. I use the events in between to assess my level of performance and measure my progress. The actual result in these events is less important.'*

If you want to achieve your next **ultimate victory**, you need to carefully select the projects in which you wish to invest your time and energy. Identify your priorities, taking due account of your goals, and **dare to say 'no'** when a project fails to meet both requirements. Deliberately refusing a customer or a project because it does not fit in with your long-term vision frees up more time and energy to devote to projects that do match that vision. So remember: set priorities and stick to them!

According to hockey player **Vincent Vanasch**, this philosophy can be summed up in three core words: *'Plan, focus and discipline.'* In his opinion, it is impossible to perform at the highest level without these three things.

—— The goal must be clear; the way to reach it can still change

The world of elite sport and the business world are both highly dynamic and uncertain environments, as a result of which it can be a real challenge to work in them efficiently. The variables on which you based your plan can change rapidly, which means that you need to be able to adjust your plan quickly and efficiently. With this in mind, top performers not only have a plan A, but also a plan B and sometimes even a plan C, so that they can offer solutions to potential problems proactively. **These options help them to maintain focus in a volatile environment.**

Put simply, a top performer is focused on achieving the things that matter at any given moment. This implies that he must always be willing to adjust when the situation changes quickly and unexpectedly, and must be able to turn these developments to his advantage. A mindset that can help in these circumstances is this: 'I get up every morning with a goal for the day, but without expectations about how I will reach that goal'. This mindset helps you to be curious about tomorrow and makes you more resilient when your perfect scenario is ruined by events.

 This is something that taekwondoka **Jaouad Achab** knows all about: *'A few years ago, a new electronic scoring system was introduced at the world championships. In the run-up to the championship, we thought about the effect that this change might have on results and decided to adopt a smart approach. While everyone else was kicking with full force on the chest protector, I trained differently. Because the protector was wired electrically, we knew that a light touch would be enough to register a score. I adjusted my strategy, technique and mindset to take account of this. I tried to save energy by not kicking too hard on the protector and in this way hoped to score as many points as possible. During the competition, my competitors were surprised by my high points tally, because I seemed to be using relatively little effort. This allowed me to maintain the right distance from my opponents and improved the timing of my attacks. In other words, I became world champion by thinking smartly about how I could achieve the best score with the new electronic system. Nowadays, everyone adopts the same approach.'*

When you prepare in advance for changes without being afraid of them, fitting them into your plan and aligning them with your goal, this breeds confidence and can take your competitors by surprise. This is how top performers gain an advantage.

Jaouad Achab – taekwondo

Top performers are extremely driven and live from one challenge to the next

——— Their intrinsic motivation is legendary

Jean Kindermans was the academy manager at the Anderlecht football club for more than 15 years. He has seen many young talents grow to become part of the present generation of Red Devils.

 'When they are kids, they all want to become a professional footballer. I wanted that too. I went to school, but that was because I had to. I played football as well, but that was because I wanted to. In my opinion, the boundaries of motivation are to be found between that "had to" and "wanted to". As a coach, you don't need to motivate a player like Romelu Lukaku; motivation burns deep inside him.' Perhaps it is no coincidence that Romelu is now the leading all-time goal scorer for the Belgian national team?

What distinguishes top performers from the rest is their **intentions**. They are strongly driven to achieve their dreams and goals. Their intentions are closely linked to the 'why' of what they do, so that they do it in a more focused and more targeted way. It is a compulsion that comes from the deepest part of their being. Their dream goals are clear. The path towards them has been mapped out. You do not need to encourage them to translate their ideas into initiatives. They are determined to prove to **themselves** and to others that they can and will perform.

The Red Lions, the Belgian men's national hockey team, is a classic example of this.

 Emmanuel Stockbroekx is one of the driving forces in the Red Lions team: *'At the Olympic Games in 2016 in Rio, we reached the final after beating the Netherlands, who had won silver at the 2012 Olympics. We lost the final, having surrendered an early lead. A month after winning this silver medal – or after losing gold, as we saw it – we decided during a teambuilding that from now on our mindset would be one of no compromise. We would no longer be satisfied with winning a quarter final or semi-final. We wanted to go all the way. Gold would be our only goal.'*

After winning the world title (2018) and the European title (2019), the **ultimate victory** was achieved with the Olympic title in Tokyo (2021).

——— Dedication and excellence: a part of their identity

Top performers set **high standards** for themselves and maintain them. They attach great importance to the way in which they carry out a particular task or activity, which must match who they are and what they want. In other words, elite athletes develop a **performance identity**. This identity and the work ethos to which it is related pushes them to perform to the very best of their ability. Doing what matches our identity means that we will do it with greater determination, which increases the likelihood of success.

 Camille Laus is captain of the Belgian Cheetahs, the women's national 400 metre relay team. She tells us what she expects from herself: '*I set a very high bar for myself and that can sometimes scare others. But setting the bar high motivates me. Aiming for what seems impossible drives me on. If someone says it is impossible for us to become Olympic champions, I won't say that he is right or wrong. I just say: "Wait and see!"'*

Top performers take responsibility for the way in which they prepare and for the resulting performance. This is strongly linked to the **winner's mentality** and **total commitment** that characterizes them, both on and off the field of their chosen activity. Top performers know that they are also responsible for who they will become in the future. They keep a clear focus on their goal and work hard every day to bring it a little bit closer. In a team context, they also hold each other responsible for these standards and for ensuring that things are not taken too far.

 Fernando Oliva, the trainer of heptathlete Noor Vidts, puts it like this: '*Noor is not someone who goes around with a t-shirt saying "I am going to win". She will never say that openly, but will still do everything possible to one day win a major championship. She will think and live like a winner by devoting attention to her diet, her sleep and her mental and physical training programmes. As her coach, I would never let her wear that t-shirt, because that is not who she is. Her behaviour helps to make some things clear to me. The coach is not only there to look at technique, but also to look at how the athlete behaves as a person.*'

These high standards are a logical consequence of the ambitious goals that elite athletes set themselves. You will never be an Olympic champion if you only train twice a week. You need to challenge yourself every day in every training. In fact, you must become your own main challenger. 'Easy' training is not an option for top athletes. They train with 100 percent conviction and effort, pushing themselves and their body to the limit.

In team sports, some athletes project their own very high standards onto their team mates. This can often be motivating, but can sometimes also have the opposite effect. If you are too demanding of your team mates and insist that they adopt your approach and standards, this may lead to disagreement, disappointment and frustration. Finding the right balance and knowing when to let go is essential, so that each athlete can **focus on their own performance**.

High standards also ensure that top performers always opt for action. They know that putting things off can be harmful for their progress. This proactive mentality demands plenty of **self-discipline**. The things they need to do to get to the top are not always easy or enjoyable. Perhaps that is why most athletes do not like the word 'discipline'. Even so, this does not mean that they need to spend every minute of every day living like a monk or nun! Every top performer identifies the key moments when they need to ask more of themselves, resisting other temptations and focusing on positive actions.

Training for many hours and performing in a way that sometimes pushes the boundaries of what was thought to be possible demands a huge physical effort. Even so, the importance of the mental component should not be overlooked. Top performers differentiate themselves from 'ordinary' people by this desire to search for their own limits. **In fact, they do this with pleasure, a pleasure that comes from the pain they feel when they know they are making progress. This desire makes it possible for them to consistently perform in ways that seem superhuman or even impossible to the rest of us**.

 Judoka **Jorre Verstraeten**: *'As a top athlete, I don't think that you can take things to the limit unless you really enjoy it as well. This is a quality of elite athletes that few other people possess. I get satisfaction from pushing my body as far as it will go. And I can't imagine a professional athlete who does not enjoy the suffering and the pain. Without that, you won't get anywhere.'*

Performance and pain: they seem to be inextricably linked. It is only the top performers with massive intrinsic motivation who succeed in giving the best of themselves each day, driving their body to the very edge of endurance (Fransen, Boen, Vansteenkiste, Mertens & Vande Broek, 2018).

Seeking the boundary between the possible and the unimaginable is something that top performers will consciously do during their training. They will only feel that they are making progress when their body screams at them to stop.

Top performers are fierce competitors

—— Only number one is good enough

 Justine Henin, ex-tennis player: *'By nature, I was rather shy and withdrawn. I just loved playing tennis. I didn't go out onto the court to be appreciated; I went out there to win.'*

Top performers have a single motivating factor that drives them forward: **to be the best** in their chosen sport or business activity. Their urge to give expression to their talent is all-consuming. They do not aim for top ten or top five; they are only interested in the highest spot on the podium. To get there, they need to set intermediary goals (as we have already discussed), but that highest spot is always the final goal. The podium might be the Olympic Games, or a world or European championship. Or it might be the Forbes 100. These top performers are occupied each and every day with achieving their goal, with becoming number one. This passionate desire is present from an early age and develops throughout their career. Top performers do not train to be picked for the squad or to spend most of their time sitting on the substitutes bench. They train to be a star on their field of play, the best in the world. This fierce ambition spurs them on in every training session and every game.

Pascal Kina, former coach of the Belgian national women's hockey team, finds it easy to identify top performers: '*I know athletes who are training hard so that they can go with the Red Lions to the Olympic Games in Paris in 2024. And I know other athletes who are training hard to become the best player they can possibly be by that date. These two mindsets are totally different and therefore training is also totally different. Every training should be about becoming the best. And that is also the attitude that every player must take out onto the field. Not to be a star just once, but to be the best in the game every game. This approach changes their way of looking at things. They watch others so that they can improve themselves and are open to the feedback of their coach and fellow players.*'

—— Challenge mindset

'Do you want to bet that…' These are simple words, but they have a strong trigger effect that unleashes the **competitive animal** in top performers. For some people, competition has negative connotations and inhibits performance. For others, it is a necessary stimulus to enhance their performance. This latter type of person finds it hard to motivate themselves if there is no competition, no pressure, no real reason to concentrate or make a serious effort. Top performers have a challenge mindset when it comes to their competitors. They see these competitors as facilitators of their own performance.

You can compare it with running a race. The person running in front of you helps you to see what is possible, what is necessary to win. If someone else can do it, why can't you do it? With the right mindset, the desire to win and to be the best helps to push you forwards, rather than holding you back. The reason you want to win is not to beat others, but to discover the best that you can possibly be and to allow this to triumph. You can see this in the respect that competitors in many sports have for each other. Think, for example, of Roger Federer and Rafael Nadal. Or, in the business world, Bill Gates and Steve Jobs.

—— Poor losers

Pawns flying off the chess board after a lost game. Tearful children after a lost football game. These will be familiar scenes to most of us. It is clear from an early age which children have trouble accepting defeat. They play to win and hate losing. This is also a characteristic of many top performers when they were young.

 It will probably come as no surprise to learn that ex-footballer and coach **Vincent Kompany** is one such person: '*Everyone who knows me will tell you that I have always had a winner's mentality. But I should add straight away that it also helped me to learn more about myself. In the past, if we lost a game, some of my team mates were afraid to come into the dressing room. If someone laughed after a defeat, they knew that they would get into an argument with me. I hate losing – and still do – but over the years I have changed my response to it. Experience teaches you how to deal with setbacks. Now I say: "Big players never lose twice in a row." If I lose, my first thought is now: "I'll beat you next time." That is a much better attitude. It immediately sets a goal.*'

Even when they get older, top performers cannot stand losing. They not only take their sport ultra-seriously, but approach every form of competition in the same way. It sometimes seems as though they find it impossible to suppress their urge to win – even if they are playing with family and friends.

 Bart Swings is an Olympic and world champion ice skater in the mass start event, as well as being a world champion in inline skating. He explains just how far his winner's mentality extends: *'In reality, I am constantly engaged with my performance and with activities that are necessary to allow me to perform. I am very, very competitive. I always want to win, no matter what I am doing. That's just who I am.'*

The environment around a top performer – whether it consciously cultivates a winner's mentality or not – also plays an important role in this respect. Winners are often bad losers. Believe it or not, I am often asked by the entourage of elite athletes to help their protégés to deal better with setbacks and defeat. As a sport psychologist, I refuse to try and 'change' people in this way. If you want to be a high-level performer, you need to have an all-consuming desire to win. Helping them to deal with disappointments in a positive manner is something very different, and that is something that I will always try to do.

—— Progression = winning

Even though top performers are ultra-competitive, the motto of the Olympic Games is: 'Taking part is more important than winning'. Many of the top performers in this book have also taken part in the Olympic Games – and they all have a strong winner's mentality. However, they do not always all give the same meaning to the word 'winning'. Winning does not necessarily mean winning from someone else. Winning can also mean making progress. **Winning from themselves**.

Achieving the best performance always involves an inner battle against yourself. You need to master yourself before you can expect to master others. Top performers experience that when they do everything possible to win, they are able to use and develop their talent optimally. It has also been shown that people who want to win – and are convinced that they will win – have a mental advantage over their opponents.

 Each time she competes, **Camille Laus** runs two races: one against herself and one against her competitors: *'That is just something that is in me and it motivates me to chase down the other runners. I always want to win. But it is not about beating someone else; it is about giving everything I've got. Sport is first and foremost about competing with yourself; only then can you compete successfully with others.'*

Top performers do not enter competitions to make friends. They are there for one reason only: to give the best of themselves and perform in a way that will make history.

Top performers do not have a brake. **They do not slow down, even when they know that victory is almost certain**. The desire to make progress and to improve pushes them to keep on going. This is never done with the intention of humiliating their opponents, but is a response to a powerful inner impulse. They know their personal records and improving these is always a goal in its own right, irrespective of the race result. So even if they are well ahead, they will still move up a gear and give every last drop of effort. At such moments, their new mission is to avoid feeling afterwards that they might have been capable of more.

Top performers are prepared to make difficult choices

SUCCESS IS LIKE AN ICEBERG

SUCCESS

MONEY

FAME

What people see

What people do not see

DETERMINATION

DEDICATION

FAILURE

HARD WORK

SACRIFICE

DISCIPLINE

DISAPPOINTMENT

PRESSURE

—— Conscious decisions

It is sometimes difficult to achieve your goal without making tough choices. Will you be willing to do it? That is a question that colours the daily reality of every top performer, although it often escapes the public's notice. Their whole life is geared to the delivery of top performances but this frequently implies the need to confront **difficult decisions** from an early age. There is an old adage which says that 'to choose is to lose' – and in some ways that is true. You don't believe me? Just ask any top performer…

 Ex-tennis player **Justine Henin** decided to break all ties with her father when she was still very young: '*When you decide as a young and talented player to aim for a professional career, this does not mean that you are going to be happy every day. I have had difficult moments in my life, moments when I needed to make hard choices. I decided to leave home, because I had serious relational problems with my father. We were not in agreement about what I should do and this put me under a lot of pressure. I felt that he was holding me back. When I now look back on that decision, I have no regrets. But I wouldn't recommend everyone to take such a step. Not everyone has the desire, the courage or the possibility to do something like that. Of course, it would have been great if my mother had lived for longer and if I had had a better relationship with my father. But that's not what happened. That's life, and you have to accept it and move on.*'

Elite athletes opt to follow their dream from an early age, but they often combine this with a course of studies. In this way, they prepare themselves for life after their sporting career. Making the right choices at the right moment can be a difficult balancing act.

 Kristel Taelman gives guidance to elite athletes who want to combine their sporting activities with a course in further education: '*The ones who are smart are those who dare to make a long-term plan that takes account of the different phases of their life. They try to achieve balance between sport, family, school and their own needs. They can see the big picture that is made up by those different phases and plan a long way ahead. This is hugely important. If you don't have a long term plan, how can you know where you are going, even today?*'

Opting to follow your dream can also often mean moving to a new place associated with that dream. This has major consequences for the social and family life of top performers, necessitating the surrender of a large part of their quality time with family and friends, or even the postponement of starting a family. These difficult but necessary choices and their 'double life' as both elite athlete and student can help to make young top performers in particular more mature than their age contemporaries. They need to make decisions that will only confront their peers much later in life. Some athletes will never have the opportunity to experience life in the same way as these peers, but on the reverse side of the coin the peers will never enjoy or understand the experiences of the athletes. In other words, top performers lose part of 'ordinary' life, so that they can lead an extraordinary life. Normal experiences like your first party, a holiday with friends or your own family are exchanged for the achievement of excellence and the winning of glittering prizes. This is a price that top performers are willing to pay.

 Show jumper **Grégory Wathelet** also made this kind of choice: '*At the moment, I don't have any children, but that is something I want later on in my life. For now, I don't have a problem making these choices, because they help me to achieve my sporting goals. I am fortunate to have a partner who understands what I do and where I want to go, and she helps me to get there. Whatever you do in life, you always have to make choices, and choosing is losing. It is not easy, but that is how things are in professional sport.*'

Top performers know why

At some point in their career, almost all top athletes ask themselves whether it is really worth all the effort to carry on. This question can arise when they reach a particular sporting milestone, but it can also happen at moments when things are not going well. The secret is not to let yourself be dragged down into a dark hole, but to take your time to reflect and set new goals. Getting the proper mental guidance can help elite athletes and top performers in the business world to find a new direction, which can give a boost to or even extend their career.

Asking the right questions at such an important moment in your career can help to kick-start a run of new successes, allowing you to reach previously unknown heights.

 Hockey player **Emmanuel Stockbroekx** has experience of this: '*Three years ago I thought seriously about stopping, but eventually decided to carry on. Because of that decision, I won almost everything that a hockey player can win. I became a world champion and a European champion, and all because I decided at a crucial moment to continue. By nature, I am a fighter, someone who never gives up. Each time I thought about stopping, I realised that there were certain obstacles in myself that I was unwilling to confront or of which I was even unaware. As far as my future is concerned, I will continue to question myself and ask, for example, whether I need to talk further with Ellen or have a conversation with the coach. Taking my development into my own hands has been key to my career.*'

Some athletes have longer careers than others. To a large extent, this depends on the sport. A show jumper can carry on well into middle age, but that is not the case for, say, a footballer or a snowboarder. However, there can also be variations within the same sport. In football, goalkeepers tend to last longer at the top level than outfield players. Having said that, in contrast to 'ordinary people', there is no fixed retirement age for athletes. The choice about when to stop is largely in the hands of the athlete themselves. Experiencing great pleasure from your sport can be a strong motive for carrying on. On the other hand, the desire to develop other aspects of your life can be a strong motive for stopping. The importance of team performance – and the wish not to harm it – can also be a reason for saying farewell to your team mates: a good team player has the courage to stop when he knows his role has been played out. Sometimes, however, the decision to end your career is forced upon you; for example, as a result of persistent injury.

 For **Seppe Smits**, the pleasure he gets from snowboarding is central to his decision to carry on: '*As long as I enjoy doing it, I will not be ready to hang up my snowboard. As long as I feel fit and my body is up to the job, I will continue to learn new tricks and will enter competitions with the same enthusiasm and will to win as in the past. Of course, results also play a part. If your results are poor for three years in a row, this obviously gives you pause for thought and lowers your motivation. No, you need to keep getting decent results.*'
He further explains that his awareness of the relative shortness of a snowboarding career makes the pleasure he experiences more intense with each passing year. '*I think that's why the second time I became world champion felt better than the first. It was six years later and I was still at the very top of the sport. That's a really great feeling. And if I could do it again, that would be ten years after the first time....*'

—— Life after professional sport and fear of the return to 'normal'

Research has shown that to a greater or lesser extent the majority of athletes have negative feelings about the transition from top performer to ex-top performer. Preparing properly for this transition can help to give athletes a **feeling of control** over the situation, so that they can make a fresh start in an efficient and well-planned manner, moving forward at their own pace and under their own conditions.

This is something that **Vincent Vanasch** has also thought about: '*I am still following my training as an osteopath. That means an extra five years. Sometimes it is difficult, but I can still combine it with my hockey. When I am ready to end my professional career, I don't want to feel boxed into a corner with nowhere to go, simply because I failed to keep my options open.*'

Being consciously active with the preparation of their second career can help athletes to deal with the uncertainties that are an inherent part of their profession. At any moment during training or competition they can be hit by an injury that can move their sporting career in a completely different direction overnight. Having a plan A, plan B and even a plan C is a necessity, not a luxury.

Scientific research has confirmed that athletes with a strongly developed identity as elite athletes have more problems with the end-of-career transition back to normal life and take much longer to adjust. Developing interests outside of sport during your career makes this adjustment less abrupt and more fluid. Studies have shown that this 'second career' approach is increasingly being adopted by elite athletes (Park, Lavallee & Tod, 2013).

Even so, many professional athletes remain frightened by the prospect of 'normal' life. Whichever way you look at it, athletes are extraordinary people who lead extraordinary lives. They experience things that are difficult to compare with the experiences of ordinary people. For example, there are not many everyday experiences comparable with giving expression to your unique talent in front of a crowd of fifty thousand cheering spectators.

 Hockey player **Vincent Vanasch** understands this: '*That is what worries me most. Missing those moments just before the start of a game, when the adrenalin really kicks in. I don't know where else I will be able to get a feeling like that. Professional sport gives you sensations that are difficult to equal in normal life. I know that I am very fortunate to have had these unique experiences and it is difficult to explain to others, because it is all so personal.*'

Out of balance

In our way of thinking about the development of high performance attitudes, there is an important basic principle that we wish to clarify. If you want to display and use these attitudes in the best possible way, it is important to realise that:
— you need to find a balance between showing either too much or too little of a particular attitude;
— the context in which you wish to perform will determine to a significant degree the opportunity and suitability of displaying particular attitudes.
On the page 'Coach yourself', you can use the dashboards to indicate whether or not you display the different aspects of the relevant chapter's attitude 'too little', 'optimally' or 'too much'. In this way, we hope to stimulate your self-insight.

Experience shows that before you can consistently display an attitude in an optimal manner, you will sometimes get things out of balance. This is not a problem, as long as you recognise the imbalance and adjust it to reflect the situation you are in. So that you are able to recognise your imbalanced behaviour, we will provide you with a list of the most common characteristics that indicate the display of too much or too little of the attitude.

Too little motivation to perform & work smart

You lack dreams and goals towards which you can work.

You are immediately distracted by thoughts or your environment, so that you constantly change your plans and goals.

Your efforts are determined by external factors, such as money, fame or the approval of others.

You take things as you find them, without setting priorities or goals.

You notice that you lack determination, resilience and a sense of responsibility.

You are easily satisfied with the results of your performance.

You lack the urge to do better and better.

You hope that everything will fall into place and are not prepared to make difficult decisions in support of your goal.

Too much motivation to perform & work smart

You are so focused on a single goal that there is no room for other goals.

You set the bar for yourself so high that your goals are no longer realistic.

Your motivation turns into obsession, so that your thoughts about your goal become frenzied rather than calm and well-considered.

You work non-stop without pause to achieve your goal, so that you become mentally and physically exhausted.

You are never satisfied with your performance and always want more, so that you seldom derive pleasure from what you do.

You work in such a focused way that you develop tunnel vision, thereby losing sight of all other aspects of your life.

You would give up everything to reach your goal, even the most important people and things in your life.

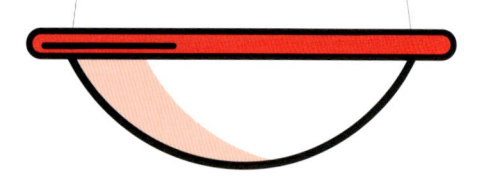
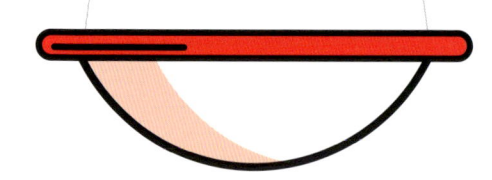

Coach yourself!

—— Describe your next ultimate victory!

STEP 1 Give yourself a score for the following aspects of this attitude.

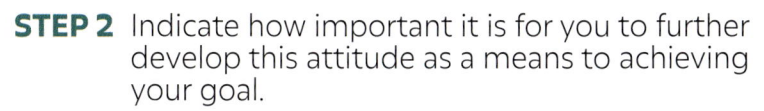

- I make plans to achieve my dream.
- I am a smart worker, doing the right things at the right time.
- I am intrinsically motivated and love facing new challenges.
- I have a winner's mentality and will do everything necessary to succeed.
- I am prepared to make difficult choices.
- I know where I want to go and have the determination to get there.

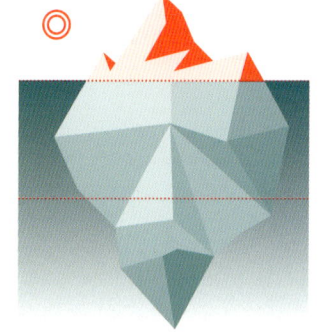

STEP 2 Indicate how important it is for you to further develop this attitude as a means to achieving your goal.

0   **10**

(unimportant)   (very important)

STEP 3 Identify your challenges and your levers. (See part 2.)

—— My challenges:

—— My levers:

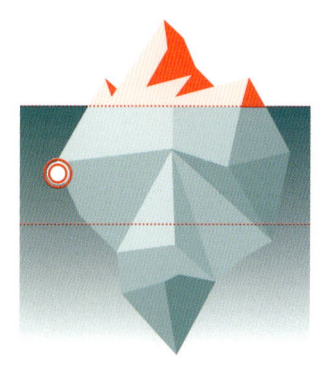

STEP 4 Identify your mental skills that will help you to deal positively with challenges. (See part 3.)

—— How will these mental skills help you?

STEP 5 Name the concrete actions you will take on the road towards your ultimate victory.

LEAD
& MAKE OTHERS BETTER

ATTITUDE 2

LEAD
AND
MAKE
OTHERS
BETTER

'My leadership competencies have evolved over the years. It requires self-leadership during your years of puberty to be convinced of what you are doing, to follow your passion with 100 percent commitment and to block out all distractions. In time, this self-leadership develops into the sharing of experiences with others around you, with the aim of making them better. In the national team, I work closely with the other keepers, because healthy competition is a driver that will allow me to develop and become an even better player. If my competitors get stronger, I know that I will need to push my boundaries further, if I want to retain my position as first keeper. It is a question of mindset.'

—— **Aisling D'Hooghe**, hockey player

Definition

'Lead'

We describe this as an attitude through which a person possesses the necessary skills to be a good leader for themselves and has the ability to encourage others in a positive manner to perform optimally and to achieve both individual goals and successes in a team context.

'Make others better'

We describe this as an attitude through which a person stimulates the development of others, regarding the resultant competition as a driver for further self-development and not as a threat.

Characteristics of top performers with this attitude

— Their self-leadership develops into authentic leadership.
— They surround themselves with a top team, based on mutual trust.
— They are emotionally intelligent and invest in mutually beneficial relationships with others.
— They believe in shared leadership as a way to make the team stronger.
— They regard competition as an opportunity for self-development.
— They help others to raise their game and progress to a higher level.

Top performers develop from self-leadership to authentic leadership

—— Self-knowledge and self-reflection

According to the ancient Greek philosophers, **self-knowledge** is the beginning of all wisdom. That is as true today as it was in ancient times. If a high potential wishes to blossom into a high performer, she must first know herself through and through. Self-knowledge is not inborn, but develops as a result of the unique human ability to reflect on our own being: our own feelings, our own thoughts, our own behaviour and its effects on others and the environment around us. This is a complex process for our brain and demands both a wide-ranging vision and powers of concentration.

The ability for **self-reflection** develops over time and can be stimulated by our environment and our upbringing. Parents, teachers and coaches can tap into this ability by asking children questions about their behaviour, their feelings and their effects. If you grow up in an environment that encourages every form of self-reflection, you will probably be more inclined to self-reflect more easily in later life.

Our interviews with elite athletes suggest that they possess a high degree of self-knowledge. Like all of us, this self-knowledge was not innate, but is a consequence of (amongst other things) self-reflection. More than other people, elite athletes need to look at the 'full picture'. During their self-analysis, they must assess the many different elements that can have an impact on their performance: their physical and mental skills, their intra- and interpersonal skills, their drivers, their value patterns, and so on. They not only know their body completely, but also know their qualities, potential pitfalls and challenges in the mental domain and in their relationships with others.

 Thibaut Vervoort, basketball player: '*As an elite athlete, you must be mentally strong enough to accept the role given to you by the coach, even if this does not correspond entirely with the image that you have of yourself and your qualities. It is important to carry on believing in these qualities and to display them whenever possible. In basketball, I was able to translate this insight into action: by focusing on my qualities, I developed a powerful motivating force inside of me, the kind of force that leads to the best performance.*'

Daniel Ofman developed the Core Quality Quadrant Model, a simple model that is used to encourage self-reflection in individuals as a means to increasing self-knowledge, and this in many different contexts, ranging from school children through business executives to professional athletes.

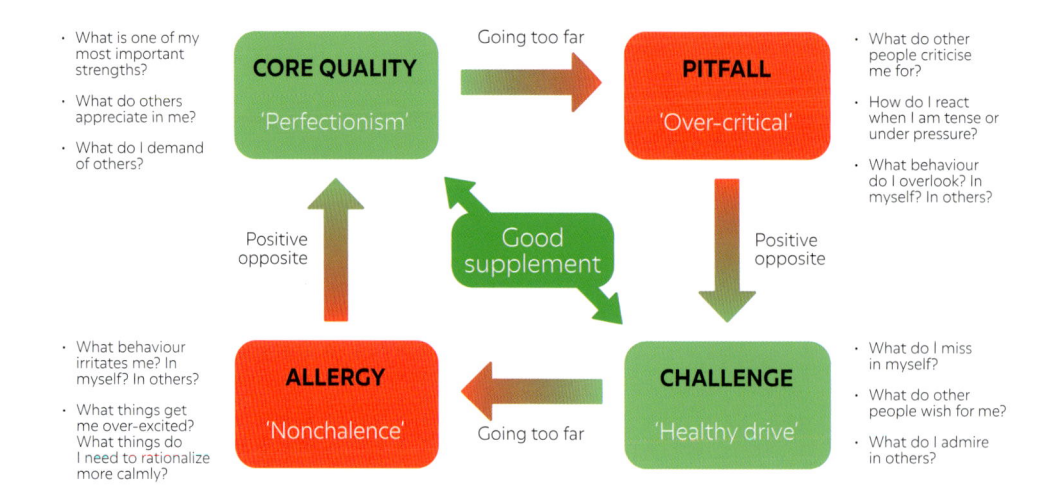

- What is one of my most important strengths?
- What do others appreciate in me?
- What do I demand of others?

CORE QUALITY
'Perfectionism'

Going too far

PITFALL
'Over-critical'

- What do other people criticise me for?
- How do I react when I am tense or under pressure?
- What behaviour do I overlook? In myself? In others?

Positive opposite

Good supplement

Positive opposite

- What behaviour irritates me? In myself? In others?
- What things get me over-excited? What things do I need to rationalize more calmly?

ALLERGY
'Nonchalence'

Going too far

CHALLENGE
'Healthy drive'

- What do I miss in myself?
- What do other people wish for me?
- What do I admire in others?

To illustrate this model, we will use a core quality that we come across every day in our work with top performers: perfectionism. For many top performers perfectionism is a red thread that runs through the entirety of their career. It is what distinguishes them from others and stimulates them to give 100 percent every time. They hate half-measures. Of course, this can also be a pitfall, because it can cause them to be unnecessarily over-critical: if you expect perfect results every time but fail to get them, this can lead to disappointment and self-doubt. For them, the challenge will be to find a healthy form of drive that shifts the focus from results to the process. This balance will be a good way to supplement their perfectionism. There is nothing wrong with trying to achieve perfect results, providing you realise that enjoying the process and making progress are also important.

As a sport psychologist, but above all as a person, I have seen that it is impossible for someone to know themselves 100 percent. But that is not necessary to achieve a great performance. Each new day gives a new colour accent to your life: you meet new people, you find yourself in new situations, you do some things with passion, you do other things unwillingly, and so on. In addition, life is a progression of transitions: from young adult to new parent, from employee to manager. These transitions allow you to discover new aspects of yourself, so that your self-knowledge will increase. This, in turn, will give a boost to your self-confidence and the way in which you conduct yourself when you consciously experience each new sensation and event, prompting reflection about yourself, about the impact of your thoughts and feelings on your behaviour and, above all, about what happens when you lose control over all these things.

Top performers have learnt to analyse and reassess themselves constantly. In this way, they monitor and stimulate their development. They do this with great honesty, because they realise that deep self-knowledge can make all the difference to their performance. They know that there will be moments in their career when they will be under extreme pressure. At such moments, they will only be able to give the very best of themselves if they have sufficient self-knowledge and self-control. This is why knowing yourself is so important as you travel the path that leads to your **ultimate victory**.

Kevin Borlée, one of the key figures in the Belgian Tornados 400 metres relay team, also speaks of the importance of self-knowledge and of doing the right thing for yourself: '*At major tournaments there are moments when I feel under great pressure. I accept that pressure and don't run away from it. I know that for me the best way to deal with it in a positive way is to remain as calm as possible. But sometimes that is difficult to reconcile with being part of a team. Every athlete deals with pressure differently. For example, some like to talk about it, but that is not what I want. At such moments, you need to know yourself really well as an athlete and must dare to stand up for what you need personally. Even when you are surrounded by other athletes, you need to retain control over what is happening around you. You need a filter. Between races, I like to listen to music. This allows me to sit in my own bubble and close myself off from the rest. At that moment, I decide for myself if there is anything I want to discuss and with whom.*'

Research among tennis players has shown that self-awareness – and, in particular, self-insight – are crucial for dealing with pressure in a positive manner. Players with greater self-insight can reduce their stress levels when they really need to. By reducing these levels, they become more resilient at difficult moments in their matches. In other words, self-insight has a positive impact on their performance (Cowden & Meyer-Weitz, 2016).

From self-control to self-leadership

When, as a result of self-reflection, your self-knowledge increases, the need to further develop yourself often grows automatically. Having greater insight into the challenges and potential pitfalls creates a feeling of greater self-control, which also gives a boost to your **self-confidence**.

For example, when someone says that she is aware that she displays her emotions 'too' forcefully in a particular situation in which she feels unfairly disadvantaged – for instance, if a referee seems to be showing bias towards her opponent – she will need to do everything possible to learn how to control those emotions. In other words, she will want to change her reaction and therefore her behaviour, because she has probably experienced that a lack of emotional control has a negative impact on her performance. Investing in mental training that will teach her how to regulate her emotions will increase her feeling of self-control and have a positive effect on her self-confidence.

This can be illustrated perfectly in the person of **Vincent Vanasch**. The International Hockey Federation has chosen him as the world's best keeper on more than one occasion. He owes his nickname 'The Wall' to the way in which he protects his goal and directs the other defenders around him. Anyone who has seen Vincent play will know that he exudes self-confidence, positive energy and calm. In turn, this not only has a positive influence on himself and his fellow team members, but also intimidates opponents. At the same time, he also prepares for each penalty shoot-out in great detail. He analyses the rival players and tapes the most important details about their style of play onto his hockey stick.

This feeling of control contributes towards Vincent's self-confidence during this crucial phase of play.

In other words, a stable level of self-confidence is an important factor for developing greater self-leadership. And it is a high level of **self-leadership** that is one of the most distinguishing features of top performers. They act on the basis of their self-knowledge and their personal drivers, which allows them to achieve the self-direction and self-motivation that is necessary for a great performance.

Self-leadership stimulates people to take greater ownership of their tasks and work processes (Neck & Houghton, 2006). People with self-leadership skills generally have more successful careers and derive greater enjoyment from those careers (Murphy & Ensher, 2001; Raabe, Frese & Beehr, 2007).

 Self-leadership is also evident – and necessary – in other areas of life. **Kristel Taelman** gives guidance to elite athletes who want to combine their sporting activities with a course in further education. She emphasises that these athletes not only need a carefully considered and well-balanced plan to deal with this double challenge, but must also have the necessary sense of responsibility and self-discipline to put that plan into practice. *'Young people should be in control of their plan, and not their coach or their parents. Of course, the support of those around them is obviously important, but it is ownership that makes the difference and provides the key to success.'*

Internal versus external attribution

As a top performer, self-leadership also implies that you take **responsibility** for your results and also attempt to discover the reasons for poor results when they occur.

 Ex-judoka **Heidi Rakels** also believes in the importance of taking responsibility for the results of your actions: *'I have a very strong sense of responsibility. Even when I lost, I never put the blame on external factors. If I was beaten, I always gave my opponent a friendly handshake afterwards. I never felt angry towards others. I was angry with myself. It was me who had not been good enough to win. I was able to deal with this rationally. Okay, it's true that external factors can sometimes go against you, but that's just the way things are. At the Olympic Games in Barcelona I was already beaten in the second round, based on a split judges' decision. One of the judges thought that I had won; the other two thought that my opponent had won. In other words, it was a close call, but it went against me. As soon as I left the mat, my entourage began to moan about the unfairness of the decision. But what was the point? I had lost – and that was that. But through the repechage I still had the chance to fight for Olympic bronze, something that I had worked and trained for during the past four years. This was a moment when I needed to retain my focus. So it was me who now said: "What's done is done. I'm going to fight for third place instead." I knew that it wouldn't help me to get locked into a negative spiral. I could think about "what might have been" later on. For now, I needed to concentrate on winning the matches that would get me the bronze. And that is what I did! For me, this was an example of real personal leadership, because at that moment the others around me did not have the right attitude.'*

In Heidi's position, most people's reaction would be like that of her entourage: 'This is not fair!' And there is no shame in such a reaction. At moments like these, it can often seem safer to protect your own ego by putting the blame on external factors. In contrast, true top performers remain objective in their evaluation. They seek the reasons for their failures primarily in themselves and are less inclined to blame external factors. In other words, top performers know themselves well enough to be able to accept an occasional defeat and see this as a motivation for working even harder. **They do not need to protect their egos, because they know exactly what they are capable of.**

—————— It's not just luck

Although top performers are willing to take responsibility for their failures and results, it was nevertheless noticeable in our interviews with them just how often they use the word 'luck'.

Heidi Rakels says that she was lucky to be in the right place to meet the right people at the right time, both in her sporting career and afterwards in the business world. Her company Guardsquare is a successful software business and in 2019, Heidi named ICT Woman of the Year, because in contrast with many other start-ups, Guardsquare was profitable from the start. *'My partner and I both wrote programmes in our spare time. My partner wrote one particular programme that focused on quality and offered it for free. Because it was immediately a gigantic success, we decided to commercialise it. We had to work hard and, of course, we needed to continue having a focus on quality. For me, our product always needed to be made better and better.'*

So was it pure luck that Heidi Rakels won Olympic bronze and later set up a company worth millions? Or was it the result of her work ethic, her proactivity and her self-leadership? Did her focus on the things that she could influence and control make her such a successful entrepreneur or was it all down to chance?

Good luck is always useful, but it does not form the basis for consistent high-level performance. In this respect, we agree with the athlete **Camille Laus**, who believes that you **make your own luck**:

'My mother always says that perhaps I was lucky to meet certain people in my career, but that I created most of my opportunities through the strength of my own personality. For example, I was already training with Jacques Borlée when I was offered a job. I took it because Jacques knew that I was professional and had studied. I always say that I have been lucky, but my mum is right: I earned those chances through my own efforts.'

Top performers succeed in building a strong team around them

While it is true that top performers can only reach their personal 'summit' if they have sufficient self-knowledge, they also need to surround themselves with others who can help to make them even better. Whether you are an athlete or a businessman, you will never get as far alone as you will with a team.

—————— If you want to go fast, go alone.
If you want to go far, go together. (African Proverb)

I can still remember the visit I had from two young and ambitious athletes at the beginning of 2018: *'We want to start up a 4 × 400 metre relay team for women.'* The Belgian Tornados – the men's relay team – were their inspiration: *'They have been putting Belgian athletics on the world map for years and we are convinced that we can do the same. We don't yet have a team or a coach, but we want you to be our sport psychologist.'* **Camille Laus** and **Hanne Claes** convinced me immediately. Even though they did not yet have a plan, their dream was clear. And they knew that they needed to build up a team around them, so that they could be surrounded by the right people who could help them. In this sense, the creation of the Belgian Cheetahs is a story of collaboration. And it is a successful story. Within a year and a half of their formation, the Cheetahs ran a top time in the world championships and qualified for the Olympic Games in Tokyo.

Put simply, top performers possess a high degree of **charisma** that they can use to make others enthusiastic for their project, so that they can get the right people on board their own particular train.

Ex-tennis player **Dominique Monami** remembers how she found the right partner to make her sporting dream come true: *'My ambition was to win a medal at the Olympic Games. I realised I could double my chances if I played both singles and doubles. I contacted Els Callens to share my ideas with her. We quickly decided that it was the best thing for both of us. Our preparation for the Games was short but super-efficient. We reached the semi-finals of the US Open and just before we set off for Sydney we had a three-day long team building session. To deal with the pressure at an event like the Olympic Games, you need real self-leadership. We went into a kind of isolation, so that we could get to know each other better, especially at the emotional level. We thought about the things that might go wrong and how we could help each other when that happened. We looked at everything in detail. We discovered differences in our characters, but also similarities. Els and I were a good match for each other, because we are both calm by nature. We both need to be calm inside our head. We still each did our own thing, but we could also support each other effectively.'*

—————— Top performers as strong leaders

Once they have surrounded themselves with the right team members, coaches or assistants, top performers give a strong lead that breeds confidence and responsibility. They help others to grow and allow the spotlight to also be turned on the performance of these others. They give credit where credit is due. These are the kinds of leaders for whom others are willing to go through hell and high water. **Philip Mestdagh**, the former national coach of the Belgian Cats, is just such a leader. I had the pleasure of working with him for more than eight years. He was able to take our team to a higher level, thanks to his **own unique leadership style**.

How does he explain his success as a leader? *'I always try to be myself. When I am with the national team, I never put on an act. The way I am with the players is the same way I am with my family and friends at home. At the same time, I also take a great deal of time and effort to find assistants with the right competencies, because it is super-important to have confidence in the advice that my experts give me. By displaying my confidence in them, I get energy and cooperation in return.'*

This shows that top performers do not necessarily need to be the best in everything. As leaders, they need above all to make sure that they have **the right people in the right places around them**. They take seriously the expertise provided by these people and challenge them to come up with the best possible solutions. In short, they invest in strong relationships with the members of their team.

As the CEO of Guardsquare, **Heidi Rakels** is sometimes asked the following question: *'What are you best at?'* Her answer: *'Actually, in nothing! My partner is better at programming and the other members of our team are all better at their specialties than I am. In other words, I am surrounded by exactly the people I need! Is this by chance? No, I think I have good intuition and can assess people quickly. However, it took time before I learnt to trust this intuition and became assertive about following my gut instincts. When I was a judoka, I went in search of good trainers. Sometimes I ended up with the wrong people, but was too young and lacked the courage to say that I wanted to change. Gradually, I came to realise that for me it is very important to have control. And it is the same in business. In our company, I let the team do what they want for around 90 percent of the time, but I need to have the control to change things for the 10 percent when I do not agree with them.'*

Although top performers surround themselves with the right people and give these people their trust, they still regard themselves as being fully responsible for the end results of their actions. **Ultimate responsibility** for their projects rests with them and them alone, and they blame no one else if things go wrong.

By now, it should be clear that top performers think and act on the basis of a growth mindset. Their starting point is an assumption that they can continue to develop with their team and as a team, thereby stimulating everyone around them to engage in a process of constant positive evolution. As a coach, this is also the approach adopted by **Vincent Kompany**. He has filled his coaching staff with specialists and, most importantly, people he trusts. Vincent wants to grow with his team to become the best football coach in the world. He wants to learn from the people around him and he uses his network to share knowledge and opinions with other experts at home and abroad. If possible, he brings these experts to the club, so that his colleagues can also continue to improve in their own fields of expertise. In this way, the team as a whole continues to grow. Moreover, top performers like Vincent expect others to act in the same proactive manner and with the same amount of passion as themselves. This expectation is their way of pushing people to stretch their boundaries even further. In short, **they lead by example**.

Top performers are emotionally intelligent and have strong emotional connections with others

As already mentioned, top performers make use of their self-knowledge to build up a strong team around them. At the same time, they also possess the talent and the strength of character to develop flourishing long-term relationships with the people in this team.

The **emotional intelligence** of top performers is higher than that of the average person. This is often the result of their curiosity about what other people are feeling and how they act. Top performers show a genuine interest in others and ask them a multiplicity of questions on all kinds of different subjects. In this way, they gain insights into the emotions, motives and desires of a wide range of people. This is all based on the top performer's genuine wish to understand and support (important) others, such as their team members.

 Hockey player **Aisling D'Hooghe** tries to adjust the help she offers to best suit the individual needs of the person she is dealing with: *'When I can see that a player needs help, I try to put myself in their position. I ask myself what I can do that will help her most. It is then a question of using your intuition and finding the right balance. I can help some players to relax by talking about everyday things or by telling a few jokes. With others, I know that the important thing is to listen actively to their worries and suggest ways to alleviate them. I vary my approach to reflect the personality of the player concerned.'*

In our interviews it was noticeable that most top performers are able to express themselves easily and fluently. When they are talking to others, whether individually or in a team situation, they have the knack of finding the right words to touch a chord with their listener(s). What they say has a powerful effect: setting things in motion, offering a solution, providing inspiration... Thanks to their empathy and other social skills, top performers have the ability **to unite people around a common goal** and increase the likelihood of reaching that goal successfully.

—— Increasing people skills by taking an interest in your team members

Although there is currently no conclusive scientific evidence, it seems likely that the emotional intelligence and social skills of top performers are not (wholly) inborn. On the contrary, they continue to develop as their life progresses.

 Hockey player **Aisling D'Hooghe** explains how you can improve your emotional intelligence simply by having an interest in and a knowledge of basic personality theory: *'Over the years, a number of different sport psychologists have worked with the Red Panthers. These experts have helped us to understand that every team member is different and that these differences can actually be strengths for the team as a whole. Precisely for this reason, it is important to get to know each other, to connect with each other, to learn about and respect each other's motives. We all*

react in different ways. Over the years, I have come to realise and accept that not everyone thinks and acts like I do. As a result, I have learnt to adjust to others, but without losing my own identity. This helps me to be a better team mate.'

—— Being able to press people's buttons

Because of their greater self-knowledge and self-control, top performers can deal better with their own emotions than others. In addition, their emotional intelligence also allows them to better anticipate the emotional reactions of their team mates. As a result, this makes it possible for them to react more adequately than the average person in certain situations.

 As a keeper, hockey player **Aisling D'Hooghe** emphasises just how crucial this skill can be: '*The most important thing is to learn how to recognise when the team is starting to play less well. If you can do this, you might be able to prevent the opponent from dominating the game or even scoring. Once you can recognise that moment, the rest is relatively easy. Basically, it means that you need to know yourself and your team mates sufficiently well, so that you know how to spur them on to redouble their efforts. Some team mates like it if I give them a lot of information. They regard this as something to hold on to and pull themselves up on. For others, you need to give them as little information as possible, because they are at their best when they can freestyle.'*

In his book *Emotional Intelligence*, Daniel Goleman describes how this kind of intelligence can be the key to success. His research revealed that in almost 90 percent of cases the difference between a good leader and an average leader is to be found in their level of emotional intelligence. In the past, employees in the business world used to be promoted to managerial positions as a reward for their good task performance. But just because you are a good programmer, this does not mean that you will automatically have the skills necessary to lead a team as a project manager. In other words, too little attention was paid to the emotional intelligence of these potential people managers.
This was a mistake: a manager with too little emotional intelligence and underdeveloped people management skills can have a negative impact on his own and his team's level of job satisfaction.

Thanks to a better understanding of the importance of emotional intelligence, in recent decades this situation has changed for the better. The current generation of leaders are now expected to be good at personal leadership. They provide this **leadership on the basis of their strengths rather than power**. They do not need to be experts in their chosen fields of activity, but they must have excellent people management skills. They must generate commitment amongst the members of their company or team by asking their opinions about the importance of their roles and the way they carry them out.

In elite sport, for example, we see that athletes are having an increasing say about their training schedules and are increasingly consulted about their opponents and the best game plan to beat them. In this way, existing leaders develop the self-leadership of (other) athletes, which immediately creates a lever for the emergence of new leaders.

Are you introvert or extravert? A thinker or a more emotional type? My experience over the years has led me to believe that everyone is capable of 'connecting' with others. Some people will first need to overcome their shyness. Others will need to control their natural enthusiasm. Some will be able to offer empathy and a listening ear. Others will be able to use their expertise to bring people together and motivate them.

—— Unconditional belief in the team and its members

Top performers might not always be aware of it, but they generally possess a **level of charisma that is far above the average**. Their words and their body language exude confidence and this **confidence** can often rub off on the other members of their team.

A word of warning, however. There is scientific evidence to show that leaders in the world of sport can have both a positive and a negative impact on team confidence and on the individual and collective performance of team members. (Fransen, Steffens, Haslam, Vanbeselaere, Vande Broek & Boen, 2016).

 A year before the 2008 Olympic Games in Peking, **Elodie Ouédraogo** was a member of the 4 × 100 metres relay team that won a bronze medal at the world championships in Osaka. This was the first medal that Belgian women had ever won at world championship level. Not surprisingly, their success created high expectations for the forthcoming Olympics. Elodie remembers how the team dealt with these expectations and consciously made efforts to boost their collective team confidence: '*After we had won a bronze medal out of nowhere in Japan, we subsequently made the click as a team. We realised that if we wanted to do something big at the next Games, we would have to do it as a team! If you don't have the four fastest sprinters in the world, you can only win by going beyond your individual limits and by giving everything you've got for your fellow team members. This is only possible if you enjoy being together and trust each other completely. From this point on, everything we did was for "the team". Every member of that team was important, and for that reason we were very supportive and protective of each other. We felt a strong bond and knew that the others would always be there for us. With a team like ours, we believed that we could do it – and we did! Today, I still work with Olivia and we have our own company in the fashion industry. The bond that we created then is still as strong as ever.*'

In her interview, Elodie – like many other athletes – also spoke about the role played by luck: '*It was only by chance that we became good.*' But if you read her testimony, it should be clear that you do not win a gold medal at the Olympic Games without having something more than luck on your side!

As already mentioned, however, team confidence can also be influenced negatively. This can happen when some members of the team start to doubt the feasibility of the project. For this reason, it is important that the team and their entourage discuss this feasibility explicitly before they start. This applies equally for individual athletes and sports. With this in mind, before each important tournament with the Belgian Cats and the **Belgian Cheetahs** we organise a workshop during which we can discuss our team goals. In particular, I can remember a crucial moment in the preparation of the Belgian Cheetahs for the world championships in Doha. As usual, the team first divided itself up into sub-groups to each create a goals pyramid. After that, the groups came together to discuss the results of the sub-groups. This revealed that there was clear disagreement about the achievable goal. What seemed feasible for one sub-group seemed impossible for another. What was the cause of this serious discussion? The feasibility of qualifying for the Olympic Games. For many of the team, the world championships was the Cheetah's first major test: how would they perform amongst the world's other top teams? Our captain, **Camille Laus**, had no doubts. For her, the position was clear: if everyone in the team performed to a high standard approaching their personal best, qualification for the next year's Olympics was near-certain. Even though some of the team were carrying injuries and some new athletes needed to be integrated into the team set-up, Camille was bursting with confidence. Her belief in each and every team member was sky-high. At first, however, she was confronted by the counter-arguments raised by the other sub-teams. Even so, she stuck to her guns and was subtly able to convince her colleagues one by one to change their opinions, using realistic and well-founded arguments. Just two weeks later, the Cheetahs wrote Belgian athletics history: they raced to fifth place in their first world championships and qualified directly for the Olympic Games in Tokyo.

When top performers express and demonstrate their confidence in the team, this has a positive impact on the team's connectedness with the team identity and helps to improve both individual performances and the team's collective performance. As far as the Cheetahs are concerned, they often run faster times for each other than when they are running in individual races. Talk about team spirit and team trust!

It is important to note that this mutual trust and confidence can be influenced and enhanced by every member of the team, irrespective of whether they have a leadership role and irrespective of whether they are a newcomer or an 'old hand'.

 Hockey player **Vincent Vanasch** told us about the impact that new blood had on the Red Lions: '*Victor Wegnez, Antoine Kina and Arthur De Sloover are players who had never lost in the national youth teams to countries like Australia. Those of us who had been around for a lot longer had had different experiences. Although the new generation were still very young when they joined the Red Lions, they played with great freedom and without complexes. Their youthful enthusiasm and confidence had a very positive influence on our team dynamic.*'

Top performers emphasise the importance of shared leadership

—— Consciously creating a positive climate

Top performers consciously try to create a **positive climate** in their environment. They do this by (amongst other things) building up positive relationships with the other people around them. This does not mean, however, that they need officially to 'claim' a leadership role. In our interviews, most of the athletes said that they don't like to feel that they are above the group and find it difficult to be in charge. Instead, they prefer to send out the right signals to their fellow team members through their own actions. In short, they walk the talk.

Sofie Hendrickx, ex-captain of the Belgian Cats, explains how personal dedication can play a role in this: '*I never consciously tried to set an example to others, but by always being there I think that the other team members knew what they could rely on me for, and what not. When I announced that I planned to retire from the national team, everyone said that I had been an inspiration. It was good to hear, but that had never been my intention. I just wanted to be a person who everyone could rely on and I always gave 100 percent for the national team. In that way, I think that I built up more credit than if I had consciously tried to be an example.*'

───── Having a sense of responsibility about your own performance and team performance

A leader will stand up for themselves and the team. This also involves questioning certain matters and suggesting appropriate alternatives. Players and staff know better than anyone else what works and what does not work, both on the work floor and on the field of play. Their input can be important for every leader or coach. This means that everyone can be of value for the team, irrespective of age. For that reason, you should not let yourself be influenced by what others might say or think about your opinions. In this respect, real leaders are willing to accept responsibility for their own words and deeds.

Hendrik Tuerlinckx has been a stalwart of the Red Dragons volleyball team for years: '*When you show initiative on the court and it works, your coach will probably be happy. But sometimes you might get a roasting, because you didn't do what had been agreed. So it takes courage to step away from the game plan and do something different. For example, during time-outs it is more difficult for younger players than experienced ones to voice opinions that cast doubt on the coach's tactics. That happened to me a few times early on in my career and it is not easy. In fact, what you are doing is telling the coach to his face that he is wrong. Some coaches – the ones who are fiercely proud of their work – can take that badly. Even so, at such moments you need to take your responsibility towards the team seriously, if necessary by further discussing it one-to-one with the coach after the game. But if you say that something is not right, you have to offer an alternative.*'

Scientific research has shown that the behaviour displayed by a leader is more important than any innate qualities they might have. This applies both on and off the field of play. The ability to develop and give expression to a 'we' feeling is crucial. This also has implications for the selection and further development of leaders. They way they behave in the team is more important than their natural presence within the team as a leader (Fransen, Haslam, Steffens & Boen, 2020).

This kind of leadership can indeed be developed. Only a very small minority of people are born leaders. Most develop the competencies that a leader needs in the course of their career. Displaying leadership can vary, depending on the situation, the context and the personalities of the top performers in question. As an athlete, you are sometimes pushed into a leadership role, even though you feel that you are not yet ready. Developing leadership in these circumstances, when it does not feel natural, takes a great deal of courage. In this respect, it is once again possible to see the interplay between the different attitudes that we discussed earlier. The development of one attitude can have a highly positive impact on another attitude.

Just as important as the need to accept **leadership roles** is the necessity to **share** those roles. Top performers realise that they cannot be everywhere and see everything. They respond to this by their willingness to share leadership. They make best use of their own strengths and give others the space to do the same.

Within the concept of shared leadership, it is possible to distinguish four different roles that can be fulfilled by different persons. The role that you take on is determined to a large extent by your innate personality and behavioural preferences. The motivational leader takes responsibility for motivational coaching; the task leader is responsible for technical and tactical coaching; the social leader is responsible for preventing the creation of sub-groups within the team; and the external leader communicates with the various professional sport stakeholders, such as the press, public and the relevant administrative bodies. The same player can carry out more than one of these roles within the team, but it is unusual for the same player to assume all four roles. As a result, there is nowadays an increasing move towards having a leadership team (Fransen, Vanbeselaere, De Cuyper, Vande Broek & Boen, 2014).

Much the same is true in the business world. The best teams are the teams with a complementary composition that allows different team members to take on different roles. These teams are generally known as self-managing or self-steering teams. Each member has his own strengths, which supplement each other cumulatively. These teams do not need a single manager to lead them. The different leadership roles are allocated to the most appropriate people and their leadership is accepted by the rest of the team.

If an employer finds herself in a function that does not allow her to fulfil her most natural preferred role, she will need to develop the behaviour and competencies that are required for this role. However, this is not easy – not even for top performers. Nevertheless, they accept the challenge and assume the necessary responsibility, identifying where and how they can have the greatest positive impact on the team.

 Vincent Vanasch explains how this works in the Belgian national hockey team: '*Most of the Red Lions are leaders in their own home teams. In the national team, some will be quicker than others to take on a leading role. That being said, we are all leaders in one way or another. We share the different responsibilities between us. As a result, everyone feels involved and we are all motivated to give the best of ourselves.*'

—— The coach's liaison

The sharing of responsibilities allows every player to make use of her strengths and to do the things that she is good at. This distribution of leadership tasks also demands a high degree of trust. There must be confidence in and of the staff on the one hand and in and of the players on the other hand. For this reason, it is crucial that the athlete-leaders should have a **close relationship with the coach** and, by extension, the rest of the coaching staff. In fact, these leaders form the bridge between the team and the staff. In some case, they can even be seen as the 'glue' that bonds the two sides to each other. They pass on comments and ideas to the staff and ensure that there are strong foundations within the team on which the implementation of the coach's ideas can be built. However, this does not mean that they are no more than the puppet or mouthpiece of either the team or the staff. Instead, their task is to facilitate the communication process. Something similar happens in the business world, where the middle managers serve as a bridge between senior management and the ordinary employees. At the same time, leaders within the team sometimes see and experience things that their coaches and managers do not see or experience. This gives them the opportunity to take the first steps that are necessary for the correction or improvement of the team. Of course, to make this possible they must have the trust of the coach or manager, which in turn implies that the latter must also be prepared to give up part of their leadership powers and share them with others.

 Steven Vanmedegael, the coach of the Knack Roeselare volleyball team, understands this: *'If I want to get something done, I first ask for the opinions of the leaders in the team. Before you can start with the full team, you need to get the experienced players on board. If you can do that, the others will automatically follow. I also regularly ask these leaders about other players and how they are feeling or progressing. I have one official captain, who has this indicated on his shirt. But I also have a second unofficial captain, who I use as and when the need arises, because I know that he wants everyone in the team to feel good. For me, it is interesting to have the option of turning to either or both of them. Because they are so different as people, they see different things. As a result, I can get them both involved in the running of the team.'*

In other words, **leadership can be borne on many different pairs of shoulders.** 'Trust' is the key word that makes this possible. This implies that you must also be willing to allow other people to have their moments in the spotlight. You trust them and feel safe enough to share the spotlight with them.

Top performers seek competition as a means to stimulate their own development

—— Growing together

As **Aisling D'Hooghe** explained at the start of this chapter, top performers do not have a problem with competition. They see the other practitioners of their sport as fellow travellers in their **developmental journey**. Making this journey is more enjoyable and more beneficial in company than making it alone. As a result, they seek out their competitors, whether consciously or not. They believe that they can grow together and help each other to reach the goals they have set. They never feel 'threatened' by others, because they know that ultimately everyone has to make their own journey in their own way.

 Jules De Sloover explains how snowboarders view their rival competitors: *'Even though snowboarding is an individual sport, we always train together in groups. I like to help others, whenever I can. Whatever the situation, I always want to motivate my friends to do better. You probably think that in competitions everyone retreats into their own little bubble but that is not the case. In that sense, snowboarding is an individual "togetherness sport". The people you compete with really play an important role in the way you snowboard and how you feel during the actual snowboarding. We are constantly giving each other tips and pushing each other on.*

Team sport and competition are inextricably linked with each other. For this reason, it is important to be able to deal with this competitive aspect; otherwise, the team's performance is likely to suffer. Top performers have the ability to put their **ego to one side** and think instead of the wider team goal. It is almost as if they board an imaginary helicopter, which allows them to view the situation from a greater distance. This encourages them to help, rather than to hinder.

For many years, **Hendrik Tuerlinckx** was a member of the Belgian national volleyball team: *'When I was selected for the national squad, I didn't always play. If I was sitting on the bench, I always tried to help the team mate who was playing in my usual position. We knew each other for more than ten years and always tried to make each other better. For example, I told him about the block options that could be used against him. After all, we both had the same goal: we wanted the team to win. Imagine, for the sake of argument, that a third player comes into the picture for our position, so that you might get dropped from the squad. If you react negatively to competition of this kind, the coach might think: "I'm not going to select that troublemaker!" Instead, he will probably pick someone who he knows is okay with sitting on the bench to help the team.'*

Competition sharpens a winner's mentality

Because of her talent, **Ambre Bellenghien**, now a top attacker in the women's national hockey team, never experienced competition as she progressed through the youth teams. The same was true during her early years with the Red Panthers: her talent always saw her through. When, however, she was not selected for the Red Panthers for the world championships in 2023 (just one year before the Olympic Games in Paris), she was forced to look in the mirror and be completely honest with herself. For the first time, she experienced doubt in her own ability and started to compare herself with her competitors. But it didn't help: *'So I decided instead to refocus on the things that I can control: my talent and my work ethic. That has now made me stronger than ever before.'*

Ambre is now grateful to her competitors, because they challenged her to become an even better version of herself. Competition can increase an athlete's motivation and improve her performance. Once again, this links in to the winner's mentality associated with top performers: they simply do not like losing. Their urge to win ensures that competition triggers their innate compulsion to never accept second best. Top performers use this to their advantage, either consciously or unconsciously. As a result, they can motivate themselves to extra effort, even at (or especially at) difficult moments. In other words, it is not only competition from other teams that helps you to improve; competition from inside your own team can have the same effect.

It has been scientifically proven that a (virtual) opponent can have a motivating effect, leading to a positive impact on performance. There is similar evidence to confirm that closing in on a rival you are chasing or pulling further away from a rival who is chasing you can likewise have a positive influence on your motivation (Konings & Hettinga, 2018). Likewise, there are studies which confirm that competing with someone who is better than you can also encourage you to raise your performance, although the difference in ability must not be too great. Even top performers who see that the difference between them and their rival is too great will be negatively influenced (Parton & Neumann, 2019).

Competition forces you to push your boundaries and prevents complacency

Facing competition not only **stimulates** improved performance in the present, but can also have a very positive impact on learning new techniques for the future. If you want to be better than the rest, you need to do things differently from the rest. Accepting the challenge posed by competition can be a kick-start for **innovation** in every sport. We will look at this more closely in the chapter on this specific attitude.

In one sense, competition forces top performers to re-invent themselves on a regular basis. It makes them train harder or perhaps even train differently. Competition also represents a challenge for athletes who are normally able to rely on their outstanding talent: without competition, it is possible that they would never feel impelled to improve further.

 Vincent Vanasch feels that as a goalkeeper he has a unique role on the field and he has also developed a special bond with the other goalkeepers in the national squad: '*The keeper is an essential pivot in the team. When you lose heavily, some players have a tendency to point the finger of blame at the keeper, rather than looking at their own performance. This is not always easy to accept. You are playing a team sport, but it often feels as though you are alone. As a result, you automatically have a connection with the second keeper. Loïc Van Doren and I train together, which makes us better and strengthens us both. I don't think that I will ever stop learning. I try to be the best version of myself that I can possibly be, although I realise that perfection does not exist. I always listen to Loic's feedback and I think that he listens to mine.*'

Scientific research has confirmed that competition stimulates the learning of new skills. Top performers have a constant need to learn new things, so that they can continue to match their rivals or even leave them behind (Passos, Araujo & Davids, 2016).

Top performers help others to raise their game

A team is as strong as its weakest link

It should be clear: top performers do not fear competition. What's more, competition also gives them a mission to make the people around them better. Even at a relatively early age, they understand that other athletes do not represent a threat, but can actually be a motor for their own further development. The higher the level of the athletes with whom they compete, the better they are able to progress themselves.

Vincent Kompany realised this early on in his career: *'I quickly understood that I wouldn't always be there or couldn't do everything on the field on my own. If my team mates performed well, we could still lift a trophy at the end of the season. But if the team and even the rivals for my position in the team did not perform well, we would win nothing. In other words, if the team performed well, even though I was not playing, I still had a chance of success.'*

Wanting to make others better has important consequences in team sports. Whereas 'ordinary' players want to keep the difference between themselves and their team mates as small as possible, for fear of not being picked for the team, top performers consciously seek to improve everyone's level of performance. They understand that it is also in their own interest that the team as a whole performs to the highest possible standard. Look at the teams that are currently at the top in their respective competitions. These are all teams where the performance of every player – and not just one or two – is outstanding. Even the substitutes bench is full of top-class replacements! These are teams that perform consistently well, time after time. Losing a player to injury or suspension will have no effect on them. Top performers will feel right at home in such a team, because they love to be challenged.

——— Team player mentality: there is no 'I' in team, but there is in win

An important condition for making a team better is that the team itself must be willing to welcome the opportunity. This requires a good **balance between leadership and coachability**. In this context, consider, for example, the phenomenon of social loafing, which can pull down the performance level of a team. An individual is guilty of social loafing when she tries to stay in the background and does less work than the rest of the team. In other words, this player surfs on the efforts of her team mates and is clearly not a team player. She does not feel any responsibility towards the team and its results.

Having said that, a form of behaviour that should not be confused with social loafing is giving your fellow team mates room to grow, so that they can also have their moment in the spotlight. As a footballer, this might mean giving an unselfish assist to your fellow striker, instead of trying to score yourself. Having a team player mentality of this kind is crucial if you want your team to grow.

Recognising and accepting that **your team is only as strong as its weakest link** is much more difficult if there are people in your team whom you would not normally consider as friends. One team that successfully made the transformation from a group of friends to an excellent team is the 4 × 100 metres relay team of Elodie Ouédraogo, Olivia Borlée, Hanne Mariën and Kim Gevaert.

 For **Elodie Ouédraogo**, the necessary change in mindset took about a year: *'Not everyone who arrives new in the team has the same agenda, and that is okay. Even so, in the beginning it was difficult. You had to keep on changing friends all the time. Then someone arrived who said that she didn't want to be friends with the rest of us. Overnight, that changed the dynamic completely! But the good thing is that even people with a different agenda eventually realise that your team is only as strong as its weakest link. I know that sounds cliché, but it's true: unless everyone is all pulling in the same direction, you can forget it as a team.'*

In your professional life as well it is also possible that you will find yourself in a team with people with whom you do not feel an immediate connection. In that case, it is crucial for the interests of the team that you put your differences to one side and focus instead on team performance and the goals you wish to achieve.

The desire to give something to others and help them to learn

What motivates top performers to make others better? Of course, there is the logical explanation that they understand that the team is only as strong as its weakest link. For most of them, however, there is something more involved than just pure logic. Our interviews revealed that elite athletes simply like sharing with others, although often they cannot explain why this is.

 Ex-basketbal player **Sofie Hendrickx** is a typical example. Making others better was already important to her during her active sporting career and is now equally important in her second career as a mentor to athletes who combine sport and studying: *'I find it rewarding to help bring out the best in someone and to create an environment in which that person can develop optimally. For me, it is very important that people feel good about themselves and are able to discover where they can go and what they want to do with their talent and the possibilities that are open to them. In today's society there is a lot of pressure on young people. It is crucial to find the right balance between committing fully to your sport and developing as a person. It gives me great satisfaction when I see young athletes blossom and grow.'*

One of the remarkable things about this desire to give is that it is largely given in the form of **feedforward** advice. Top performers often teach others important lessons – lessons that they themselves sometimes learnt the hard way – with the aim of preventing young athletes from making the same mistakes that they made. This does not mean that making mistakes is not okay. Some will inevitably happen. Even so, eliminating avoidable mistakes by sharing your knowledge is obviously a good idea.

Confronting team mates and giving feedback and feedforward

For some athletes **confronting team mates** can be difficult, whereas others find it easy. Top performers who are leaders in their team and want to make others better know that helpful confrontation is a key part of their role. They will always do this respectfully and with the best of intentions. Their sole aim is to improve both individual and collective performance. Giving feedback in a correct manner is essential for creating a safe growing and learning environment for others. The purpose behind feedback must always be to stimulate growth and development. If the recipients of the feedback can sense this, they will accept what you have to say.

Britt Herbots, a star attacker in the Belgian national volleyball team, is also a believer in the importance of feedback among team mates: *'One of the strengths of the Yellow Tigers is that we can be quite hard on each other out on the court and this is readily accepted. We are all working for the same goal and we know that we all need each other to achieve it. This means that we have to be willing to take criticism and tolerate differences in personality.'*

Experience shows that after giving feedback in the heat of the moment, it is important to later have a one-to-one conversation with the person concerned. This allows you to give context and clarification of your feedback and also shows that you treat your team mates with respect. You can be demanding, but respect and fairness are more important. Having the courage to **give feedback and feedforward with the intention of making others better** is one of the core competencies of a good leader. In the next chapter, we will look at the importance of accepting this feedback and feedforward in a positive way.

Out of balance

In our way of thinking about the development of high performance attitudes, there is an important basic principle that we wish to clarify. If you want to display and use these attitudes in the best possible way, it is important to realise that:
— you need to find a balance between showing either too much or too little of a particular attitude;
— the context in which you wish to perform will determine to a significant degree the opportunity and suitability of displaying particular attitudes.
On the page 'Coach yourself', you can use the dashboards to indicate whether or not you display the different aspects of the relevant chapter's attitude 'too little', 'optimally' or 'too much'. In this way, we hope to stimulate your self-insight.

Experience shows that before you can consistently display an attitude in an optimal manner, you will sometimes get things out of balance. This is not a problem, as long as you recognise the imbalance and adjust it to reflect the situation you are in. So that you are able to recognise your imbalanced behaviour, we will provide you with a list of the most common characteristics that indicate the display of too much or too little of the attitude.

Too little
lead &
make others better

Too much
lead &
make others better

You think too little about yourself: your strengths and points for development are blind spots for you.

You overanalyse yourself and start to have doubts.

You lack self-confidence, so that you find it difficult to lead others.

You are too full of yourself and are reluctant to accept the contributions of others, so that a distance is created between you and them.

You are only concerned with your own performance and goals and seldom look at others.

You pay too much attention to others, so that you forget your own roles, responsibilities and goals.

You prefer not to take responsibility and try to avoid all leadership roles.

You are intrusively over-present as a leader, constantly correcting others but without giving them space to make their own contributions.

You find it difficult to develop sustainable relationships with others, so that team performance suffers.

You are more concerned about others than yourself, so that you efface yourself to promote the development of those around you.

You experience the progress being made by others as a threat to yourself.

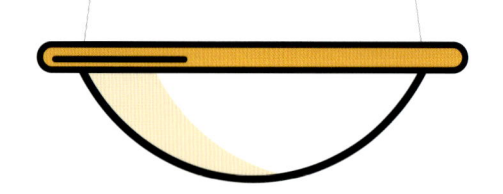
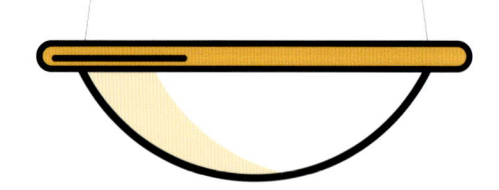

LEAD
& MAKE OTHERS BETTER

—— Describe your next ultimate victory!

....

....

....

STEP 1 Give yourself a score for the following aspects of this attitude.

- I am my own leader: I know myself, know where I want to go and I know which following steps will help me to get there.
- I am capable of building a team around me to pursue a common goal.
- I develop sustainable win-win relationships with others.
- I share leadership with others, taking account of our different strengths and weaknesses.
- I experience competition from others as being beneficial for my own development.
- I help to raise the performance of others to a higher level.

STEP 2 Indicate how important it is for you to further develop this attitude as a means to achieving your goal.

0 | | | | | | | | | **10**
(unimportant)   (very important)

STEP 3 Identify your challenges and your levers. (See part 2.)

—— My challenges: ....

—— My levers: ....

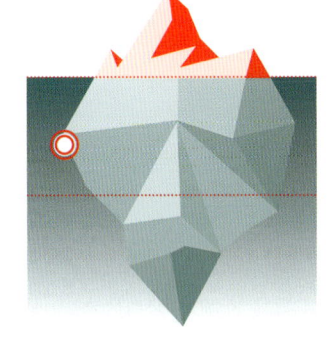

STEP 4 Identify your mental skills that will help you to deal positively with challenges. (See part 3.)

—— How will these mental skills help you?

....

....

STEP 5 Name the concrete actions you will take on the road towards your ultimate victory.

....

....

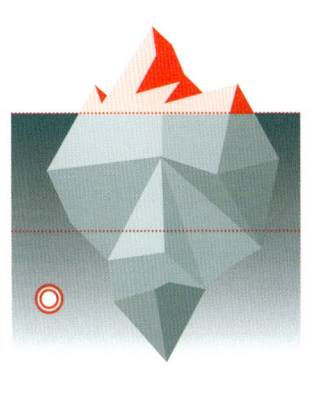

BE COACHABLE & FOLLOW

ATTITUDE 3

BE COACHABLE AND FOLLOW

'I think that you can always do better, can always improve. In my opinion, there is no such thing as a ceiling to your development. I am convinced that if you train well, carry out the required movements in the correct technical manner, are in a good place mentally and do your very best to make everything come together at the right moment, then there is no limit to what you can achieve. I am not saying that everything will be perfect, but I do believe that at such a moment you are capable of giving the very best of yourself. When that happens, magical things are possible. It is with this mindset that I am training for my next goal: reaching the final of the next Olympic Games.'

—— **Hanne Claes**, athlete

Definition

'Be coachable'

We describe this as an attitude through which someone demonstrates the willingness and the openness to improve their performance on the basis of self-reflection and advice given by others.

'Follow'

We describe this as an attitude that is characterized by a responsiveness that accepts the leadership of someone else.

Characteristics of top performers with this attitude

— They advocate life-long learning, believing that there are no limits to personal development.
— They voluntarily look at themselves in the mirror; they are curious and self-critical.
— They search proactively for feedback and feedforward.
— They can lead, but can also follow.
— They understand why they are doing something.
— They are mentally flexible.

Top performers are convinced that there is no limit to their development

—— Growth mindset and life-long learning

None of us can remember how we learnt to first crawl or walk. What characterized us as babies was our inexplicable compulsion to move forwards. Even if our initial efforts failed, we persisted. We took a breather, had a look around – and tried again. We searched for new learning opportunities and approached them boldly. **We have no recollection of whether we ever felt any doubt or fear.** We just kept on going, supported by the enthusiastic and unconditional support of those around us. Everyone was convinced that sooner or later we would 'master' what we were trying to do, so that our **ultimate victory** would become a fact. What makes this example so useful is that the process of learning to walk is regarded as a universal symbol for development and growth. Literally and figuratively.

Whether you are learning at school, in a sports club, at a music academy or even on the work floor or behind a computer in an online tutorial, it is your attitude that will determine how quickly and how completely you will absorb, process and use the information that is being offered to you. **Your mindset** and the way you think about learning really make all the difference, not only for your own development, but also for the development of others who you are mentoring.

In her book *Mindset*, the psychologist Carol Dweck describes two different kinds of mindset: the growth mindset and the fixed mindset. She argues that we all use both these mindsets, but as individuals we have a preference for one over the other.

People with a **fixed mindset** are convinced that qualities such as intelligence and athletic ability are inborn and therefore not learnable. No matter how hard you try, these qualities always remain the same and cannot be developed. As a result, people with this mindset place insufficient value on 'making an effort' and, consequently, will often neglect to develop their full potential. When they fail in a task, they see no point in trying again and again, concluding instead that the task is simply beyond their competence.

In contrast, top performers typically have a **growth mindset**. They are convinced that qualities like talent and intelligence can be developed and improved over time. As a result, they believe that no challenge is impossible and that everyone is capable of realising their full potential.

 Thibaut Vervoort, a leading figure in the Belgian 3x3 basketball team, has continued to develop himself, and not just in the technical and tactical domains of basketball: *'Personally, I devote plenty of attention to the psychological and mental aspects of professional sport. I love talking with people and elite athletes who I regard as a source of inspiration. I read a lot, watch documentaries and listen to podcasts, all with the aim of finding new insights that can help me to develop further.'*

TWO MINDSETS

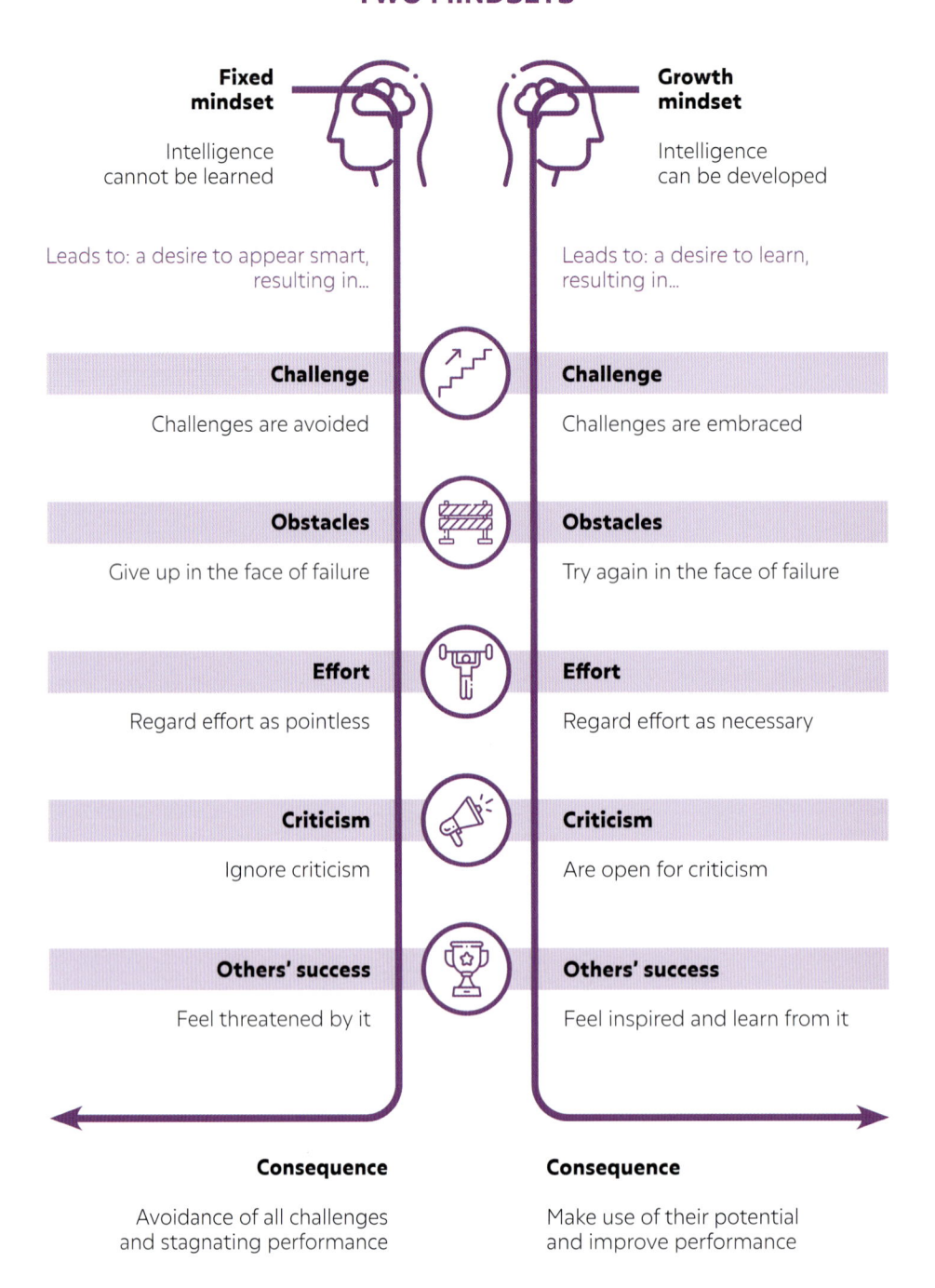

Fixed mindset

Intelligence cannot be learned

Leads to: a desire to appear smart, resulting in...

Growth mindset

Intelligence can be developed

Leads to: a desire to learn, resulting in...

Challenge

Challenges are avoided

Challenge

Challenges are embraced

Obstacles

Give up in the face of failure

Obstacles

Try again in the face of failure

Effort

Regard effort as pointless

Effort

Regard effort as necessary

Criticism

Ignore criticism

Criticism

Are open for criticism

Others' success

Feel threatened by it

Others' success

Feel inspired and learn from it

Consequence

Avoidance of all challenges and stagnating performance

Consequence

Make use of their potential and improve performance

Adapted from *Two Mindsets* (Dweek & Holmes, 2007)

Having a growth mindset ensures that top performers are constantly on the look-out for new learning opportunities. They are keen to acquire new skills and to sharpen up their existing ones. For this reason, they think about their development and search for ways that will allow them to make further improvement. They realise that they can learn not only from their successes, but also from their failures. This positive mentality continually pushes them forwards, helping them to devise innovative solutions for the challenging problems they face and further expanding their mental flexibility. **Top performers learn their whole life long.**

Scientific research has confirmed that people with a growth mindset invest more time in training than people with a fixed mindset. They love accepting new challenges, because they offer new possibilities for learning. Their constructive mindset also ensures that they show greater determination for longer periods of time and display more resilience when faced with setbacks (Kramaley & Wishart, 2020).

Having a growth mindset can therefore have a positive effect on the vision of top performers, because – as mentioned previously by **Hanne Claes** – it gives them the feeling that they have not reached the ceiling of their ability and performance.

 With her American team, **Emma Meesseman** won the WNBA and was chosen as the Most Valuable Player in the final series. In basketball, this is the equivalent of winning the world title. Emma explains how her passion for excellence and her growth mindset helped to make this possible: *'During the season in America, the games follow each other in quick succession. For this reason, the pace of training is lower than in other competitions. Although the coaches would prefer for me to rest after each training, I always like to do a little bit extra – although I usually have to insist before I get my own way. The coaches want me to rest to spare my body from the extra punishment, but I know myself very well and so I know when I need to stop. During this extra training I focus on the aspects of my game that can improve my individual performance. I really enjoy these individual sessions and I am open for anything that the coaches wish to suggest or pass on. I am convinced that this makes me a better player. And it also makes me a smarter player. If I now look back on the final, I can see me taking shots that I would never have taken in the past.'*

The mindset with which Emma trains, her desire to constantly improve and the way in which she is consciously occupied with her further development are the hallmarks of a top performer *pur sang*.

The good news for the rest of us is that a **growth mindset is something you can learn**. Through the upbringing you give your children or the manner in which you coach or lead, it is possible to influence the people in your environment in a positive way and stimulate them to develop this optimistic and pragmatic mindset.

Top performers dare to look at themselves in the mirror: they are inquisitive and self-critical

—— Self-evaluation

In the previous chapter, the importance of self-reflection and self-leadership for those wishing to achieve top performance was repeatedly stressed and the link between those two concepts was explained. If you want to perform at the highest level and constantly develop yourself further, you must also be capable of evaluating that performance critically and independently. Daring to look at yourself in the mirror and **evaluating** what you see as **objectively** as possible is part of this process. Top performers are sufficiently confident of their own ability that they can regularly focus on areas that still need improvement. They are not afraid to concentrate on these areas, because they know that this will help them to grow and perform even better.

With this search for constant improvement comes the realisation that there is no such thing as perfection. As already mentioned, there is no ceiling to growth. But there doesn't need to be. Self-development is not about complying with an **ideal image of yourself**; it is about becoming the best self that you can possibly be – and this best self will never be able to do everything perfectly. If, however, you dare to confront yourself and your shortcomings in all honesty, this will allow you to quickly take steps in the direction that will lead you to the best version of yourself. The importance of being proactively engaged with your own development and of making optimal use of these learning opportunities is something that was repeated time after time in our interviews with top performers.

In addition to critical self-appraisal, there are other ways that you can help to stimulate your own continued growth. Many top performers try to emulate what they see in other elite athletes. They **learn through observation** and imitation. Moreover, they do not limit themselves to examples from their own area of expertise, but frequently look at other disciplines or seek advice from experts. When they feel that they are approaching the current ceiling of their performance, they often analyse best practices from other sports, in the hope of raising that ceiling higher. They gather information from top specialists in other fields and check if and how this information can be amended and adapted for their own use.
Top performers also regularly reflect on their **goals**, modifying them when necessary and **identifying aspects** of their **talent and performance** that can still be better developed. They think in the long term and realise that self-scrutiny is a valuable technique that helps them to learn from their own experience.

Elite athletes need to understand the **underlying mechanisms** that can affect their performance both positively and negatively. For example, this might involve identifying the attitudes that you display too much or too little during your preparation and in competition. It is also important to remember that you should also self-analyse after your best performances, so that you can discover why you did so well.
For this reason, top performers assess both their individual and team **performances over a full cycle**: not just the competitive events, but also the preparation leading up to those events. In other words, you need to question yourself regularly about the actions you have taken today that can lead you towards your **ultimate victory** tomorrow.

Top performers go proactively in search of feedback

——— Proactively seeking expertise

In both the business world and the world of sport, the concept of the 'personal development plan' is still very much standard practice. The purpose of making such a plan is to trigger the individual concerned to self-reflection and action. Sadly, however, analysing your talent and points for further development in this manner is all too often seen as a necessary evil. The majority are too busy with other things and prefer to lose as little time as possible completing what is usually a pro-forma document rather than a real plan.

The conversations conducted in relation to PDPs often take place within the context of a **performance management** cycle. Based on the conviction that there is no limit to your growth and following deep self-reflection on your performance, you discuss with your coach or manager your current position, where you want to go and how you can get there. This is the moment when your coach or manager gives you feedback about your results, the way you do things and **how you can improve**. The main purpose is not so much to 'score' your performance, but also to highlight the steps that you still need to take and how this can best be achieved.

Although such conversations are crucial to the process of self-development, it is not always necessary for them to be formalised. Both in sport and in business, talking in an informal setting can sometimes work better, since it reduces any feelings of pressure and increases the willingness to accept feedback.

Even so, it will surprise no one that **learning to accept feedback** is also a **growth process** in its own right. It requires a certain degree of self-confidence to see the message contained in both feedback and feedforward. You must be able (and have the courage) to see that you have a good basis, but that some things need to be done differently, if you really want to reach the top. For truly outstanding performance, you need to develop the skills that will allow you to push your boundaries to their limits. The feedback from others helps you to identify those skills. Nevertheless, many people still experience feedback as an attack rather than constructive criticism, so that it feels more threatening than self-reflecting on yourself.

 Athlete **Hanne Claes** admits that even top performers need time to come to terms with this aspect of their coachability: *'Learning to spontaneously ask for and accept feedback is something that I have developed over the years, thanks in part to Ellen. In the beginning, I used to avoid feedback, because as a child I had always felt the need for confirmation. This is still an area of improvement, but I have learned – and am convinced – that feedback is necessary if I wish to continue developing.'*

The insight that uncertainty or doubt can sometimes be a by-product of feedback is important and should not be ignored. These are the growing pains that are inevitably associated with the process of self-development. You can compare this with muscle pain. Training hard and searching for your body's limits is also discomforting at first, both physically and mentally. However, recognising this discomfort as an indication of where you still need to do more work can also offer support. And if you do that work, after time the discomfort fades. Daring to **confront uncomfortable situations and truths about yourself** is never easy, but it is a necessary precondition if you want to be a top performer. We will look at this further in the chapter on innovation.

—— Learning from others

Top performers are inquisitive and go in search of people who can teach them something. They dare to ask questions and collect opinions. Strong opinions of your own are something that only you can develop, but those opinions will be much richer when you test them against the opinions of others that differ from your own.

For this reason, top performers who are willing to be coachable look at feedback in a fundamentally different way from others who are not happy to be coached. The growth mindset and curiosity of top performers, combined with their desire to improve, means that they will proactively go in search of feedback. They see this **feedback as a learning opportunity** and do not experience it as threatening.

Scientific research has also confirmed that people with a growth mindset experience critical feedback as more valuable than people with a fixed mindset (Cutumisu, 2019). This means that even though the story of a person's self-development might not necessarily be one of unbroken progress, top performers approach each new day with the intention of learning something new and moving another step forwards, however small. They absorb feedback and information from their environment like a sponge, even when it is not directly targeted at them.

 Antonia Delaere is one of the key players in the Belgian Cats and has been part of the team for many years. *'When you join the national team as a very young player, you come with the intention of learning a lot and you listen to everyone around you. Although my role in the team has now changed and I am now regarded as one of the experienced players, I still keep my eyes and ears open all the time. I still want to learn from everyone, even players who are younger than myself. When the coach gives feedforward or feedback to one of my team mates, I always try to see how that might be applied to myself.'*

A top performer wishes to continually improve in all aspects that relate to his chosen activity. Most of the elite athletes who we interviewed for this book have built up **a team of experts** around them for this purpose. They work together in a structured manner with a sport physiotherapist, a nutritional expert, and a fitness trainer, but this team can be temporarily expanded to include other experts in function of specific development needs.

 Fernando Oliva is a top athletics coach: *'As a coach, I learn every day from exchanges between people from different fields of expertise, but also from the athletes I train. Adopting a "Pharaoh" attitude as coach – in other words, "my way or the highway" – makes no one better.'*

Top performers never learn and develop in isolation, but through interaction with their entourage. This entourage forms an important part of the athlete's journey towards high-level performance and, in the end, their **ultimate victory**.

Measuring is knowing. This realisation now permeates all levels of society, including the business and sporting worlds. For example, you might collect details about how many hours per week you spend on e-mails and social media as a means to increase your efficiency. Or, as a hockey coach, you might get instant feedback about the amount of possession, number of shots, etc. of your team. In addition, coaches are nowadays supported by video analysts, who send through images on their i-Pads to illustrate passages of play, while medical data for individual players can be analysed to evaluate their levels of fitness, effort and performance. The coach can then use all this substantiated information to make decisions that can increase an individual's or a team's chances of winning.

In other words, technology is now an indispensable tool for increasing coachability. Figures that show in black and white an athlete's level of performance at any given moment in comparison with that athlete's best recorded level of performance cannot be ignored. Correctly measured statistics are an objective yardstick that force every sportsman and woman to face up to often unpleasant facts.

In professional sport, video analysis helps elite athletes and players to learn from themselves and from others. It can also help them to prepare for a confrontation with a particular opponent, without ever having faced that opponent before. The images give them an idea of what to expect. Moreover, the use of images as a learning tool for top performers is an excellent way to give feedforward. Of course, images of events and training can also be used to give feedback, but our proactive vision argues that giving feedforward is the better of the two options.

In the top teams that I guide as a sport psychologist, video images are used not only for tactical analyses, but also to give feedback or feedforward relating to the seven attitudes highlighted in this book. This can be done at both the individual and the team level. Image fragments are selected from game and event recordings in which certain attitudes were inadequately, excessively or optimally displayed. During workshops, the players are divided into small groups and watch different clips, which they are then asked to analyse. Having done this, they then show three clips to the rest of the team, on which they would like to concentrate during future training sessions. These clips might illustrate attitudes that were poorly displayed and that therefore need to be improved in subsequent competition. Equally, they might demonstrate the right attitudes that need to be perpetuated and, if possible, further strengthened.

In this manner, technology is used as a way to actively involve athletes with their own attitudes and development, both individually and as a team.

It seems likely that in the years to come technology and data tracking will be used even more. This will be a welcome development, providing we do not lose sight of 'what' we are measuring and 'why' we want to measure it.

——— Accepting feedback

Actively going in search of feedback from others, experts and even computer-generated sources is an important first step. However, the following step – which is of crucial importance in the learning process – is often overlooked: that feedback needs to be accepted and acted on.

Being given feedback and immediately thinking 'That is not true' will get you nowhere. **Accepting feedback** often requires you to look deep inside yourself. You must be prepared to make yourself vulnerable and to say that it is okay if there are some things that you are still not doing well enough. There is nothing wrong with admitting this to yourself. On the contrary, in time it will make you better, smarter and stronger.

Our ability to accept feedback often depends on how easily we think that we can implement it. If your boss gives you feedback on your presentation tomorrow and says that he feels that it would be more powerful for you to do this presentation in a completely new language, you will probably think: 'This is never going to happen!' And you would be right. Learning a language is a process that takes weeks or even months. And it can be years before you can speak it fluently.

This applies equally to mental training: it is a slow rather than a fast trajectory. You can certainly make rapid progress in a matter of weeks, but it will again take months or years before you have mastered the necessary techniques fully.

 Athlete **Hanne Claes** shares her vision on feedback: *'I find it more difficult to be given person-related feedback than sport-related feedback. Feedback over my technique or my tactics during a race is much easier to accept than feedback about my personality or attitude. This second kind of feedback is more confrontational, so that there is a greater likelihood that I will take it "personally". To deal with this in a positive way, I have learned to regard myself as a rough diamond: something that needs to be polished before it can truly shine.'*

Feedback and feedforward are both more quickly accepted when they are communicated in a positive way. This does not mean that feedback should consist entirely of compliments, but the comments and criticisms should be formulated in a positive manner. There is a world of difference between 'That's the hundredth time you have done it wrong and you still don't understand!' and 'Next time try it like this'. The first way is much less likely to be well-received, accepted and implemented. The second way will stimulate the desire to change and to master new skills and techniques. In other words, athletes require **constructive criticism** if you want to help them to become the best they can possibly be.

Top performers decide whether to follow – or not

Leaders and followers are inextricably linked with each other. After all, without followers there can be no leaders. It is the former who give a right of existence to the latter. Of course, the reverse is also true: we cannot speak of followers when there are no leaders.

Top performers alternate these roles, depending on the context. In some contexts, top performers opt to act as leaders, whereas in other contexts they are willing to make themselves coachable. Think, for example, of team leaders in cycling. For the entire season they are the number one figure in their team and all the other team members ride in support of them. But once the selection of the national team for the world championships is made, all this changes. Undisputed leaders in their own team now need to serve as water carriers for the team leader chosen by the national coach. And they are willing to do this because they all have the same higher goal: to win the race and have a world champion in their ranks!

Regrettably, the attitude that persuades people to be followers when the circumstances demand it is far too often painted in a negative light. Most of us like to see ourselves as leaders rather than followers. Followers are somehow seen as being less than leaders and nobody really wants this stigma. But how can you ever grow to become an excellent leader unless you first develop the qualities that are necessary to be a loyal follower? How can you understand how a team functions and what your followers need, if you have never been a follower yourself? Practical experience suggests that in an organisation it is better to find yourself somewhere in the middle between these two roles: if you want to perform well, you need to be flexible and demonstrate the attitude that is most required of you in the given situation.

 Britt Herbots puts it like this: '*One of the qualities of our Belgian volleyball players is the fact that we are "good foot soldiers". If they tell us to go left, we go left. If they tell us to go right, we go right. We follow what our leaders tell us and do it to the very best of our ability.*'

In other words: **there can be no good leadership without good followership.** The ability of the followers to perform their role correctly is just as important for success as the ability of the leaders to perform theirs!

Philip Mestdagh is the coach who turned the **Belgian Cats** into a high performing team. As an excellent leader, he is the first to say that he did not do this alone and that every player and every member of the team staff made a contribution. One of the main building blocks for success behind the Cats' historic qualification for the Olympic Games was the coach's firm belief that if you want to perform as a team, the different roles and responsibilities must be made crystal-clear, must be accepted by all – and must then be carried out exactly as agreed.

Once you are on the field of play, as a player you have no control over what spectators think about your performance or about you as a person. For this reason, top coaches expect that you will concentrate fully on the matters over which you do have control: your allotted role in the team. You must embrace this role, carry out the specific tasks given to you by the coach to the best of your ability, and do this with the right attitude. Finding this 'right attitude' will depend to a large extent on the demands of the context. On one occasion you may need to show more leadership. On another occasion you may need to display more boldness and initiative. **The more members of the team who understand, accept and execute their role, the greater the chance that the team will perform like a well-oiled machine.** Nothing illustrates this better than one of the crucial matches during the European championships when the Belgian Cats won bronze. During that game the coach decided to give one of the team's best players a purely defensive role, a role of the kind that most players would regard as 'thankless'. He did this to keep the opposing team's key player out of the game. If you want one of your own players to 'sacrifice' themselves in this way, how you communicate your intentions as a leader is crucial. You must explain the need for this role to the player in question, but also emphasise to the rest of the team that the perfect implementation of your plan will make all the difference. This will stimulate your player to rise above herself in her special role.

By constantly reminding your team of the importance of their roles, by explaining precisely what you expect of them and by showing how this will all contribute towards a positive team result, you can create the necessary clarity and ensure that your players embrace their roles and remain faithful to them. This will help the team to perform well at important moments on their road to success. As a sport psychologist, I have also seen instances where players find it difficult to accept the role given to them and have sometimes decided to leave the team for this reason. When that happens, it is right to express regret but the decision of the player in question must be respected, especially if it results in her missing, for example, a European championship. Not everyone is suited to the role of water carrier, even though this role is crucial. When a player realises that she is not ready to accept such a role, it is indeed better that she decides to help the team in a different way by being honest and having the courage to step out of the project.

The importance of the relationship between leader and follower

 Noor Vidts is a rising star in the world of the heptathlon. She describes her relationship with her coach as follows: *'There is mutual respect and trust between me and my coach. That trust was created and persists because my opinion counts and he is willing to listen to me.'*

As already mentioned, top performers proactively search for information that can help to improve their performance. They ask the advice of others, but also engage in self-reflection. They are open to constructive criticism and different opinions in the form of feedback and feedforward.

Our interviews with leading athletes revealed that in general top performers deal with this feedback and feedforward selectively. They listen and ask questions, following which they think critically about the answers they receive. They then consciously decide whether or not they agree with these answers and will implement the advice they contain. The relationship of the top performer with the giver of this advice has a strong influence on these decisions.

Trust, positive intention and expertise are the key words for determining a top performer's level of coachability. Whether as an athlete or as an employee, it stands to reason that most of us will be more open to coaching if our coach, manager or leader has these qualities. Top performers will only accept advice when they have full **confidence** in their coach. This confidence is the foundation on which the relationship can be further developed.

In this regard, the top performer's perception of the coach's **intentions** is also important. They must believe that the coach's feedback is being given with **positive intent**. If they do not believe this, they will not follow the advice. Once again, respect is key. Top performers will only accept a 'no' if they respect their coach and believe that he means well.

Expertise is the final building block in a strong relationship between coach and top performer, and its significance should not be underestimated. A coach can acquire expertise though his own scientific and academic background, through rich practical experience or through his own career as a former athlete. Some top performers have a preference for a particular kind of expertise, but the most important thing is that expertise in some form is available within their team set-up. Even when the three core conditions – trust, intention and expertise – are present in the relationship between coach and top performer, the athlete will continue to reflect critically and proactively. Using targeted questions and well-founded opinions, he will assess and re-assess the reliability of the advice he is given.

Thinking critically about feedback and deciding whether or not to follow it is a competence that develops with the age and level of expertise of top performers.

In this respect, scientific research (Barker-Ruchti, Rynne, Lee & Barker, 2014) has identified three phases in the development of an Olympic athlete. These athletes are often thrust into a professional elite sport environment at a relatively early age, frequently before they are 20 years old. In this first phase, they are mainly concerned with learning how to behave in this new environment. Young athletes of this kind are less inclined to challenge their coach. On the contrary, they accept what he says and try to implement it. In the second phase, the athletes are now familiar with their environment and become more demanding. They think more carefully about what works for them and what doesn't, and no longer follow the coach's advice blindly. In the third and final phase, the athletes know as well as (if not better than) the coach what is best for them and they are willing to take responsibility for their own actions. If they feel that the coach is not making the right decision, they say so and propose an alternative. The athletes interact consciously with their environment and seek to influence it. The length of time between these different phases varies from athlete to athlete.

 Noor Vidts: '*During the long jump at the world championships in Budapest, Fernando said: "Keep your run-up the way it is now". I had the feeling that the distance needed to be shortened, and so I changed it. This resulted in a better jump. Afterwards, Fernando said: "What I really like is the fact that you were able to make the decision yourself." This testifies to the level of trust in our collaboration. I can always discuss things with my coach and am actively involved in the final decisions we agree. At the same time, this helps me to take decisions independently when the situation requires it.*'

During the first phase, it is also important for the athlete to establish and retain a degree of **autonomy**. The coach can certainly guide the athlete during the introductory years of his sporting career at the professional level, but the athlete must also display a degree of self-leadership, since this is essential if he wants to develop more independently from the coach in later years. This may sound self-evident, but it can be a challenge for some athletes if they are (already) too coachable and have too much respect for the coach. Top performers spend countless hours with their coach, not just in training, but also in travelling to competitions and events. The closeness of this relationship can be both a strength and a challenge, depending on the people involved.

Top performers need to understand 'why' before they will follow

Let's take a closer look at the reasons why top performers are so critical. It is self-evident that top performers need to spend many hours of effort and practice before they can become an expert in their chosen sport or activity. Expertise is something that needs to be built up over time. It does not happen overnight. Analysing how top performers acquire this expertise is now a separate branch of performance science. The idea that you need ten thousand hours of practice to become an expert is not new. However, in recent years this concept has been adjusted, so that there is now a greater **focus on the quality rather than the quantity** of the hours of practice. It is the quality of your training or learning experiences that determine just how quickly you become an expert. The better the quality, the faster your progress.

Consider, for example, the internships of students in the business world. The purpose of these internships is to allow young men and women to take their first steps in developing expertise. It is the concrete content and not the number of their hours of training that will determine their level of expertise by the time they leave the host company. Interns who do lots of routine administrative work or (even worse) are made responsible for the daily coffee breaks and lunch orders will have had little or no opportunity for high-calibre learning. They will therefore arrive on the labour market with a lower level of expertise than other students who were allowed not only to observe experts at work, but also to take their own first tentative steps under the experts' guidance.

Ericsson (2007) carried out research into the way in which expertise is developed and the importance of the quality of training in the developmental process. He discovered that performance is not only the result of innate talent, but that the secret to excellence is also to be found in deliberate practice.

Deliberate practice is a highly structured activity that has the improvement of your performance as its specific goal. This requires continued evaluation, feedback and (self-) reflection. If you want to practise deliberately, you first need to be very clear about the expertise you wish to acquire. At the same time, the learning trajectory needs to be geared to your current level of expertise and to the next level (which Ericsson called the zone of proximal development). The learning tasks always go slightly further than your current level. Deliberate learning also demands a high degree of motivation, without which it will be difficult to make the efforts and sacrifices that acquiring expertise makes necessary. Last but not least, the practice trajectory must be monitored by an experienced teacher or coach, who can give effective feedback.

In addition to deliberate and high quality training, **knowing why** you do something is another crucial factor in helping you to reach the expert level. You need to be consciously aware of how and **why your actions** fit into the learning loop. Loop learning is a reflective form of learning. The very act of thinking carefully about your own learning process helps top performers to learn faster and therefore make progress more quickly.

Top performers learn in **three loops**. In the first loop they learn **what** they have to do. This involves observing and imitating the actions of others. In the second loop they learn **how** these actions work. This means that they no longer simply copy someone else's actions but adjust those actions to suit their body's own requirements. By understanding how actions work, they can implement them more effectively. In the third loop they ask **'why'** questions about the actions. Understanding why they need to practise specific actions helps top performers to internalise the process.

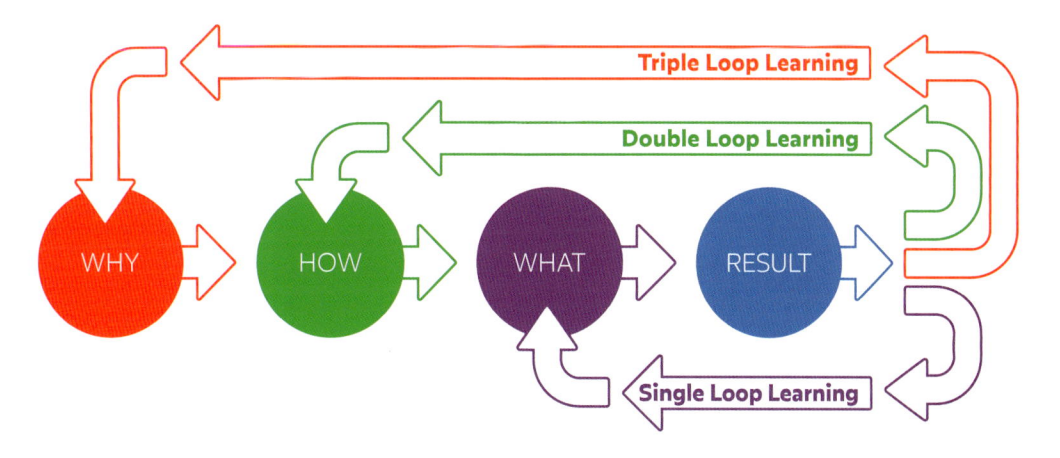

Engelbart, *Improving our ability to improve*, www.almaden.ibm.com/coevolutiory/pdf/engelbart_paper.pdf.
Simon Sinek, Start with WHY, www.startwithwhy.com.
Masterson, Clegg, Fung Federal Health Futurs, l.usa.gov/RLqa7b

 Kevin Borlée is a convinced loop learner: '*Our training sessions are always consultation moments. I don't just do things because I am supposed to do them. I need to understand. I need to know why we are adjusting certain aspects. This allows me to approach the training with a conscious focus and in this way I can make progress faster.*'

Learning something new is never easy, but if you know why you are learning it your willingness to learn and accept feedback will increase.

Top performers are mentally flexible

Whenever I mention the concept of 'flexibility' in the world of professional sport, many people immediately associate this with the physical abilities of the athlete. They think spontaneously about stretching or yoga techniques that will help to make the body more supple

However, flexibility is about much more than physical attributes. Top performers also need to possess **mental flexibility**. The world is evolving all the time and new technologies are constantly pushing us forwards. The popular cliché that 'standing still means going backwards' seems to get truer and truer with each passing year.

As an HR manager, I have seen restructuring plans follow each other in quick succession and as a sport psychologist I have witnessed how football managers are sacked one after another as the season progresses. Whether in the world of business or the world of sport, individuals and often entire teams need to **continually adjust to changing circumstances** if they wish to perform to the highest standard.

This means that they are constantly challenged to be flexible. This mental or cognitive flexibility can be described as the ability and the willingness of our brain to adapt our way of thinking and our way of behaving in response to new, changing or unexpected happenings. Top performers have a high degree of this **mental flexibility**. They learn faster and adapt more quickly to changes, new people and new situations. They approach challenges from a number of different positions and develop a number of different solutions for problems. They are more easily able to put themselves in other people's positions, which allows them to be more tolerant of mistakes. In this way, their mental flexibility can have a positive impact on their relationships and their efficiency.

 Basketball player **Thibaut Vervoort** is well aware of the importance of mental flexibility: '*When you join a new club, it is essential to find out everything you can about the habits, customs and culture of both the club and the country. I am currently playing for a club where only a few of the players speak minimal English, so that it is difficult to have deep conversations with my team mates about subjects like emotions. This means that when I am in a bit of a dip, I need to find other ways to pep myself up. Going abroad to play forces you to understand people in a different manner, to look at how and why they do things in a different way. The more you learn to understand a people and their culture, the more you can place their behaviour in its proper context and assess it critically.*'

Some people can adjust and **adapt more easily** than others. Personality, age and intelligence all have an influence on mental flexibility. There is also an element of 'the survival of the fittest' involved. Athletes, coaches and managers who desperately cling on to the old methods that have brought them success in the past are by no means guaranteed to be successful in the future. It may require additional effort to **think flexibly** and deal with new situations and people, but it always provides new **learning opportunities** that can lead to improved performance.

Cognitive rigidity is the opposite of mental flexibility. It has a number of different gradations, but if you wish to continue growing you will need to let go of your old certainties and embrace new people and new situations, rather than seeing them as a threat.
However, you need to be careful! Too much mental flexibility can also have a downside. Someone who instantly adopts all the latest trends and constantly changes his plans without communicating this properly makes it very difficult for his environment to follow him. In the sporting world, this can damage team performance. Imagine, for example, that a volleyball coach sees during the pre-match warm-up that the opposing team are planning to adopt a system different to the one he thought and therefore he decides to adjust his own strategy at the last minute. However, his players have trained all week in a particular formation that will now

need to be changed in a matter of minutes. Will they be able to cope with this new situation? If they can, it will be a triumph. If they can't, it will be a disaster. It is at moments like these that a coach needs to be able to assess the mental flexibility of his team.

Conclusion? If you want to adapt optimally to any situation, you need to find the right **balance between mental flexibility and mental stability**.

In the first chapter, we looked at the transition that elite athletes need to make at the end of their active sporting careers. For most of them, this means closing one chapter of their life and starting a new one, in which the development of new competencies will be necessary. Without good mental flexibility they will not succeed. Fortunately, the majority do not find themselves in this unenviable position, because a very high proportion of top performers have a growth mindset: learning new things and striving to become the best possible version of themselves is embedded in their DNA. At the end of their career, all that changes is the context in which the new learning now takes place.

Out of balance

In our way of thinking about the development of high performance attitudes, there is an important basic principle that we wish to clarify. If you want to display and use these attitudes in the best possible way, it is important to realise that:

— you need to find a balance between showing either too much or too little of a particular attitude;
— The context in which you wish to perform will determine to a significant degree the opportunity and suitability of displaying particular attitudes.

On the page 'Coach yourself', you can use the dashboards to indicate whether or not you display the different aspects of the relevant chapter's attitude 'too little', 'optimally' or 'too much'. In this way, we hope to stimulate your self-insight.

Experience shows that before you can consistently display an attitude in an optimal manner, you will sometimes get things out of balance. This is not a problem, as long as you recognise the imbalance and adjust it to reflect the situation you are in. So that you are able to recognise your imbalanced behaviour, we will provide you with a list of the most common characteristics that indicate the display of too much or too little of the attitude.

Too little
be coachable & follow

Too much
be coachable & follow

You believe in 'I am who I am' and use this as an excuse for not changing.

———

You only trust your own knowledge, insights and experiences and are not open to the opinions of others.

———

You never accept other people's feedback and never think about how you might do things differently.

———

You cannot make yourself vulnerable and put the blame for failures on others or external factors.

———

You find it difficult to accept all forms of leadership from others. You cast doubt on everyone and everything.

———

You find it difficult to function in a team or to accept a particular role and the responsibilities that go with it.

———

You find it hard to adapt to new situations and people, so that you have trouble integrating.

Your thoughts and actions are totally dependent on the people around you, so that you lose all sense of your own identity.

———

You attach more importance to the knowledge, insights and experiences of others than you do to your own.

———

You listen to everyone who gives you feedback, causing you to doubt your own opinions and actions.

———

You make yourself vulnerable and put the blame for failures squarely on yourself.

———

You always accept whatever others have to say, without assessing it critically.

———

You behave too subserviently in a team and accept all the roles and responsibilities given to you, even if they do not match your abilities.

———

You constantly adjust to new situations and new people, so that you always put others first to the detriment of your own position and interests.

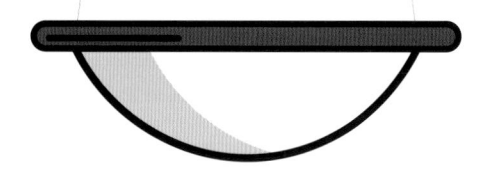
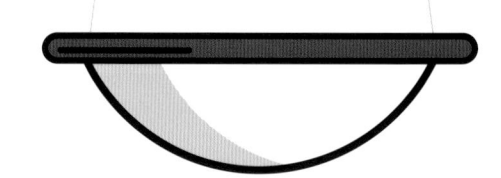

Coach yourself!

Describe your next ultimate victory!

....

....

STEP 1   Give yourself a score for the following aspects of this attitude.

- I am convinced that there are no limits to my development potential.
- I am capable of self-criticism and can identify my own strengths and points for further development.
- I search in a proactive manner for feedback and feedforward.
- I can accept the leadership of others but decide for myself whether to follow them or not.
- I am fully aware of my learning process and know why I develop certain aspects and not others.
- I am mentally flexible and can adapt easily to new people and new situations.

STEP 2   Indicate how important it is for you to further develop this attitude as a means to achieving your goal.

0									**10**

(unimportant)   (very important)

STEP 3   Identify your challenges and your levers. (See part 2.)

My challenges: ....

My levers: ....

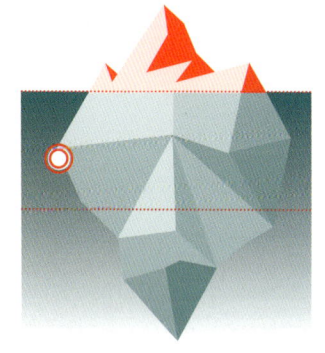

STEP 4   Identify your mental skills that will help you to deal positively with challenges. (See part 3.)

How will these mental skills help you?

....

....

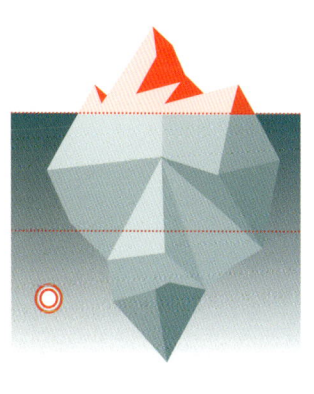

STEP 5   Name the concrete actions you will take on the road towards your ultimate victory.

....

....

ATTITUDE 4

INNOVATE, DARE AND REPEAT

'I am only 21, so I have plenty of room for further improvement. Why am I already a Red Devil and playing for one of the top clubs in the Premier League? Because ever since I was young I have had the courage to try new things and to keep on repeating them until they work. I dare, I create and I learn. That makes me different – and I like being different.'

—— **Jeremy Doku**, footballer

Definition

'Innovate'

We describe this as an attitude through which a person develops the ability to view a situation from different perspectives and to think creatively and innovatively about how to provide solutions.

'Dare & repeat'

We describe this as an attitude that is typified by a person's willingness to step repeatedly out of their comfort zone and to take the necessary risks that will increase their chances of achieving sustainable success.
Both these attitudes are further characterised by openness and a readiness to deviate from the standard plan, preferring instead to follow intuitive insights that make it possible to seize any opportunities that present themselves.

Characteristics of top performers with this attitude

— They dare to be themselves.
— They trust their own intuition.
— They are creative and open to new ideas.
— They are prepared to leave their comfort zone and proactively seek new challenges.
— They take calculated risks.
— If something fails, they try again until it succeeds.

Top performers dare to be themselves

—— Be yourself, everybody else is already taken

Being completely yourself is never easy. It requires a certain amount of vulnerability. We make ourselves vulnerable to others, giving them the chance to criticise who we are as a person. By revealing our true selves – warts and all – we run the risk that we will not receive everyone's approval.

Of course, we human beings are also social creatures; we want to be part of a group. And, consciously or unconsciously, we adopt certain aspects of the groups to which we belong. Think of the different groups in which you move each week. You behave differently at home than at work, and differently at work than in your sports club. Different contexts appeal to different aspects of your personality, but remaining relatively close to who you are in all circumstances will be the key to performance in each of your different environments.

 Jeremy Doku, a rising star at Manchester City and for the Red Devils, views it in these terms: *'If you are being yourself but, as result, you see that you do not fit in with the group, you should not think that this is your fault. Just find other friends who appreciate you as you are. End of story.'*

The fear of being rejected by others will be less strong when you are completely yourself. Moreover, **daring to be yourself** will ultimately give you access to groups in which you truly feel fantastic. These groups, as Jeremy Doku says, appreciate you for who you really are, and not a version of yourself that you hope others will like. In this respect, realising and accepting that not everyone will want to go along with your story is important. **We all have our own unique journey towards our ultimate victory and it is inevitable that some people will not like the route you have chosen to follow.** By remaining true to yourself, your feeling of control will gradually grow, allowing you to exude greater self-confidence and perhaps convince or even inspire more different people to join you as you head towards your goal.

In other words, daring to be yourself means accepting yourself as you are and basing your further **development on your own strengths and qualities**. You need to be 100% authentic.

 Basketball player **Thibaut Vervoort** explains how he got his nickname: 'must see TV': *'On the 3x3 circuit, it is often said that my style of play is not like anyone else's. I always give 110 percent, dare to take important shots at key moments and play better the more pressure I am under. I believe that is why I was chosen by the International Basketball Federation as an ambassador for our new and rapidly growing sport.'*

Consider, for example, the matter of powerful emotions. Your powerful emotions and the way they can influence your performance could potentially form a stumbling block as you move towards your **ultimate victory**. But instead of trying to push these emotions to one side – thereby effectively denying a part of who you really are – try instead to embrace them, control them and convert them into your greatest strength. These powerful emotions can help you: they set you apart from others. Discovering how you can develop them represents an important step, not only in your process of self-fulfilment, but also in your journey towards your **ultimate victory**.

The sport world and the business world are both dynamic environments in which people are constantly looking for new innovations. The purpose of innovation is to gain an advantage over your competitors. Your uniqueness as a person is such an advantage – and one that no one can imitate. Being more than or different from everyone else can give you an important competitive edge. Remember, however, that your uniqueness consists of both strengths and weaknesses. Learning how to use them effectively to your benefit will put you ahead of the rest.

——— Stand for what you think and what you do

In his book *The Five Dysfunctions of a Team*, **Patrick Lencioni** sets out the basic principles that a team must follow if it wants to perform outstandingly. He also stresses how important it is to be authentic and vulnerable in your relationships with others. In his opinion, a team can only be high-performing when the team members have full confidence in each other and succeed in breaking through what he calls artificial harmony.

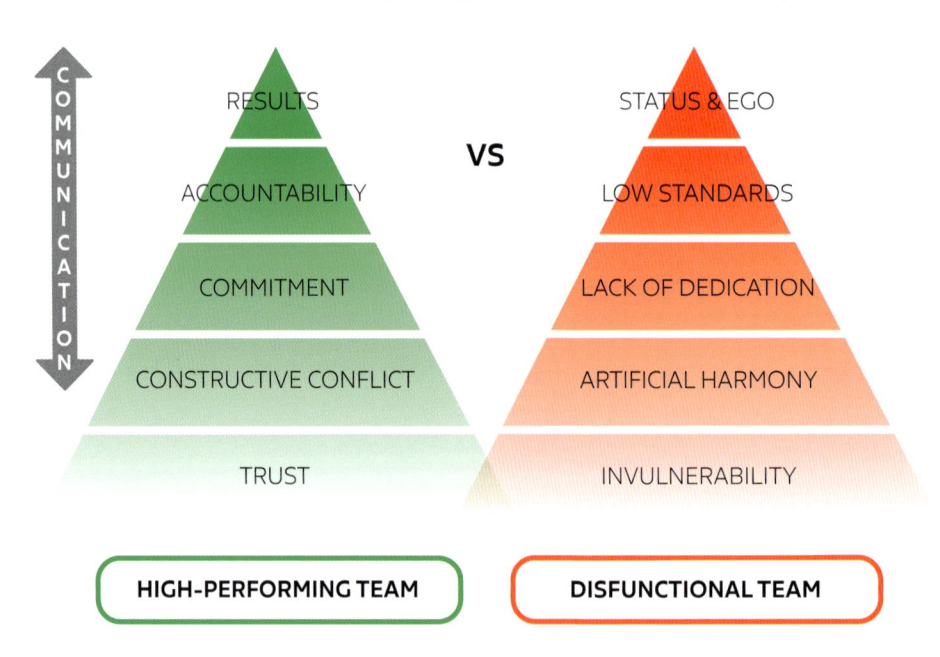

Artificial harmony can be described as a condition in which the members of a team create a 'fake' form of unity and do everything they can to preserve its illusion. Within this artificial harmony, the players do not dare to talk about important themes for fear that their opinions will be misconstrued by the other team members. This lack of mutual trust has a negative impact on team performance. In reality, it is the opposite approach – daring to express your opinions, disagreeing with others and having fierce but respectful discussions – that leads to better decisions at the team level.

Whether you are active in the world of sport or the world of business, just open your diary and check the number of team meetings that you are expected to attend. These meetings are collaborative moments that are intended to bind, inspire, motivate and activate the team members. Far too often, however, you will note that such meetings have the opposite effect.

Perhaps the meetings seem pointless because they are not used effectively to communicate about previously taken decisions? Or because they are a one-man show, dominated by a single person? The origin of these and every other reason for this kind of disillusionment is to be found in the more general state in which the team is locked: a state of artificial harmony. Artificial harmony arises when no one is prepared to make themselves vulnerable.

Artificial means false, not real. Each team member erects his own wall, behind which they hide. They do not dare to be themselves or to stand up for their opinions. As a result, the relationships within the team are largely superficial. Consequently, the level of commitment will also be lower, which will be reflected in the quality of the end results.

But it doesn't have to be like that. When sufficient trust is present within the team, everyone will dare to be themselves. In this way, constructive conflicts will be able to develop, during which all the players will feel free to express their true opinions. This increases the level of commitment and accountability of the entire team and will help to ensure that its individual members are all pulling in the same direction.

This is what distinguishes top performers from the rest: they have the necessary courage to be themselves in all possible circumstances, even when they feel that the context and the environment in which they find themselves will expose them to many significant challenges. In short, **They stand for what they think and do.**

 Jeremy Doku also understands the importance of being yourself at all times: '*After my first game with City, I didn't feel good about my performance. I came to the conclusion that "I wasn't myself". I hesitated too much, thought too much about what people would think of me. In the next game, I decided to play to my strengths. After all, that was why Pep had brought me here from Rennes. In the next game I showed much more what I am made of.*'

The message is clear: be yourself, be true to your core values, principles and ideas, and have the courage to stand up for them at all times. By acting **authentically**, you increase the likelihood that you will be genuinely appreciated by the environment in which you find yourself. This will require you to make yourself vulnerable, but this can also serve as a source of inspiration for others. Because you are being fully yourself, this will make them feel comfortable, so that they can have the confidence to be fully themselves as well.

Top performers trust their intuition

We seldom have more difficulty finding the right words than when we try to explain to others the choices that we have made on the basis of a certain gut feeling: our intuition.

There are different versions of the definitions of the words 'intuition' and 'instinct'. There is still no clear consensus about what they mean and their processes are hard to explain. We can see that animals and children are often in closer touch with their intuitive sense and that as we get older we learn how to suppress this sense, because reason and logic increasingly take a more prominent role in our daily functioning. Even so, intuition continues to ensure that we can deviate from the 'plan' or what is normal, when we feel that this is necessary. In this way, intuition brings us back closer to our authentic self. And it is this willingness to act intuitively that gives top performers their uniqueness and sets them apart from the rest. **When intuition takes over, magical moments can result, both in the sporting arena and on the work floor. At such moments, we create, innovate and excel**.

Recent research into the elite youth teams of top football clubs in England has revealed that these clubs attach great importance on the extent to which their young players display creativity. The physical differences between players get smaller as they get older, so that creativity becomes an ever-greater determining factor in achieving a superior level of performance (Hendry, Williams & Hodges, 2018).

As already mentioned, it takes courage to be yourself all the time and to deviate from the agreed plan. It also takes courage to trust in the reliability of your intuition. Experience and past successes based on intuitive choices are important in developing this trust. And just as your **ultimate victory** is not only about winning gold medals, so these past intuitive successes are not only about performance. Remaining true to yourself is also a success, even if it is not objectively measurable.

 Jeremy Doku: '*At my best, I play and decide "in the moment". I observe and feel what is happening and adjust accordingly. I don't like planning. That puts a brake on me, causing me to think too much, so that I lose part of my creativity and speed.*'

Our experience with elite athletes has taught us that those who rely heavily on their intuition are also the most observant and perceptive. They instantly pick up any changes in their environment and, thanks to their powers of empathy, are highly receptive to the emotions of others. For example, they can sense when people in their immediate surroundings are tense. Subtle changes of this kind are not noticed by everyone, but they generate in top performers a certain kind of feeling, which gives them a stronger connection with the emotional side of their character, in which they are prepared to trust.

Of course, it is possible that you will feel safer if you put your faith in logic and figures or if your intuition tells you that you should not deviate from the plan. It also needs to be remembered that intuition is not everything. In a top team it is important to have a balance between individuals who are highly creative and can think out of the box and individuals who are more predictable and conservative.

But one thing is certain: if you are going to follow your intuition, make sure you follow it 100 percent. **Have the courage to give it everything you have got and believe that you can make the difference by being yourself.**

Top performers are open to new ideas and are creative

Some players can read the game quicker than others. According to **Pascal Kina**, coach and sporting director of the La Gantoise hockey club, this game insight – also referred to as 'vista' – is the combined result of the player's passion and ability for the sport in question. Top performers are often passionate about their chosen sport from an early age, as a result of which they unconsciously 'record' endless hours of sporting observations in their head. As children, they watch the games of their heroes on television. Later, they play their own games and, thanks to video analysis, can even replay fragments of them. The attitude of displaying courage – daring to be themselves – will be a decisive factor in determining whether a player can effectively show and develop game insight. Courage is also necessary to give expression to your insight and creativity at key moments in the game.

 Thibaut Vervoort: '*Basketball and 3x3 basketball might seem like the same sport, but their respective rules mean that they are played totally differently. The 3x3 concept pushes you continually to make fast decisions. You can only do this effectively by playing to your strengths and daring to use them. In 3x3, you can't hide behind four other players and this helps to stimulate creativity and a willingness to take risks.*'

Creativity of this kind is crucial for developing yourself and your potential. Using new equipment, applying new techniques, copying ideas from other sports: these are all part of the development process. If you want to keep ahead of your competitors, you need to be a trendsetter in your sport. Of course, following the rules of that sport will always be necessary, but this should not prevent you from occasionally trying to colour outside the lines. That is what makes others really sit up and look!

Research involving Olympic athletes has shown that they are creative and innovative. This helps them to stay one step ahead of their rivals. You simply cannot do what everyone else does and expect that your performance will be better than all the rest (Phillips, Davids, Renshaw & Portus, 2010).

Before you can introduce innovation and creativity into your sporting or working environment, it is, of course, crucial that you have first fully mastered the basics of your sport or profession. In other words, the people who introduce innovations are often experts. They set the tone for others, allowing them to keep ahead of the game. It can sometimes seem as though innovation comes easily and naturally to these experts, but appearances can be deceptive. Certainly in professional sport, what the top performers do often seems very simple, but in reality their 'simple' performance is the result of years of dedicated training. To make exceptionally difficult things seem simple requires an exceptionally high level of performance.

Top performers also bring new innovations into their sport in different ways. They do not easily accept the status quo and are constantly on the look-out for creative solutions to the challenges that face them. Thanks to their growth mindset, they regard these challenges as opportunities, not threats.

Vincent Vanasch, the best hockey keeper in the world, does this kind of thing regularly. When he, Jérémy Gucassoff and the staff of the Red Lions realised that there were no real rules to determine the maximum length of the keeper's stick, they decided to use a longer stick during penalty shoot-outs. This was a huge success, since other countries were not prepared for dealing with this changed situation. The international federation eventually introduced new regulations for stick length. As Vincent says: *'When you are at the top, it is necessary to constantly reinvent yourself if you want to stay there.'*

The challenge for top performers is to find the right balance between innovation on the one hand, while retaining a firm hold on the basics of their sport on the other hand. If you want to build further on your talent, you always need solid foundations and at some point it becomes difficult to keep on building and innovating. Finding this right balance is not always easy, certainly in a society that increasingly places the focus on individualisation and uniqueness. This often leads 'simple' to being negatively equated with 'everyday'. **So be warned: do not make things unnecessarily complex for yourself. The simplest solution is sometimes the most efficient one.**

Top performers leave their comfort zone and enjoy the discomfort

As already mentioned, elite athletes are constantly searching to push the boundaries of their sport by introducing new innovations. At the same time, this allows them to push their own personal boundaries. **It takes courage to step out of your comfort zone in this manner, so that you start to feel discomfort instead.** This is not simply a question of physical discomfort – for example, because you are pushing your body to its limits – but also mental discomfort, because everything feels unfamiliar or because there are some things that you still do not dare to do fully.

Before we look in more depth at the ways in which athletes leave their comfort zone, it is also important to understand the context in which this takes place. **The first precondition is that your environment is actually prepared to let you step outside your comfort zone and learn new things**. In other words, the context must be sufficiently safe to allow you to experiment, with the risk that you might at first fail. You must be given the necessary time to practise and grow. In these circumstances, the coach must place emphasis on the process, not on immediate results. Only then will you be able to search for your limits in safety. In contrast, it is very difficult to leave your comfort zone in an environment that punishes daring and innovation. Without the support and understanding of those around you, combined with a belief that the learning process is more important than short-term outcomes, you will not get very far.

Scientific research has also confirmed that innovative and creative behaviour is displayed significantly more in environments that encourage such behaviour (Vaughan, Mallett, Davids, Potrac & Lopez-Felip, 2019).

Let us assume, then, that your environment is safe and supportive. What exactly is the comfort zone that you now wish to leave? In practice, there is no such thing as a single comfort zone. Everyone has a different comfort zone. For one person, speaking to a large audience might be well inside their comfort zone, whereas for someone else this is a cause for instant panic. In other words, we all have our own individual comfort zone and it is evolving all the time. But whatever its boundaries, you will need to step across them regularly if you ever want to stimulate your personal development.

It therefore follows that learning new things and leaving your comfort zone are closely linked. Inside your comfort zone, you learn relatively little, precisely because you seldom do anything new. When you leave that zone, you come into what is known as the stretch zone. This is where you learn the most new lessons. The stretch zone is still a safe learning environment and one that gives you a positive feeling while you are experimenting. Leaving your comfort zone can often feel strange, so it makes sense to take small steps at first. In other words, you gradually stretch your comfort zone. Taking big steps risks bringing you too quickly into the so-called red zone, which leads to stress. If you are overstressed, you will learn nothing. It is just as fruitless as taking no steps at all.

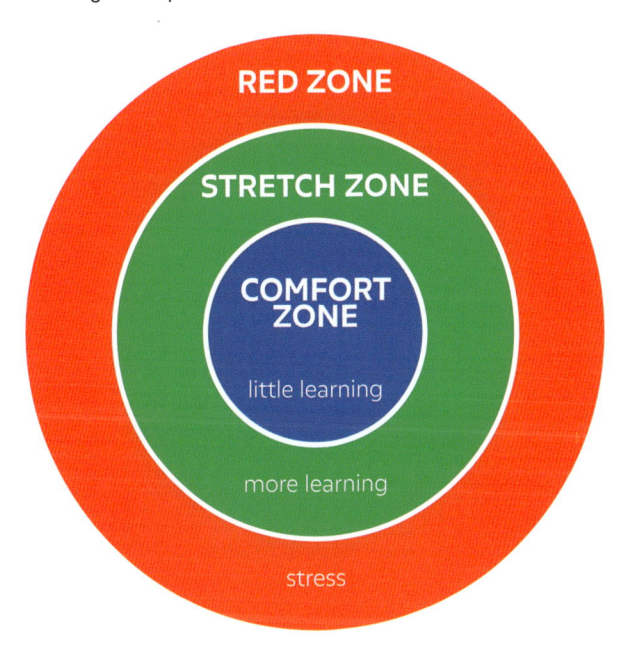

Think back to how your learnt to ride a bike. At first, you probably began with a walk bike or a three-wheeler. Then it was time for your first proper bike, but with stabilisers. Once you were ready for the stabilisers to be taken off, your parents still ran behind the bike with a hand on the saddle, to help you keep your balance. Gradually, they let go of the saddle for short periods, so that you could get used to the feeling of riding alone. Perhaps you sometimes asked them if they were still holding on, because you were not yet fully convinced that you could ride solo. Inevitably, there were moments when you fell, but this did not stop you from getting up and trying again... With small variations, this is the process that most of us went through. But one thing is certain: our parents did not buy us a racing bike and immediately expect us to climb Mont Ventoux! This would have been far beyond our capabilities and might have put us off cycling for life.

Feeling too much stress and anxiety can be a sign that you have entered your red zone. In this zone you are too far from anything that makes you feel comfortable, so that negative emotions start to dominate your thinking. This, in turn can have a negative impact on the outcome of your actions. Of course, it does not have to be like that. Experiencing the right kind of tension can also generate positive emotions.

 Snowboarder **Seppe Smits** knows when he is in his stretch zone – or risks leaving it: '*For me, being daring means turning fear into adrenalin. But there is only a certain level of fear that you can convert into adrenalin in this way. Perhaps some people can convert more than others, but I know that I have a certain limit and when I feel too afraid to try a new trick I know that I have reached that limit.*'

If we look more closely at ways you can enter your stretch zone, it becomes clear that top performers have two preferred methods for doing this. They seek either physical or mental discomfort.

 As far as pushing mental boundaries is concerned, hockey player and Red Lion **Emmanuel Stockbroekx** has noted that his comfort zone has expanded over the years: '*I now no longer have a problem with many things that I used to find uncomfortable. For instance, talking to Ellen about the challenges that I was facing at certain moments in my career required me to make myself vulnerable. At first, it felt uncomfortable talking to a relative stranger about personal things, but not anymore. And the process has more than proven its worth in the long run.*'

To take steps towards your **ultimate victory**, it is crucial to increase your comfort zone by doing things in your stretch zone. But remember that you can only achieve your **ultimate victory** if, at some point, you are prepared to leave that comfort zone.

Top performers take calculated risks

Leaving your comfort zone is easier when you know yourself through and through. This brings us back to the importance of self-knowledge and self-confidence, which we discussed in chapter 2.

In his book Think and Grow Rich, Napoleon Hill describes the six basic fears. These fears prevent us from stepping out of our comfort zone, because each fear is associated with certain risks and possible consequences:
  — the fear of material loss or losing what you now have;
  — the fear of criticism and the opinions of others;
  — the fear of physical pain and illness;
  — the fear of rejection or not being liked;
  — the fear of getting old, losing your youth and deteriorating both physically and mentally;
  — the fear of death.
If you can identify the origin of your fear, you should be able to cover the associated risks. Let's return to the example of giving a presentation to a large audience. If your anxiety is

rooted in your fear of being rejected, it can be a good idea to practise the presentation on your family and take account of their feedback. Alternatively, you could record yourself and assess how you come across to others, making any necessary adjustments. Techniques like these increase your self-knowledge, which in turn should increase your self-confidence about giving the presentation.

One or more of the six fears play a role for all of us in our (un)conscious decisions to remain in our comfort zone. But if you want to achieve your **ultimate victory**, you must overcome these fears and leave the zone anyway. Top performers try to step out of their comfort zone every single day. They do this by taking risks, but they are calculated risks: reckless behaviour is not part of who they are.

 Heidi Rakels is a former judoka who founded the company Guardsquare with her husband. The company has won numerous awards and in no time became a trendsetting reference in the field of mobile application security. Heidi has clear views when it comes to risk-taking: '*We think we are risk-averse, whereas others think that we have taken lots of risks. What typifies us, however, is our way of thinking: we always ask what we must do to maximise our chances of success. Once we have decided this, we cover the risk as best we can, so that none of our decisions are reckless. There is always balance.*'

Heidi shows us here just **how important it is to find a balance between seeking and taking risks on the one hand and remaining true to your basic plan on the other hand**. When you are part of a team, it is even more important not to take headstrong and impulsive decisions. And, in essence, most of us are part of a team in one way or another: at work, in our family, when playing sport, and so on. In these circumstances, the decisions we take as individuals have an impact on the team, so that you need to bear this in mind when assessing the risks.

For example, it is not a good idea to surprise your team with something new and unexpected that has not been previously discussed. If you do this, it can have negative consequences for the cohesion of the team over time: your decision to deviate from the plan without consultation might encourage others to do the same, creating a snowball effect of individual initiatives that leave the agreed team plan in tatters. One possible solution for this is to appoint certain players as 'risk-takers' at crucial moments. For example, the **Belgian Cats** have two world-class guards or play-makers. Each of them has her own strengths, which the coach can seek to exploit, depending on the needs of the game and the qualities of the opponents. One of these guards is excellent at rolling out the agreed game plan and keeps to the structure and vision set out by the coach. The other guard is more creative and plays more intuitively, so that she is brought in by the coach at moments when the game plan is clearly not working. When this happens, the Cats need something different, something out of the box, a player who can shake things up depending on the actual situation she sees in front of her. This way of playing is riskier than sticking to a game plan, but it has helped the Cats out of tight corners more than once.

Making clear agreements in the team can help to avoid confusion as a result of deviation from the normal plan. Involving those around you in assessing the risks involved with any such deviation is also a very good idea. This allows you to use both your own experience and the experience of others to evaluate what might go wrong, how and with what consequences.

Your environment plays an equally important role with regard to the perception of risks. Taking risks is only really dangerous when top performers are not surrounded by the right people or when they rely on bad advice.

A study that examined the training and performance of professional gymnasts concluded that an environment that regularly encouraged them to ignore pain led to more injuries. They were persuaded to take risks in pushing their physical boundaries, but in more cases than average their body could not take the additional strain (Cavallerio, Wadey & Wagstaff, 2016).

One of Napoleon Hill's basic fears is fear of physical pain. This is a type of pain with which elite athletes are familiar. Their body is one of their most important weapons, which means that they need to treat it with care. That being said, in the search for game-changing innovations, it will always be important to search for the limits of your body and dare to push them a little further each time.

From our interviews, it is apparent that young athletes are not always aware of the risks that professional sport involves. They often have their first major injury before they realise that they are not invincible and have limits to what they can do. Dealing with injuries will be discussed at more length in the next chapter, but estimating the likely risk of injury is an important aspect of our 'dare' attitude. Making a poor estimate can have far-reaching consequences for the rest of your career.

 Snowboarder **Seppe Smits** explains how his vision on risk has changed over the years: *'I now try to train in a more structured way and take more calculated risks than in the past. In snowboarding, you learn by experience what kind of person/ rider you are, how you can best train, what are your strengths and weaknesses. I try to build on this experience. I now take far fewer risks in training than in the old days. I have learnt to understand that I don't need to do reckless tricks to achieve a high level of performance.'*

In essence, Seppe is here emphasising the coherence that needs to exist between the attitudes 'Work Smart' and 'Dare'. In his case, achieving this balance has resulted in two world titles.

Top performers dare to try again, even if they failed at first

Imagine: you have thought carefully about all the possible risks and have still decided to try something new. As a result, you take your first step outside your comfort zone. What happens? You fail! What is your immediate reflex: try again or give up?

If you have the growth mindset that we discussed earlier, it is better to try again. Learning is a process of ups and downs. Having said that, **trying again after a failure demands courage.** Your entourage has often witnessed this first failure, which for some people makes the second effort even more difficult. And let's be honest: the idea that there will be others who like to see you fail is all too real! Even so, it is important that you do not give up after a first failure. Try and distance yourself slightly from the situation and refocus on your goal. Remember that you want to push your boundaries and achieve your **ultimate victory**.

Jeremy Doku, footballer: *'When a dribble doesn't work, I make an instant analysis. What went wrong? But because I know that dribbling is my strongest point, I know how to adjust – and so I try a new dribble at the next available opportunity.'*

When we think of top performers, we think of experts in their chosen fields. They are authorities and trendsetters who cannot be ignored. But when you look at their careers, you can often see that these are the people who had the courage to make the most mistakes. The only difference between them and everyone else is that they refused to give up. They would not allow their mistakes to put a brake on their development and they used the lessons of failure to stimulate their further growth.

Our interviews with elite athletes made clear that they are not perfect; far from it. They have all known setbacks, some more than others, but they never let this stop them from pursuing their goal. We have already mentioned that experience can help you to evaluate the level of risk when you plan to leave your comfort zone. **Failures are also experience** and these essentially 'negative' episodes often contain a treasure trove of useful information. Above all, they tell you what you should avoid and what you should do differently in future.

In summary: being daring means having the courage to start again when something does not work first time around. Even experts were beginners once upon a time. **It is sheer guts and determination that transforms the beginner into an expert**.

Out of balance

In our way of thinking about the development of high performance attitudes, there is an important basic principle that we wish to clarify. If you want to display and use these attitudes in the best possible way, it is important to realise that:
   — you need to find a balance between showing either too much or too little of a particular attitude;
   — the context in which you wish to perform will determine to a significant degree the opportunity and suitability of displaying particular attitudes.
On the page 'Coach yourself', you can use the dashboards to indicate whether or not you display the different aspects of the relevant chapter's attitude 'too little', 'optimally' or 'too much'. In this way, we hope to stimulate your self-insight.

Experience shows that before you can consistently display an attitude in an optimal manner, you will sometimes get things out of balance. This is not a problem, as long as you recognise the imbalance and adjust it to reflect the situation you are in. So that you are able to recognise your imbalanced behaviour, we will provide you with a list of the most common characteristics that indicate the display of too much or too little of the attitude.

Too little
innovate, dare & repeat

Too much
innovate, dare & repeat

You fail to stand up for your ideas, feelings or values, because you are afraid of what people might think, say or do.

———

You think more in terms of difficulties and obstacles than opportunities.

———

You never act or take decisions on the basis of your feelings and instinct.

———

You cannot make yourself vulnerable and put the blame for failures on others or external factors.

———

You are afraid of making mistakes and never deviate from the agreed plan.

———

You prefer to play safe, rather than take risks.

———

Once you have failed at something, you do not have the courage to try again.

You do not think about what you say and do, and take no account of the consequences of your action.

———

You jump from one idea to another, without thinking any of them properly through.

———

Your feelings and intuition prompt you to take impulsive decisions.

———

You are reckless and deviate constantly from the agreed plan.

———

You take so many risks that you jeopardise yourself, others and the level of your performance.

———

Your volatile nature prompts you to deviate from the agreed strategy too quickly.

———

You are over-confident and make the same mistakes time after time.

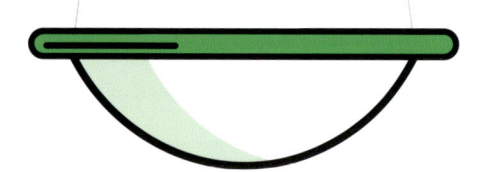
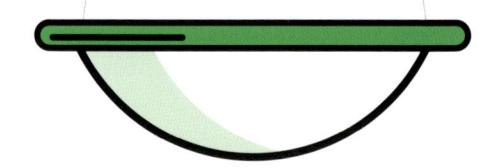

Coach yourself!

—— Describe your next ultimate victory!

....

....

STEP 1 Give yourself a score for the following aspects of this attitude.

- I dare to be myself and stand up for who I am and what I think.
- I dare to trust my feelings and intuition.
- I am creative and open for new ideas and new ways of thinking.
- I regularly leave my comfort zone.
- I take calculated risks.
- I am not discouraged by failure and dare to try again.

STEP 2 Indicate how important it is for you to further develop this attitude as a means to achieving your goal.

0 ▢▢▢▢▢▢▢▢ **10**
(unimportant)   (very important)

STEP 3 Identify your challenges and your levers. (See part 2.)

—— My challenges:

....

—— My levers:

....

STEP 4 Identify your mental skills that will help you to deal positively with challenges. (See part 3.)

—— How will these mental skills help you?

....

STEP 5 Name the concrete actions you will take on the road towards your ultimate victory.

....

....

De Sloover Jules
SNOWBOARD

Silver at the Olympic Youth Games, 1x gold, 1x silver, 1x bronze at the Europa Cup for Big Air, 1x silver at the Europa Cup for Slopestyle

@julesdesloover

Delaere Antonia
BASKETBALL

Olympian, 7th place in Tokyo, Member of the Belgian Cats, Participation in the world championships, 2x bronze at the European championships and European champion

@antonia_delaere

Vidts Noor
ATHLETICS

Olympian, 4th place in Tokyo, World champion, indoor pentathlon, Silver and bronze at the European indoor championships, pentathlon

@noorvidts

Monami Dominique
TENNIS

Bronze at the Olympic Games, Belgian Sportswoman and Sports, Personality of the Year for 1998, Successful entrepreneur

@domimonami

Doku Jeremy
FOOTBALL

Red Devil, participation in world and European championships, Player for Manchester City

@jeremydoku

Jaques Heleen
FOOTBALL

Ex-Red Flamer (national team), Winner of the Superleague, Ex-coach Red Flames youth teams, Head coach Club YLA

@heleenjaques

Swings Bart
ICE SKATING AND INLINE SKATING

Olympic champion (ice), World champion (ice and inline), European champion (ice and inline)

@bart_swings

De Greef Stef
FENCING

Multiple Belgian champion, Participation in world and European championships

@stefdegreef

Pieters Thomas
GOLF

Olympian, 4th place in Rio, Winner of the World Cup of Golf, First Belgian winner of the Rolex series (Abu Dhabi championship)

@thomaspietersgolf

D'Hooghe Aisling
HOCKEY

Olympian, 1x silver and 1x bronze at the European championship, Participation in various world and European championships

@aisling2121

TOP PERFORMERS

Achab Jaouad
TAEKWONDO

Olympian, 5th in Rio, World and European champion, Multiple Belgian champion

@achabtkd

Henin Justine
TENNIS

Olympic champion, Multiple Grand Slam winner, Successful entrepreneur

@justineheninacademy

Degraef Margo
TABLE TENNIS

Silver at the European youth championship, Multiple Belgian champion

@margodegraef

Hendrickx Sofie
BASKETBALL

Ex-captain of the Belgian Cats, Bronze at the European championship, Multiple Belgian champion

@sofiehendrickx8

Boon Jill
HOCKEY

Olympian, Ex-Red Panther, participation in various European and world championships, Silver at the European championship

@jillboon

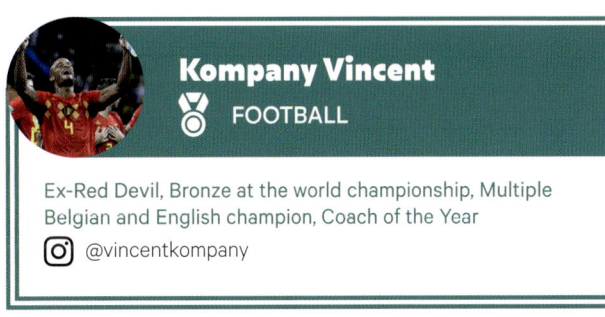

Kompany Vincent
FOOTBALL

Ex-Red Devil, Bronze at the world championship, Multiple Belgian and English champion, Coach of the Year

@vincentkompany

Darcis Steve
TENNIS

Olympian, Finalist Davis Cup, Coach of the Belgian Davis Cup team

@darcis_steve

Vervoort Thibaut
3X3 BASKETBALL

Olympian, 4th in Tokyo, Bronze at the European Games

@thibautvervoort

Rakels Heidi
JUDO

Bronze at the Olympic Games, Gold, silver and bronze at the European championship, Multiple Belgian champion, Successful entrepreneur

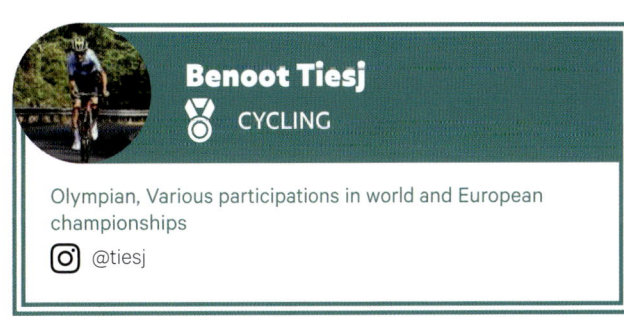

Benoot Tiesj
CYCLING

Olympian, Various participations in world and European championships

@tiesj

Bolingo Cynthia
 ATHLETICS

Olympian, 7th in Tokyo (4 x 400m) with the Belgian Cheetahs, Silver and bronze at the European championship, 5th at the world championship, Multiple Belgian champion

 @cynthia_bolingo

Devos Laurens
 TABLE TENNIS

Multiple Paralympic champion, 2x gold and 1x bronze at world championship, Multiple European champion

 @devoslaurens

Saive Jean-Michel
 TABLE TENNIS

Olympian, Silver and bronze at the world championship, Gold and silver at the European championship, Chairman of the BIOC

 @saivejean_michel

Ouédraogo Elodie
 ATHLETICS

Olympic champion, Bronze at the world championship, Multiple Belgian champion, Successful entrepreneur

 @elodie_ouedraogo

Lecluyse Fanny
 SWIMMING

Olympian, 8th place in Tokyo, Bronze at the world championship, Gold, silver and bronze at the European championship, Belgian record holder at various distances

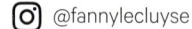 @fannylecluyse

Wathelet Grégory
 SHOW JUMPING

Olympian, bronze in Tokyo, Gold and silver at the European championship

 @watheletgregory

Campenaerts Victor
CYCLING

Bronze at the world championship, Gold and silver at the European championship, World hour record holder 2019-2022, Multiple Belgian champion

 @campenaertsvictor

Vanasch Vincent
HOCKEY

Gold and silver at the Olympic Games, Gold and silver at the world championship, Gold silver and bronze at the European championship

 @vincvanasch21

Gérard Joachim
TENNIS

Paralympian, bronze in Rio, Multiple Grand Slam winner, Multiple Belgian

 @joachimgerard10

Ballenghien Ambre
HOCKEY

Member of the Red Panthers national team, Bronze at the European championship

@ambre_ballenghein

Nikiforov Toma

 JUDO

Olympian, Silver and bronze at the world championship, Silver at the Olympic Youth Games, Gold, silver and bronze at the European championship

@nikiforovtoma

Herbots Britt

 VOLLEYBALL

Member of the Yellow Tigers national team at world and European championships, Bronze at the European youth championship, Multiple Belgian champion

@brittherbots4

Laus Camille

 ATHLETICS

Olympian, 7th in Tokyo (4 x 400m) with the Belgian Cheetahs, Participation at various world and European championships, Multiple Belgian champion

@camillelaus

Stockbroekx Emmanuel

 HOCKEY

Olympian, silver in Rio, World champion, Gold, silver and bronze at the European championship

@emmanuel_stockbroekx

Borlée Kevin

 ATHLETICS

Olympian, 4th in Tokyo (4 x 400m) with the Belgian Tornados, Gold, silver and bronze at the world championship, Gold, silver and bronze at the European championship, Multiple Belgian champion

@kevborlee

Tuerlinckx Hendrik

 VOLLEYBALL

Ex-member of the Red Dragons national team, Participation at various world and European championships, Multiple Belgian champion, Assistant coach to the Red Dragons

@hendriktuerlinckx

Meesseman Emma

 BASKETBALL

Olympian, 7th in Tokyo, WNBA winner and Most Valuable Player, Gold and bronze at the European championship

@emma_meesseman

Smits Seppe

 SNOWBOARD

Silver at the Olympic Games, European champion, Silver and bronze at the world championship, Big Air and gold and bronze for Slopestyle

@seppe.smits

Verstraeten Jorre

 JUDO

Olympian, Bronze at the European championship, Gold at the Judo Grand Slam, World Cup winner

@jorreverstraeten

Claes Hanne

 ATHLETICS

Olympian, 7th in Tokyo with the Belgian Cheetahs, Participation at various world and European championships, Multiple Belgian champion

@hanne.claes

BE RESILIENT

& BOUNCE BACK

ATTITUDE 5

BE RESILIENT
AND
BOUNCE
BACK

'I sometimes go to bed with something worrying me... but when I wake up the next morning I only have opportunities in my thoughts and that gives me tons of energy. I simply can't get up with dark clouds hanging over my head. My greatest strength is my reset button. I wasn't born with this, there has been a trajectory. To develop this attitude, you first need to fall and learn how to get up again. That's the only way to do it and it takes time.'

—— **Vincent Kompany**, ex-footballer and coach

Definition

'Be resilient & bounce back'

We describe this as an attitude through which someone deals in a positive manner with the challenges and setbacks of life. Optimism, determination and persistence are behavioural characteristics that typify this attitude.

Characteristics of top performers with this attitude

— They are mentally tough and not easily knocked off course.
— If they fall, they immediately stand up again, thanks to their determination to succeed.
— They are able to convert setbacks into something positive.
— They use the pressure they experience to grow.
— They know how to manage their emotions and turn them to their advantage.
— They deal in a positive way with injuries and illnesses.

Top performers are mentally resilient

Everyone is searching for balance in their life: physical balance, mental balance, family and relational balance, work-related balance... All these different forms of balance are interconnected with each other and therefore we also try to keep their totality in balance, because this gives us a pleasant feeling of control, achievement and peace of mind. That being said, finding and maintaining this balance is far from easy. Our daily reality is full of challenges and situations that can quickly disturb our balance. Think, for example, of a promotion at work. Great news, but it also throws up new challenges that can (temporarily) knock your overall balance off course! Perhaps you will find yourself in a new team and are expected to develop new competencies, as well as working more overtime, which will all have an impact on your family life. Every event, no matter how small, always has an impact on our balance in one way or another, generating emotions and thoughts that will influence our future behaviour, whether consciously or unconsciously.

In my work as a sport psychologist, I have had countless conversations about 'mental strength' and what it actually entails. It is a subject about which there are many theories and difficult definitions, but in my opinion people are mentally strong when they possess the necessary skills to quickly rediscover their balance whenever it is lost. Most of us usually manage to achieve this, but some achieve it quicker than others. **The faster you are back in balance, the greater your mental strength.**
This is something in which top performers excel. They have the ability to consciously experience the effects that specific events have on them and are trained to convert the associated thoughts and emotions into something positive. In this way, they quickly return to their normal high level of performance. This positive channelling of thoughts and emotions by engaging their mental skills is the key to maintaining balance in their life and career.

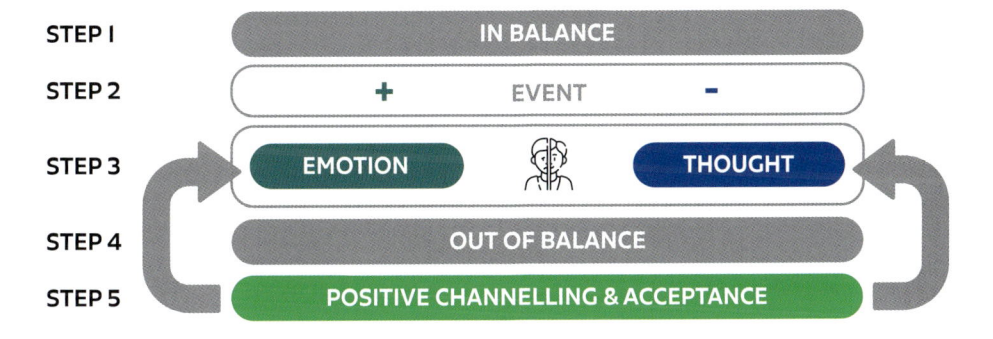

STEP 1	IN BALANCE	
STEP 2	+ EVENT −	
STEP 3	EMOTION THOUGHT	
STEP 4	OUT OF BALANCE	
STEP 5	POSITIVE CHANNELLING & ACCEPTANCE	

Be careful, however! Losing your balance is not something that is always negative. True, it can make you feel uncomfortable, but discomfort can also be necessary to achieve your personal development. It gives you the opportunity to question what you are doing, and how. In other words, it gives you the chance to grow. Sometimes, we even deliberately create this imbalance: a life lived in constant perfect balance would soon risk becoming monotonous. This is one of the reasons why we sometimes consciously step out of our (balanced) comfort zone and, once again, this leads to growth. **In this way, the cycle of balance, imbalance and growth is kept... in balance!**

Top performers learn how to rise after every fall and show determination

In life, we frequently experience setbacks that knock our well-ordered existence off course. These setbacks cannot be avoided; they are an inevitable part of being alive.

 Jean-Michel Saive: *'No matter how hopeless the situation seemed, there was never a single point in my career that I felt was lost before it was played.'*

In contrast to people who stay in their comfort zone, top performers will significantly increase the likelihood of experiencing setbacks because of the attitudes they adopt: their dedication, their dynamism, their desire for self-realisation, their daring and their need for constant renewal all ensure that they frequently find themselves in new and even uncomfortable situations.

Even so, the importance of the challenges and setbacks faced by a top performer during his journey to his **ultimate victory** is often overlooked. The focus tends to be on his successes rather than his failures. It is success that stays in people's minds. In some ways, this is a pity, because we can learn more from a top performer's disappointments than from his triumphs. This is something we will look at further in the second part of the book.

A feeling of failure is generated when something does not go as planned, when you fall short of your goal, or when you lose an important game or tournament. The emotion associated with failure gives you pause for thought and encourages self-reflection. You ask yourself how things might have gone differently. What was missing that denied you success? This self-reflection makes you stronger, because it allows you to **learn from your mistakes.**

—— Overprotection hinders development

People who achieve exceptional results have often known exceptionally difficult moments during their childhood and/or youth. This teaches them at an early age that there is only one way to respond to setbacks: **stand up, dust yourself off and keep on going.**

 Ex-tennis player **Justine Henin** also went through a very difficult period as a child and she believes this helped to shape her future. *'My mother died when I was only twelve. Back then, children were never kept in the picture about their parents' illnesses. Even so, as a child you are not blind. You can feel things and sense that something serious is going on. Throughout that period I was terrified that my mother would die. When it finally happened, there were months when I wasn't interested in anything, not even tennis. Nothing seemed to have any point. Fortunately, I came to realise that I couldn't carry on like that and I soon turned a corner. I understood that life is a gift, but one that you have to work for. I asked myself the question: "What do you really want to do? Right now, my life is difficult but how can I use this event to get something positive out of it?" I really suffered as a child, but I made a conscious decision to live the rest of my life to the full. Of course, I would have preferred it if my mother was still alive today, but it was through her death that I came to realise that there were certain things that I wanted to, had to and could develop. Without our family tragedy,*

perhaps I would never have developed them. This does not mean that things were not still difficult afterwards, but I had learned to stand up whenever I got knocked down!'

Justine's testimony moved me deeply. She is certainly not the only person ever to have suffered such a loss and in my professional life I have come across other young and not-so-young athletes who have had similarly traumatic life experiences. Fortunately, it is not necessary for everyone to go through such difficult periods if they want to develop strong mental powers of resilience. On the other hand, too much protection, so that we are shieled from setbacks and failures, can stand in the way of personal growth and the development of this kind of resilience.

'Adversity causes some men to break, others to break records.'
—— William Arthur Ward

In today's society, we are easily inclined as parents – with the very best of intentions – to protect our children as much as we possibly can. This is something I often hear from the elite sport coaches with whom I work closely. Much more than in the past, they say, they are now asked increasingly by the parents of young athletes to justify their decisions. And it is the same in the educational world, where teachers are also increasingly asked by parents to avoid or modify 'difficult' situations. Again, this is done with the best of intentions, but it has the effect of denying their offspring crucial learning opportunities. **At the same time, every form of overprotection leads children to think that they are not allowed to fail.** This in turn denies them the chance to learn positive lessons from their setbacks. It is only through setbacks that we learn how to do things differently; how to better prepare for the next time; how to ask for help; how to work with others; and how to boost resilience.

All top performers have failed repeatedly before they finally became successful. What's more, they continue to make mistakes even after success has been achieved. In fact, it is the way that they are able to deal with setbacks that allows them to be regarded as top performers: **learning from your failures and carrying on regardless is what separates the winners from the rest.** A learning curve never goes straight up in an unbroken line of success!

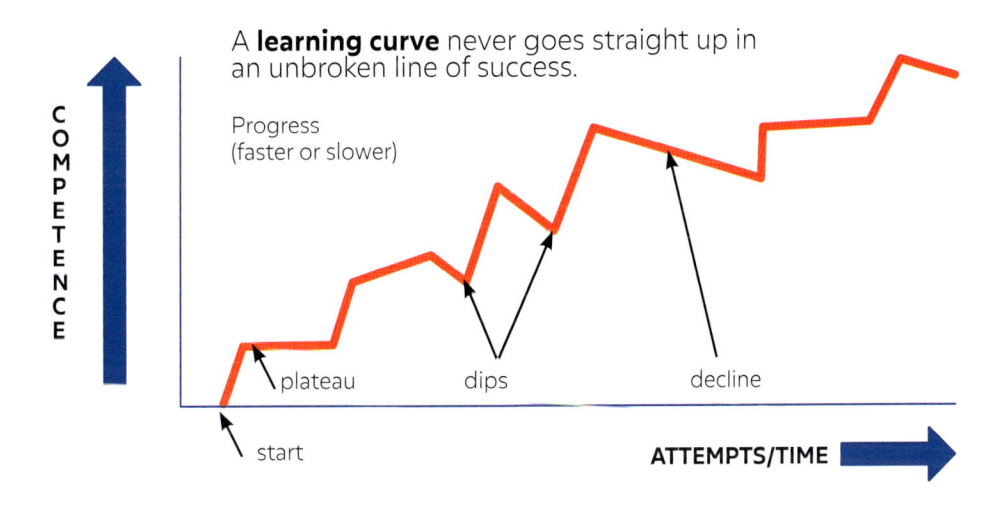

A **learning curve** never goes straight up in an unbroken line of success.

Progress (faster or slower)

COMPETENCE

plateau   dips   decline

start

ATTEMPTS/TIME

Show jumper **Grégory Wathelet** shares this opinion: *'Setbacks help you to become a better athlete in the future. Also a better performer and a better person. If you have always had things easy in life, you are more likely to fall apart when you are finally confronted with a setback. When that happens, such people are inclined to blame everyone and everything around them. To them I would say: stop moaning, look at yourself and get on with it!'*

In my experience, those who are not able to consistently produce top performances have a tendency to cast themselves in the **role of victim**. They are quicker to ask 'Why me?' They blame their failures on others, fate or bad luck. When this happens too often, it can even lead to a condition known as **learned helplessness**: repeated confrontations with negative and (in their mind) uncontrollable situations result in them no longer trying to change the circumstances in which they find themselves, even though they are capable of doing it. It is precisely for this reason that it is so important to stop and consider these situations and to reflect on the effect of your actions on them. At the same time, you need to look forward as well as back: how can you influence future situations so that they turn out more positively? **Taking ownership and accepting responsibility** for both your successes and your failures is the only way to make lasting progress.

——— The half full glass

Optimism also plays a crucial role in dealing with setbacks. The good news is that you learn to see the glass as half full rather than half empty! It is all a question of mindset, changing something that seems to be negative into positive thoughts. Try to imagine how different your life would be if you were to assume that everything will always work out well. That you would always land on your feet. If you can think like this, it's easier to be more daring. If you do eventually face a setback – and at some point you certainly will – you will be more inclined to regard it as a momentary blip, an inevitable but ultimately insignificant part of a much bigger and more positive whole. This allows you to remain calmer and think more clearly.

Perhaps this also explains why many top performers regard themselves as being lucky. They have developed this optimistic feeling and positive mindset, so that they are convinced that the universe works with them and not against them.

In his book Learned Optimism, the psychologist Martin Seligman describes how optimism can have a positive influence on our lives and how you can learn an optimistic approach to life. His concept of 'learned optimism' emerged from his analysis of the scientific study of the opposite phenomenon of 'learned helplessness'. He asked why some people are never helpless. The answer, he concluded, was optimism. Just as importantly, he argued that this optimism can be acquired by looking at our setbacks in a different way and responding accordingly. For this purpose, he developed a simple ABCDE model, which you use to conduct a dialogue with yourself after an unwanted event or setback.

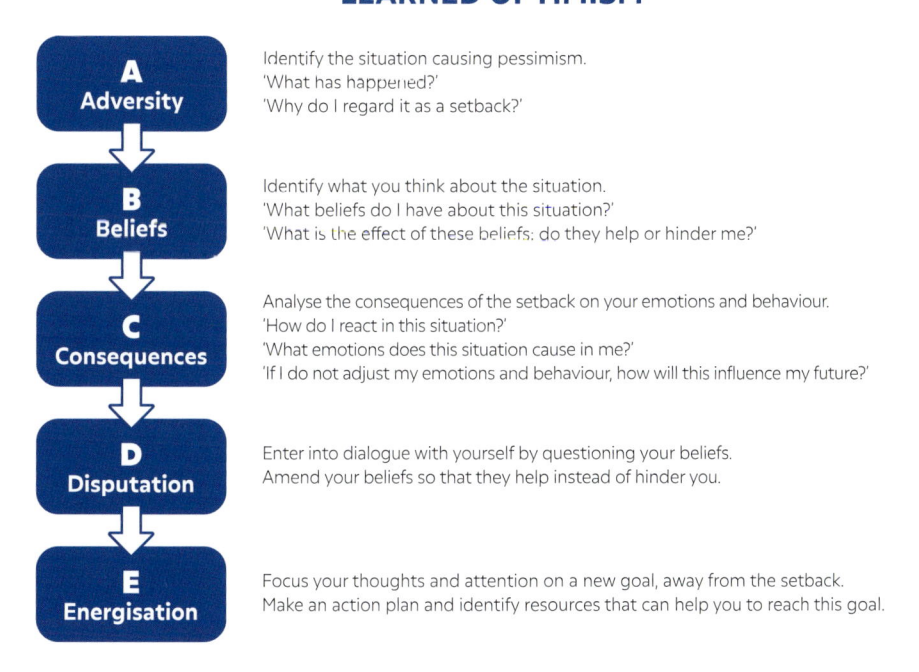

A — **Adversity**
Identify the situation causing pessimism.
'What has happened?'
'Why do I regard it as a setback?'

B — **Beliefs**
Identify what you think about the situation.
'What beliefs do I have about this situation?'
'What is the effect of these beliefs: do they help or hinder me?'

C — **Consequences**
Analyse the consequences of the setback on your emotions and behaviour.
'How do I react in this situation?'
'What emotions does this situation cause in me?'
'If I do not adjust my emotions and behaviour, how will this influence my future?'

D — **Disputation**
Enter into dialogue with yourself by questioning your beliefs.
Amend your beliefs so that they help instead of hinder you.

E — **Energisation**
Focus your thoughts and attention on a new goal, away from the setback.
Make an action plan and identify resources that can help you to reach this goal.

In other words, pessimism and optimism seem to be linked to our beliefs. In the chapter on the 'Be Coachable and Follow' attitude, we have already discussed the power of our own beliefs. If these are limiting, Seligman claims that we can call them into question and remodel them through a process of internal dialogue.

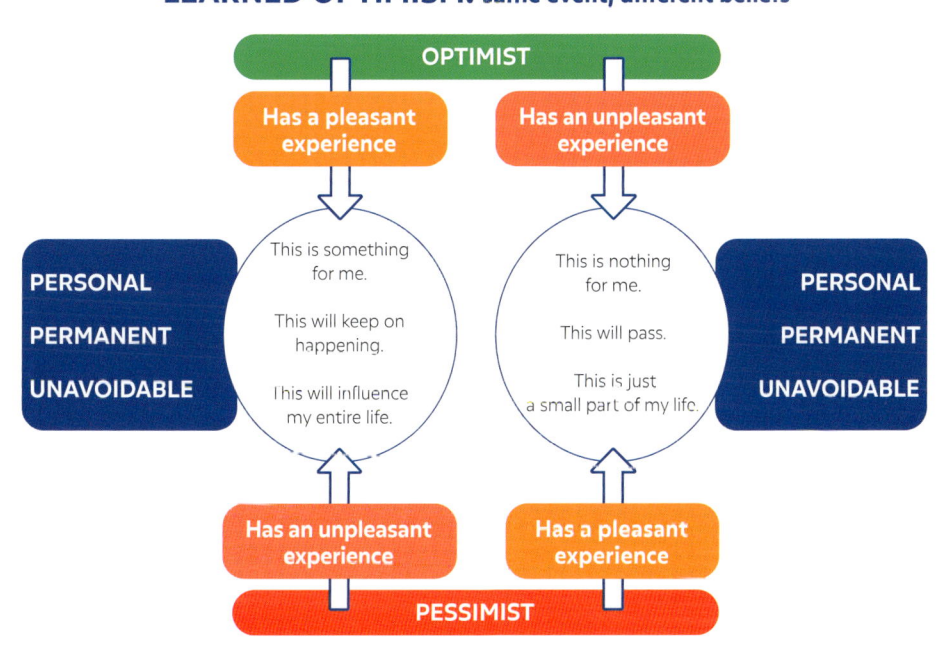

LEARNED OPTIMISM: same event, different beliefs

OPTIMIST

Has a pleasant experience → This is something for me. This will keep on happening. This will influence my entire life.

Has an unpleasant experience → This is nothing for me. This will pass. This is just a small part of my life.

PERSONAL PERMANENT UNAVOIDABLE

Has an unpleasant experience

Has a pleasant experience

PESSIMIST

Changing your mindset and becoming more optimistic is something that only you can do for yourself. Finding the right reasons for both your successes and failures plays an important role. You can do this, for example, by asking the following questions:

— Realistic goal or not: given the situation, was your goal feasible?
— Internal or external influences: what was my own role in the success or failure?
— Control: how much control did I have over the situation and could I have influenced its outcome?
— Focus: was I focused on the situation's possibilities or its limitations?

In essence, you need to convince yourself that optimism will take you much further than pessimism. Reflecting on successes and failures by taking a step back, analysing the situation and the results objectively, and identifying the key influencing factors will help you to draw the right conclusions.

At the same time, it is also important to set goals and make promises to yourself. **For instance, you can promise not to give up when things get difficult.** You can prepare yourself mentally for these difficult moments by devising a trick or mantra that you can use when the moment arrives. If you are a basketball player and today all your shots are missing, say that in this game you want to be the best defender instead. In the attack, you sometimes need a little bit of luck to succeed, but defending is more about your attitude and determination.

—— Instant gratification, self-control and perseverance

Switching from pessimism to optimism and setting personal goals requires a good deal of perseverance. As you press on resolutely towards your goal, it is not easy to voluntarily delay the pleasure of instant gratification. This perseverance, together with self-control and determination, form the key to a successful career.

In our consumer society, it is not easy to avoid the temptations of **instant gratification**. As a result, there is a growing tendency towards a preference for less rewarding but more direct benefits than for more valuable but delayed future benefits. Modern technology and social media both play a major role in this: when all the world is available to you at the click of a mouse, it is a serious challenge to postpone 'jam today' in favour of 'jam tomorrow'. What's more, this relationship between instant gratification and technology forms a vicious circle: the more technology offers us what we want when we want it, the more used we become to getting everything handed to us on a plate, without the need to make an effort. It is instant gratification of this kind that sometimes forms a major block to developing an attitude of perseverance.

Top performers have learned that if you want to be consistently successful to a high standard there is no such thing as instant gratification. Training hard for dozens of hours a week is what gets them to the top. They don't take the lift; they take the stairs. And like all of us, on the way up they sometimes need to pause and take a few steps backward. They realise that these backward steps are part of the process, learning moments that can help them to move forward again more quickly: *reculer pour mieux sauter*. They don't need a lift, because they know that in the long run it will get them nowhere.

 Bart Swings, skater: *'Discipline is choosing between what you want now and what you want most.'*

'Persistence pays off', says a Belgian proverb. And persistence, perseverance and determination are all things you can learn. They have nothing to do with intelligence or innate talent.

 Taekwondoka **Jaouad Achab** is a world champion and a three-times European champion. Even so, his career did not always run smoothly: '*I came to Belgium when I was 18 years old. In Morocco I could only take part in small regional tournaments, which bore no comparison with the standard here. It took me years of hard work to close this ability gap and eventually I reached a level that allowed me to win every contest that I took part in for over a year. When I was first selected for the European championships in 2014, I immediately won gold. I did the same at the world championships in 2015, as result of which I climbed to the number one position in the world ranking. Then my coach left and suddenly I was lost. I felt really low and for more than a year things went from bad to worse. From hero to zero. I eventually accepted the reality of the situation and I now have a new trainer. Together, we have worked hard to get me back to my old standard – and with success. The result was a new European title.*'

When you have been challenged from an early age to evolve and develop at a level that is just above your own, you learn far more than when you work at your own level or an even lower one. If, for example, you found secondary school fairly easy, so that you didn't have to make much effort to get a good report, you may find it hard when you step up to the more demanding university level. In contrast, students who found things difficult at secondary school will have probably developed a method of study that allows them to adjust more quickly to the heavier university curriculum. They are also more used to working hard to achieve the results they want. Similar examples relating to the development of this kind of perseverance can also be found in the sporting world. Some boys and girls are more physically mature than others. In my experience, these early maturing athletes have more chance in the short term of being picked for the better teams, clubs and national selections. They are bigger and stronger, which in most sports works to their advantage at that age. This means that the late maturing athletes have to compete against the physical superiority of their age contemporaries. Because they cannot do this physically, they have to do it by learning to be smarter and more determined. Each time they lose a game because they are (still) not strong enough, they analyse why and learn to keep on going. Maybe next time will be better. As a result, their physical disadvantage yields a mental advantage – especially when they mature fully, so that the physical playing field is level.

Of course, it is not possible for every imbalance to be made good by determination and mental resilience. There is always a process of natural selection at work, not only in sport but also in the academic and business worlds. Even so, the same principle still applies: if every setback can be seen as a chance to learn, this gives people the opportunity to move their studies and/or careers in a new, better and sometimes different direction. Consider the case of **Victor Campenaerts**. He left swimming because of his physique: he was too small. He then became a triathlete and later a professional cyclist, who broke the world hour record in impressive style in 2019.

As a recruiter in my earlier career and now as a sport psychologist, I still attach importance to this aspect in interviews and conversations: has the candidate experienced setbacks in his life and how did he deal with them? The level of perseverance he displayed (or did not display) in the past will be a good predictor for how he will react to future difficulties and disappointments.

Top performers turn setbacks into something positive

In 2015, the **Red Panthers** played in front of their home public as hosts for the qualifying tournament for the Olympic Games in Rio. I had already been working with this fantastic team for a couple of years and this was the moment that we had all – players and coaching staff – been looking forward to and training for so hard. A few minutes before the end of the key game, we were leading 2-1. The Belgian supporters, who were present in huge numbers for a hockey game, thought that we had already qualified and were chanting 'Rio, Rio, Rio'. The atmosphere was amazing. It was at this point that our opponents made a last-ditch tactical move: South Korea took their keeper out of their goal, so that they had an extra outfield player. After this unexpected switch, the Red Panthers started to make one mistake after another, a snowball effect that eventually led to the Koreans equalising just 35 second before the final whistle. 2-2! By now, the pressure on our side was enormous, so perhaps it was no surprise that we lost the subsequent shoot-outs. The unthinkable had happened in just a few minutes' time. Our dream was gone.

This massive collective disappointment taught me just how important it is to always be prepared for the unexpected, so that you are less surprised and more resilient when it occurs.

Since then, I have tried to help every individual player and every team that I work with to be better **prepared to face unforeseen challenges and setbacks, so that they can bounce back more quickly and more appropriately**. This quick reaction to a setback means that you can process it more easily, so that room for further action is created faster in your mind.

Developing scenarios that answer 'what if?' questions can help to set you back on the right track. This is vital, especially in a tournament where the matches follow each other in quick succession. Your ability to put setbacks and disappointments behind you will have a crucial impact on your further results.

By reacting systematically and at speed to setbacks, you develop a strategy for dealing with them. At moments of disappointment various other factors also come into play, such as tiredness, powerful emotions and external pressure, so that your brain has a lot to process all at once. Examining different scenarios in advance makes it easier to maintain your focus at this critical moment. The scenarios give you something to hold on to when your focus is slipping and gives your self-confidence a boost: you have already thought about what happens next and you have a clear plan.

 Basketball player **Antonia Delaere** underlines the importance of preparing and discussing scenarios: '*At the Belgian Cats, this is a standard workshop, something we do before every major championship or key game. The players name all the different situations that might occur and could have a negative impact on how we play. Some examples? One of our top players gets a serious injury; or we lose a big lead and are forced to play overtime; or we commit too many fouls early in the game. Next, we discuss as a team the most relevant situations and identify all the threats and even the potential opportunities that they present. After that, we describe in tactical terms how we need to react to each situation, both as*

individuals and as a team, and what attitudes we need to display. We finish off by making concrete agreements, so that everyone knows exactly what to do if such a situation arises.'

As far as the teams I work with as a sport psychologist are concerned, this ability to deal with setbacks and to develop strategies that help to carry you through the difficult moments has often made the difference between winning a medal and going home empty-handed.

Of course, you can plan for the perfect game, but you need to remember that achieving this perfection is unlikely. We are all human and we all make mistakes that can sometimes torpedo even the most carefully prepared plan.

 Thibaut Vervoort, 3x3 basketball player: *'You can take and make a thousand shots in training, but when the game starts that is exactly the shot that you miss. Why? Because in the game various other factors come into play.'*

The important thing is how you react when you make a mistake. You need to know what to do and you need to show the right attitude. Planning in advance for these moments can help you to still achieve the performance that is expected of you.

Top performers can take pressure and use it to grow

Whether you are nervous or relaxed by nature, at some point we all find ourselves in situations where we come under great pressure. This usually happens at crucial moments, when the consequences of your actions are regarded by yourself as having a defining influence on your future.

To deal with this pressure effectively, it is important to understand why the body reacts so strongly to the situations we perceive as threatening. First and foremost, this is an evolutionary reaction. When humans were still living in caves, the world was full of danger. The only way to survive was to react quickly. If you were cornered by a wild animal, you had two choices: fight or flight. The stress level generated by situations of this kind was so great that it immediately activated a physiological reaction directed by the sympathetic nervous system. This sent a boost of adrenalin through the body, making it possible to develop extra strength that allowed prompt reaction to the threat, either by running away or standing to fight. Nowadays, of course, situations that demand a fight-or-flight response are (thankfully) few and far between. In our modern lives, stress usually increases gradually and the **body's physiological reactions are milder**: butterflies in the stomach, a faster beating of the heart, a dry mouth, increased sweat production, a widening of the pupils, and so on. If you can recognise these changes and can convince yourself in a rational manner that your body is preparing itself for something important, there is a greater likelihood that you will respond **positively** to that something.

For elite athletes,, attempting to qualify for the Olympic Games is a stress moment of this kind. The pressure they feel is huge, because they are on the verge of fulfilling their dream. How they interpret this stress and how they deal with the resulting pressure will decide whether they win or lose.

Too little pressure and too much pressure are both damaging. **To achieve top performance, you need to find the right balance of pressure**. Consequently, you need to develop different techniques that will allow you to increase or decrease your pressure level in a positive way at the right time. If, for example, you feel constantly under too much pressure, it is possible that your nervous system will move into overdrive, so that even the most banal situations seem dangerously threatening. This is not a healthy situation and certainly not conducive to a good performance. At the other end of the spectrum, if your sympathetic nervous system is too slow to react, you will never be able to take advantage of the physiological reactions that pressure generates.

This applies to all of us, but is even more crucial for top performers. People who experience little pressure – at school, giving presentations, talking to their bosses, etc. – have seldom needed to raise their game. In contrast, top performers are constantly setting the bar higher, increasing the pressure in a way that makes the difference between good performance and truly outstanding performance.

 Laurens Devos is a table tennis player who won gold twice at the Paralympic Games. He explains how he dealt with pressure: *'Ever since I was young, I have wanted to prove myself. This was the result of my experiences with people who didn't believe in me, just because I have physical limitations. This taught me how to deal with pressure. Before the final in Rio I felt tense. I had played the same opponent five times in the past and four times I had lost. I also lost the first two points of the match, because I deviated from my normal game. Fortunately, I took a deep breath and said to myself: "Laurens, concentrate and just do what you have to do". I stayed calm and switched back to my normal style of play – with success! Winning the final gave me an incredible feeling. I didn't go to Rio expecting gold, so that I didn't feel under too much pressure. It was different at the next Games in Tokyo. This time I had a title to defend. I was only sixteen when I won in Rio. Five years on, everyone expected me to win again, but that was by no means certain. There was much more pressure on my shoulders. Fortunately, I am one of those players who thrives on pressure. It makes me work harder and forces me to become more focused. As a result, I kept on searching for the right stress balance, which gave me the self-confidence to believe that I could do it again. And I did! Gold in Tokyo for a second time!*

To perform in an optimal way you will, depending on your personality, need to find ways to either raise or lower the pressure. **In the end we all have an ideal level of pressure with which we perform at our best.**

Why is it that some people feel constantly under pressure and others seldom have that same feeling? In the book *What Business Can Learn From Sport Psychology*, Dr. Martin Turner and Dr. Jamie Barker argue that the explanation for this difference is to be found in the difference between having a threat mindset or a **challenge mindset**. Experiencing pressure activates one or the other. A challenge mindset sees pressure as an opportunity, as something we feel capable of meeting and overcoming. In contrast, a threat mindset sees pressure as a danger, as something we do not feel capable of meeting and overcoming.

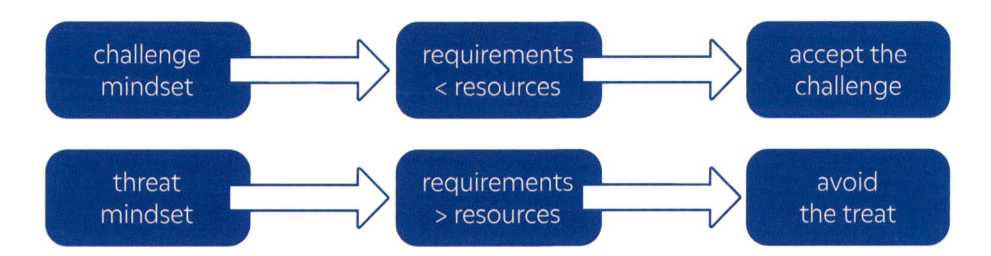

It is possible that in the same situation you might first find yourself with one mindset, before later switching to the other mindset, as the result of a choice you have made or something that has happened. This is something that you often experience in competitive sport. For example, if your lead over your opponent is shrinking fast, this can trigger a change of mindset. In these circumstances, you need to make a conscious decision to remain in the challenge mindset. You can do this by talking to yourself positively, thereby giving your self-confidence a boost, which in turn helps you to move up a gear, so that your opponent remains at a 'safe' distance behind you. But if this doesn't happen, there is a chance that you will freeze and slip into a threat mindset. Your level of performance drops and you get the feeling that you no longer have the situation under control.

 Noor Vidts, heptathlete: *'When my stress level starts to rise, so that doubts and negative thoughts start to enter my mind, I always try to replace these thoughts with the words " I am here to enjoy myself". In this way, I remain in control of my thoughts and feelings.'*

Once again, your toolbox – the scenarios you have prepared and the mental training techniques you have learnt in advance – can be a great help when these moments of doubt occur. **Proactively working to deal with pressure will make you more resilient in the long run.** It increases your feeling of control, so that you can cope with stress more easily.

The earlier that top performers learn to deal with pressure, the greater the likelihood that they will one day be able to achieve their ultimate dream. This will not be possible for those who have never (yet) experienced pressure. When you feel pressure, irrespective of whether you are playing against a weaker opponent or a stronger one, it creates multiple learning moments that will later help you to master such pressure. Over time, these learning moments are crucial: at vital points in your career, the resilience to pressure that you have built up can make all the difference.

—— The underdog

From our interviews with elite athletes, it was clear that some of them prefer to start a match or an event from an **underdog position**, believing that this gives them an advantage. And indeed, there are numerous examples in sporting history where an outsider has beaten a red-hot favourite. Every game has to be played and every race run, so the result is always uncertain. How can pressure play a role in this?

If you are in an underdog position, you feel less stress than your opponent. The expectations of your entourage and supporters are lower: as an underdog, they think you will lose, so that you know you will not disappoint them, whatever happens. But if you win, you give them a fantastic story! Consequently, the focus of an underdog is winning. By contrast, the favourite has everything to lose. He is expected to win, so if he doesn't his entourage and supporters will be disappointed. The pressure on him to avoid this is high, so that the favourite's focus is not losing.

Scientific research has shown that athletes who set goals that are focused on achieving a particular outcome are more successful than athletes who set goals that are focused on the avoidance of a particular outcome. This applies to both process goals and result goals. Playing the ball in two touches may seem the same as avoiding playing the ball in three touches, but formulating this goal in the first manner gives a greater chance of success (Li et al., 2011).

As already mentioned, the **favourite's role** adds extra pressure onto the shoulders of athletes. Favourites are burdened with very high levels of expectation. To be successful, they need to be able to cope with these expectations and not crack under the pressure. They must avoid setting the bar unnecessarily high and must not start doubting their own abilities. In team sports, boosting team confidence and cohesion can be a good way of dealing with these matters. Loyalty to the team gives the players something else to focus on, which relieves the pressure on them as individuals. Being able to rely on the support of a team means that you retain your focus and positivity at the moments of greatest pressure.

 Elodie Ouédraogo, Olympic 4 × 100 meters champion, knows from personal experience the impact that pressure can have on performance: *'If you are running alone, you only have yourself to fall back on. This was something I often found difficult to handle and, as a result, I underperformed. Not because I wasn't physically capable or not ready, but because I allowed doubts to creep in to my head. I gave those doubts no room when I was running in a team. You don't have the idea that 'everything is down to me' when you are in a team. You are part of a group and have a specific function within that group. You can certainly be the decisive factor if you run well, but you are never the sole decisive factor if things go wrong. That's not the case when you run as an individual. The honour is for you alone, but so is the failure. Perhaps for this reason, I think that you get over failure more quickly as a team. Because you are all in the same boat, it is mentally easier.'*

If you want to perform to the highest standard, you therefore need to look at pressure differently. We recommend that you **accept the pressure**, and sometimes even embrace it, **so that you can learn from it and turn it to your advantage** as you progress along the path to your **ultimate victory**.

Thibaut Vervoort, basketball player: *'The best compliment you can get is to be called a "sniper" or a key player. The key moments are the best moments in the game, the moments when everything comes together. I prepare for such moments by training hard, going as physically deep as I can, and by visualising mentally that I play well when those moments arrive.'*

Top performers experience emotions, but do not let them determine their behaviour

Emotions and sport go hand in hand. Even when you are not in the stadium and are 'only' watching on the TV at home, you still feel as though you are a supporter. Images of elite athletes who burst into tears of joy or disappointment after their game or event call up the same emotions in their fans. This emotional aspect (and commitment it involves) is why so many of us love watching sport.

But no matter how strong the emotions felt by top performers, they will do their best to ensure that they have the least possible impact on their performance. At key moments, they need maximum mental stability. Consequently, they keep a tight control over their emotions and don't allow themselves (and their behaviour) to be carried away by them.

 Britt Herbots, a veteran of the Yellow Tigers volleyball team, knows the importance of keeping your thoughts and emotions in check: *'During a game I always try to think in problem-solving terms: where are the opportunities, what can I change to up my game... things like that. I find it more difficult after a disappointing game. Then you feel rotten all evening and sleep badly. You keep on thinking about all those missed opportunities – and that's not good. It increases the chance that you will head into the next game with doubt in your mind. "Don't give me the crucial ball, because last time I missed". If you start thinking that way, things are guaranteed to go wrong again. After a bad game, I make sure that before I go to sleep I take a moment to talk to myself: "Don't exaggerate. Don't blame yourself. Turn the page. New day. New game. Let's go"'*

Because they can **control their emotions, top performers are able to use them cleverly to their own advantage**. Of course, they can also feel frustration during a match, but they will not let it affect their accuracy or their game insight. They have learned how to channel their emotions in a positive way. Consequently, they can convert their frustration into energy that allows them to run faster, compete more fiercely or create more chances.

—— Emotional permeability

As well as being useful, emotions are also infectious. This applies to both positive and negative emotions. Positive people often have a positive effect on those around them, while negative people have a negative effect. This is the result of a process known as **emotional permeability**, which is the extent to which we are able to pick up other people's emotions and allow them to have an influence on our own emotions and, indirectly, on our performance. Some people have a high level of emotional permeability and are able to detect small emotional signals in their environment that others might miss. The impact of emotional permeability also varies from person to person.

Emotional permeability is also an important factor in the workplace. For example, it can have a huge impact on the performance of a team. If someone has a negative mindset, this can be picked up by a colleague with high emotional permeability, who in turn will think and act more negatively. In this way, a single person can have a harmful influence on the entire group. But the opposite is also true. If you understand how emotional permeability works, you can use it strategically to positively influence both your own performance and that of your team.
When we are coaching elite athletes, we like to use the metaphor of a raincoat. You can wear a jumper in the rain and get soaking wet or you can wear a raincoat and watch the raindrops run off you. Emotions work in the same way. With a 'raincoat', you are better protected against the emotions of others. Everyone in your team experiences emotions and deals with them in their own way, but you pull on your raincoat, so that by the end of the day you are not drenched in other people's thoughts and feelings.

The principles of emotional permeability and emotional infection can be seen at work in the **Belgian Cats**. The Cats recently won the women's European basketball championship with a team comprised of top players, each with her own different and unique personality. Part of the reason for their recent success is that they have learnt to accept and complement each other's differences. The team members try to influence each other and use their emotions to strengthen themselves and the team. However, this means that the players sometimes need to pull on their raincoat, so that they can put the emotions of their teammates to one side, when they need to maintain a strong focus on the team's performance.

At the same time, the players on the substitutes' bench also have an important role to play. These replacements act as a mirror to reflect the emotions they can see out on the court, so that they can influence those emotions in a positive way. If the game is a tough one, with plenty of tension, the bench tries to exude an air of calmness and control. In this way, they can help during the time-outs to reduce the pressure on the players who will go back out onto the court. It is also agreed that the replacements will only give positive signals to the on-court players. Displaying too much stress and negativity initiates a downwards spiral and therefore needs to be avoided at all costs. In other words, the Belgian Cats' bench creates a safe environment, a bubble in which the players can take both a physical and a mental breather, allowing them to refocus before the game resumes.

Joe Dispenza is a neuroscientist and bestselling author. In his most recent book, *Becoming Supernatural*, he explains how emotions can help you to change your reality and your future. By making clever use of your emotions, you can achieve the results that you want. For example, he says that at work you don't need to wait until you are promoted before you can start to feel competent. It is by first developing and displaying your own feeling of competence that promotion will logically result. Instead of waiting for a moment (like a promotion) when a certain feeling will be generated, generate that feeling yourself at a time of your own choosing, so that you can become the manager and orchestrator of your goals.

In short, ignoring or suppressing your emotions has a counterproductive effect. This applies as much to elite athletes as it does to the rest of us. It is much better to accept your emotions, channel them and convert them into positive energy that will launch you on your way towards your **ultimate victory**.

Places at the top are few and far between. This means that they are much sought after. Think back to the iceberg metaphor on which our coaching model is based. The top layer, which is reached through the optimal and consistent display of the seven key attitudes, is only small, but it is the most visible part of the iceberg. Consequently, top performers, both in the business and the sporting world, are constantly in the limelight – and in the wind. As a result, their position in this (small) top layer is vulnerable. They are continually evaluated and judged by others, many of whom have only superficial knowledge and information for making these evaluations and judgements. This is something in which the media plays an important role. After every performance, dozens of new reports appear, both positive and negative. Nowadays, these are multiplied and magnified by social media, creating a tsunami of opinions about a single person: the top performer.

 Britt Herbots, volleyball player: '*We are not heroes. We are just normal people, who have good days and bad days like anyone else. We, too, have emotions.*'

Not all top performers have the same ability to deal with the **pressure created by the media**. They each need to decide who are the important people in their lives, the people whose opinions really count. The opinions of all others can then be safely ignored, avoiding the waste of vital energy.

People in the top performer's entourage can also be affected by the things that are said or written about them. In fact, they often take criticism harder than the top performers themselves, which can have a further negative impact on performance. And even if the articles have no direct effect on the top performer and his immediate entourage, family and friends can also be hurt by negative comments in the media.

 Ex-tennis player **Justine Henin** was confronted at an early age with what others wrote and said about her: '*It was sometimes difficult to deal with the criticism. When you win, you are a hero. When you lose, you get all kinds of rubbish thrown at you. Sometimes this involved aspects of my personality rather than my game and I was constantly being compared with Kim [Clijsters]. In the end, I decided to stop reading articles about myself.*'

The media can make or break a top performer. But so too can the people around them. One week the coach tells the world that you were the hero. The next week he might leave you out of the team. What separates top coaches and top businessmen from the rest is the fact that they discuss their decisions with the players or employees concerned. **If you want to bounce back stronger and better than ever before, you need to know the areas where you are expected to improve – and this can only happen by identifying these areas with your coach or manager.** Once you have this information, you must deal with it positively and start putting its lessons into practice. Again, you should not regard such decisions and discussions as a personal attack: they are an opportunity to learn. And if your coach and manager does not take the initiative to discuss these matters with you? Take the initiative yourself, but do it respectfully.

Top performers know how to deal positively with illness and injury

 Grégory Wathelet, show jumper: *'Being motivated when everything is going well is easy. Staying motivated when things are not going well – that is the real challenge!'*

In the sporting world, there is a popular wisdom which says that there are two kinds of athletes: those who are injured and those who have not yet been injured – but soon will be. This implies that injury is an inevitable part of being an athlete. In other words, as an athlete you must accept and be prepared that at some stage in your career you will need to go through a recovery process, if you wish to get back to a high level standard of performance. Likewise in the business world, there are various factors than can put you 'out of the game' for quite some time. **It is how you deal with these setbacks that determines whether you will remain a top performer or not.**

Top performers in the world of sport and the world of business achieve outstanding results and therefore have a high sense of their **own worth**. They know that they are one of the best in their chosen field and link this to their identity as a person. No longer being able to do what they are so good at doing can have dramatic consequences for their self-image. For that reason, it is important – both in sport and in business – to devote sufficient attention to the mental component of injuries and illnesses. Proactively preparing top performers will help to limit the length of time that they are out of action and ensure that they are stronger than before when they eventually return. Challenging them to learn new things during their enforced lay-off period is a useful way to keep them motivated. Making their progress measurable further strengthens the beneficial effect.

It is vital that during their recovery period top performers do not feel under pressure to start performing again too soon. In this respect, the people around them play a crucial role. Everyone must accept that illness and injuries are part of life and it is important to make this clear to the top performer. **It is only by listening to their body** that top performers will be able to recover in a responsible manner and deal positively with the physical setbacks that confront them.

Starting again too quickly can also be linked to having a wrong view about illnesses and injuries. Instead of seeing them as an opportunity to learn, athletes sometimes regard them as a waste of time. This is a mistake. Although injuries can temporarily rule out sport-specific training, a period of injury is an ideal chance to become stronger in other aspects of your sport. For example, you can focus more on your mental training or do exercises in the gym to strengthen parts of your body not affected by the injury. Whichever of the many options you choose, there is certainly no need to sit around doing nothing. Having a positive image of injuries can help you to accept them more easily and give you the time you need to return to competition in optimal condition.

 In recent years, heptathlete **Noor Vidts** has been plagued by a series of injuries, but she tries to approach each new situation as positively as possible. *'I focus on what I can still do, and not on what I can't do. In consultation with my trainer, the volume and intensity of the training for each of the heptathlon disciplines is adjusted to reflect the nature of the injury. With seven disciplines to choose from, we have plenty of options.'*

In addition, it is also important during periods of injury that top performers can still feel **connected with their coach or team**. As a trainer or manager, you must avoid giving your top performers the impression that they no longer count because they are temporarily out of the game. Continue to place a focus on the things that they can still do and explain how they are still an added value for the team. This will help to counterbalance their momentary loss of identity and will better prepare their rapid reintegration into the team when they are fit to return.

This is something that the Dutch do much better than the Belgians. In the Netherlands, there a no such things as sick notes or medical controls. It is the task of managers to remain in contact with their sick or injured employees and agree with them what they can still do during their convalescence. For their part, the employees can also display self-leadership by voluntarily indicating the tasks they feel capable of performing – providing, of course, that their physical and mental condition makes this possible. It is a system that certainly increases the connectedness between the company and the individual. The subsequent reintegration of the 'absentee' is also planned carefully on a step-by-step basis, following consultation with the person concerned. This speeds up the reintegration and allows the employee to return to the desired level of performance much sooner.

What applies in the business world also holds true for the sporting world: recovery is faster and reintegration runs more smoothly if the **engagement of top performers is kept at the highest possible level during their periods of illness or injury.** Even when they are out of action, there are still ways for top performers to work towards their own goals and those of the team. This gives them the **security** and the **motivation** to come back faster and stronger than before.

Out of balance

In our way of thinking about the development of high performance attitudes, there is an important basic principle that we wish to clarify. If you want to display and use these attitudes in the best possible way, it is important to realise that:
— you need to find a balance between showing either too much or too little of a particular attitude;
— The context in which you wish to perform will determine to a significant degree the opportunity and suitability of displaying particular attitudes.

On the page 'Coach yourself', you can use the dashboards to indicate whether or not you display the different aspects of the relevant chapter's attitude 'too little', 'optimally' or 'too much'. In this way, we hope to stimulate your self-insight.

Experience shows that before you can consistently display an attitude in an optimal manner, you will sometimes get things out of balance. This is not a problem, as long as you recognise the imbalance and adjust it to reflect the situation you are in. So that you are able to recognise your imbalanced behaviour, we will provide you with a list of the most common characteristics that indicate the display of too much or too little of the attitude.

Too little
be resilient & bounce back

Too much
be resilient & bounce back

Small setbacks knock you off balance
and cause you to doubt yourself and your competencies.

———

Nothing seems to affect you; everything just slides
off your thick skin.

———

You have a tendency to attribute the blame for setbacks
in an incorrect and non-objective manner
(looking too closely at yourself or at external factors).

———

You are unstoppable and always keep on going,
even if this harms your physical and/or mental health.

———

Setbacks have a huge impact on your emotions and thoughts,
so that you cannot let go of the problem and worry
about it constantly and in a negative way.

———

You respond indifferently to setbacks,
with no emotions and no thoughts.

———

You need a lot of time to come to terms with setbacks
and to get back to your pre-setback level of performance.

———

When setbacks occur, you do not pause
to think about their cause
or what might have happened differently.

———

When you are under pressure, it seems as though your
knowledge and ability desert you, so that you underperform.

———

You never experience pressure or healthy stress.

———

What others think about your performance has a major
influence on what and how you do things.

You allow nothing and no one inside your cocoon
and attach no importance to other people's opinions.

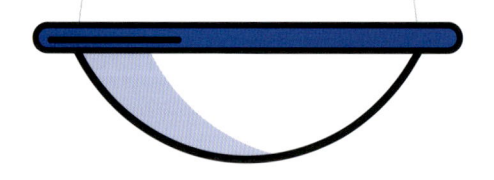
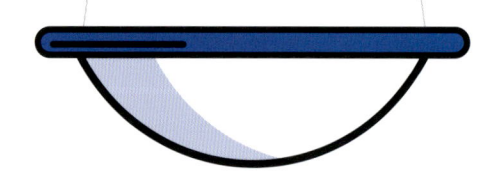

Coach yourself!

—— Describe your next ultimate victory!

....

....

STEP 1 Give yourself a score for the following aspects of this attitude.

- I regard myself as mentally resilient. I am always in control of my thoughts and emotions.
- I show determination when things get difficult.
- The way I perform is not affected by setbacks.
- I search objectively to find the reasons for my successes and failures.
- I have a positive relationship with stress and know how to control it.
- I attach most weight to the opinions of others who are important to me and do not let myself be worried by what everyone else thinks about me and my performance.

STEP 2 Indicate how important it is for you to further develop this attitude as a means to achieving your goal.

0										10

(unimportant)   (very important)

STEP 3 Identify your challenges and your levers. (See part 2.)

—— My challenges: ....

—— My levers: ....

STEP 4 Identify your mental skills that will help you to deal positively with challenges. (See part 3.)

—— How will these mental skills help you?

....

STEP 5 Name the concrete actions you will take on the road towards your ultimate victory.

....

....

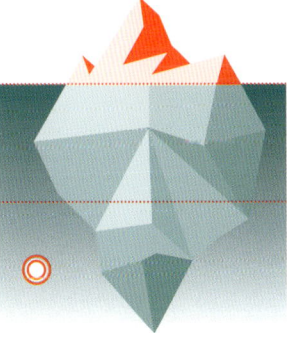

ATTITUDE 6

OPTIMAL USE AND REFUEL OF ENERGY

This chapter was written in collaboration
with P. Beschuyt, the head of Kopman

'I am well aware of the things that give me energy, but also of the things that cause me to lose energy. Even so, I am still learning all the time. My energy level is directly linked to the way I feel and perform. That is why balance is so important to me. The way you are, the way you respond to life is crucial. You attract the energy that you radiate yourself. If you radiate positive energy, other positive things will come your way.'

—— **Cynthia Bolingo**, athlete

Definition

'Optimal use & refuel of energy'

We describe this as an attitude through which someone knows how to manage their energy levels optimally by using the available energy in the most efficient way and by topping up energy reserves at the right moment.

Characteristics of top performers with this attitude

— They know the importance of balance in their life.
— They feel closely connected with their energy levels and know both their 'energy-givers' and 'energy-eaters'.
— They understand the needs of their body.
— They regard mental energy as a crucial factor in top performance.
— They gain energy from positive relationships with others.
— They give meaning to all the different aspects of their life.

Top performers are aware of the importance of balance in their life

——— Balance is crucial

We all attempt to achieve **balance in our life**, so that all its different components fit together nicely. For many people, this 'perfect' fit includes a great partner relationship, healthy and happy children, an interesting and well-paid job and enough me-time to relax, play sport and develop ourselves intellectually. And, as the icing on the cake, enough time and money to travel and see something of the world. The posts of our friends and acquaintances on social media and the vibes of today's many feel-good films all support the idea that this perfect scenario is possible. As a result, almost all of us try to achieve it, although we soon find out that it is quite a challenge!

Finding the right balance in life is something very personal. It depends on the importance that each of us as individuals attaches to the different parts of that life: our body and physical appearance, our dreams and ambitions, our thoughts and emotions, our relationships with other people, and so on. If all these different aspects are in balance, each will have the right level of priority. This gives you the pleasant feeling that everything in your life runs smoothly, almost automatically. You feel in balance, lively and full of energy, so that you are able to ensure that each of the individual aspects functions optimally.

——— The relationship between energy, balance and sustainability

Today's world is changing at lightning speed. So, too, are people's expectations. This means that finding a sustainable balance is becoming ever more difficult. In fact, it is probably the most important challenge that we face collectively as a society. It is certainly the goal of my **ultimate victory**!

To deal positively with these evolutions and expectations, you need energy. Lots of energy. Perhaps this is why the energy question has become one of the most important topics of the 21st century. Hopefully, you start each day fully charged with 100 percent energy. Depending on how your day progresses, you will need to use part of that energy at different times for the different things you need to do. If the deadline for a project is approaching, you may have to work a few hours more than on a normal day. You might even have to work during the weekend or lose some precious hours of sleep. At all these moments, you draw on your reserves of physical and mental energy. The things you are doing are useful and necessary for you to achieve your goal. If, by contrast, you had wanted to maintain a consistent balance – closing your laptop at exactly five o'clock each day – you would never have made that deadline. In other words, adjusting your balance and going temporarily over your limits can help, providing you reestablish your energy balance once the deadline has been met. If you fail to do this, so that you remain out of balance for too long, this is not sustainable and can lead to a burn-out.

Top performers distinguish themselves by the flexible way that they are able to use their energy to achieve their (life) goals. It is their **efficient energy management** that makes all the difference. In the world of elite sport, good energy management makes longer careers possible. If you draw on your energy reserves too deeply or for too long, so that you put yourself under constant physical and mental pressure, you will soon find yourself flirting with physical and mental exhaustion, so that the likelihood of injuries increases. If you are an outstanding basketball player you can play in top competitions around the world all year long and you will always be expected to perform at your best. Euroleague, WNBA, important tournaments with the national team... These competitions follow each other in quick succession, so that there are very few opportunities for rest and recuperation. Consequently, the pressure on physical and mental energy levels is high. What is often forgotten, however, is that the distance between yourself and the other important people in your life also puts a heavy drain on your emotional energy.

Basketball player **Emma Meesseman** explains the importance of making conscious choices for her personal evolution and performance: '*When I decided to take a summer off from the American WNBA, I had just had a difficult season in Europe. I felt tired, both physically and mentally. I needed a break and that summer I was finally able to make some time to take a holiday and to see my family and friends. It did me a lot of good to just lead a "normal" life for a few months. I deliberately chose to take those six weeks off, immediately prior to our preparation for the world championships. It was 200 percent the right decision – and I would do it again.*'

And she did. In the summer of 2023 Emma took another break from the WNBA, to give her more time to prepare mentally and physically for the approaching European championship. Led by a seemingly tireless Emma, the Belgian Cats won gold and Emma herself was chosen as the tournament's Most Valuable Player.

The optimal use of energy is the key to a long and successful career. True, the average length of the career for a top athlete is shorter than for a top manager, but the efficient expenditure of energy is central for them both.

——— Achieving the right balance: hundreds of conscious choices each day

Top performers are aware of the importance of finding the right balance and can identify the elements that can either achieve or upset this balance. This allows them to achieve a consistently high level of performance over a long period.

Changes and new technologies are both elements that can knock you out of balance. Think of the business world, for example, where the introduction of laptops and smartphones made necessary a radical shift in mindset. Nowadays, you are contactable always and everywhere, so that you no longer have an excuse for not giving an answer to your colleague, customer or boss within an hour. Initially, this created an imbalance for many people. It was only when it became clear that no one was expected to be available 24/7 that employees were once again able to relax at home and restore their balance. Compulsory home working during the COVID pandemic had a similar effect, with people again needing time to get used to the change and reestablish their balance.

An important element in this balancing exercise is making conscious choices. Top performers are in very close contact with their energy and make choices that will keep their energy levels in balance. This means, for example, that the choice to work late for a week to meet a deadline is a deliberate and well-considered choice, whereas the idea of being constantly available is not.

 As a professional volleyball player, **Hendrik Tuerlinckx** makes a number of conscious choices in the course of a year that have a positive influence on his performance at key moments: *'At certain times of the year, I pay careful attention to what I eat and when. During those periods, I avoid alcohol as well. I also avoid social contact, because I need rest and relaxation. It is important that I communicate all this clearly to my wife and that she understands what I am doing and why. This gives me great mental calm in the run-up to important games. I know that I have done everything I can to be ready. Even if I don't play well, I have nothing to reproach myself for.'*

Thinking constantly about your daily habits and making conscious choices about them allows you to decide where you want to channel your energy, so that you can prevent your environment from becoming an insidious energy drain. Balance can only be achieved if you actively search for it in your daily life all the time.

Do you not really know where to start and would like some quick wins? Start by thinking carefully about your diet, your sleeping habits and the amount of exercise you take. You will almost certainly have room for improvement in each of these areas and by making the right conscious choices you will be able to make progress quite quickly in the related energy domains. Saying that you don't have the time is not a valid excuse! Give priority to your balance – and your life!

Top performers are in close contact with their energy levels

—— Energy in all its forms

Interested readers will have noted from the above sections that you need an awful lot of energy if you want to live up to the expectations of your environment, continue performing to a high standard and still lead a healthy and balanced life.

Hundreds of years ago, the philosopher Descartes argued that the body and the mind were two completely separate and fully independent entities. Nowadays, we no longer accept this. We know, for example, that maintaining focus and doing what you have previously agreed upon become harder when the body is tired. Or we find it difficult to sleep when our body is still bursting with energy, because we have been sitting in an office chair all day.

Our years of experience in the world of professional sport have also confirmed the **clear link between body and mind**. You can see this in the final minutes of any game. By this time, elite athletes have driven themselves physically and mentally to their limits in their desire to achieve the very best performance. But now they start to feel cramps and their thinking becomes clouded. This is the moment when victory can sometimes slip from their grasp. When this happens, every element that might have contributed to this unexpected and undesirable result is examined critically. Were the players fit enough? Did they show the right attitudes in the right way? Were the tactics flawed or misunderstood?

By looking at all these elements separately, a crucial part of the puzzle is overlooked: namely, the overall coherence and cumulative effect of the different factors. This is what really makes the difference. And this is why we recommend a holistic approach to the human energy question.

Viewed from the **perspective of this holistic vision** and in order to make the different energy domains more tangible, the Kopman network – in Dutch, *kopman* means something like 'team leader' – has developed the Kopman Wheel, based on the insights of a team of experts, including myself in my role as a sport psychologist. The wheel divides energy into four domains – physical, mental, relational and existential – and demonstrates their interconnectedness. These four sources of energy and their relationship to each other were first identified by Kessels and Smit (2019), on whose ideas we will expand further in the remainder of this chapter.

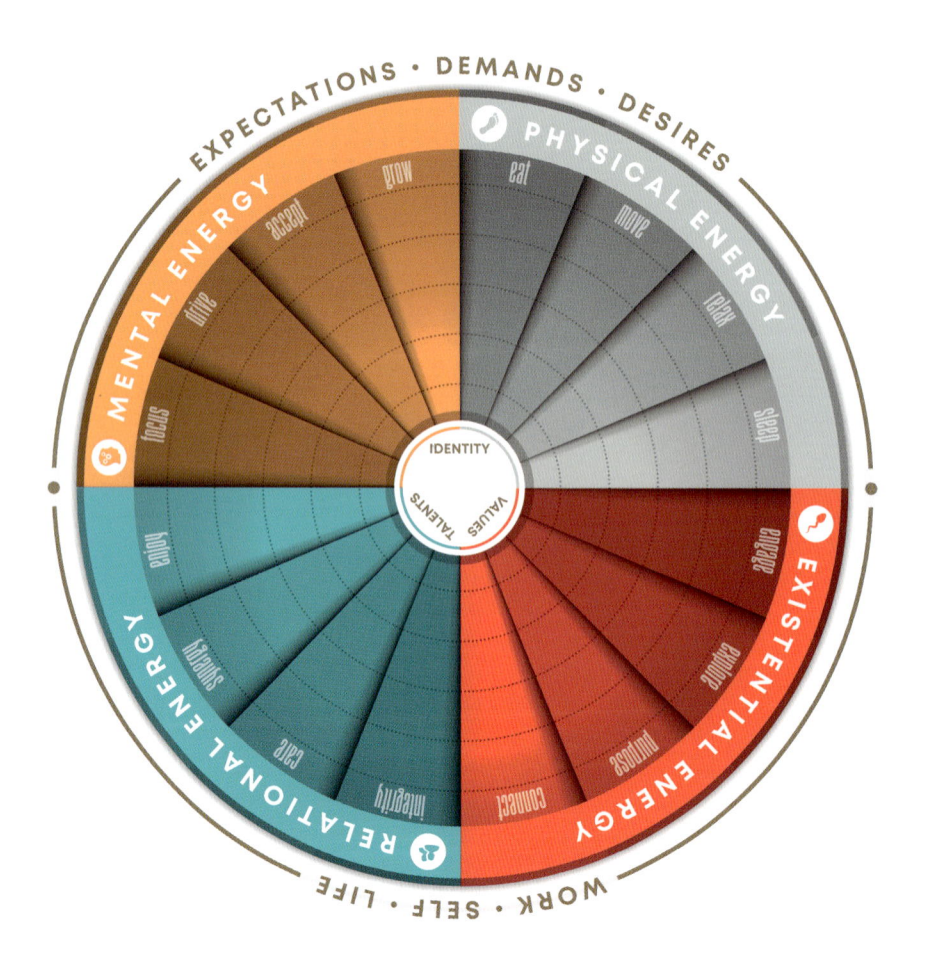

If you want to achieve your **ultimate victory**, **optimal energy management** – finding the right balance between the four energy domains – is a must. This is something that every top performer understands.

Cynthia Bolingo is an Olympic athlete and a key member of the Belgian Cheetahs relay team. She makes time each day to consciously assess and adjust her energy levels: *'I am convinced that the four forms of energy need to be in equilibrium, if you want them to have the maximum impact on your performance. In particular, you need to avoid overloading any one of the domains. It is all about finding the right balance. This balance ensures that I feel good and helps me to stay properly connected to myself. I can also benefit from this sense of inner connectedness during my races. When I feel good, my focus is at its best. My thoughts and emotions are concentrated on what I have to do and feel in order to run a good race. At such moments, I also sense the presence of pressure and competition, but I can distance myself from these intrusions, because I am so well connected to myself and others. In this way, I can make an abstraction of things that might affect my performance negatively.'*

Cynthia's testimony makes clear how all the energy domains are connected and how they can influence performance in a positive way. **In essence, the four domains are communicating vessels, which flow into each other and settle at the right level.**

By now, it should be equally clear that a long-term shortage of mental energy can result in physical problems and vice versa. A well-known example of this phenomenon is burn-out. Long-term cognitive stress eventually disturbs the patterns of your sleep and biorhythms, pushes up your blood pressure and heart rate, makes your breathing more superficial and reduces your interest in and ability for exercise. After a time, this results in physical complaints. But the opposite process is also possible. Chronic pain or chronic inflammation can have a negative effect on your mental health. In other words, you can suffer from a burn-out as a result of a physical problem or even a relational problem. In this case, the mental impact is only secondary, but this complicates both the diagnosis and the treatment. Conclusion? The beneficial effect of exercise, a healthy diet and a good night's rest on mental health should never be underestimated.

Thibaut Vervoort, basketball player: *'I get energy from many different sources: a bad personal performance, winning an important game, the goal of qualifying for the Olympic Games... But I can just as easily get motivation from a week's holiday, away from my sport. At the moment, I am playing in China. That's great! I am enjoying the discovery of a new culture and developing new ways of thinking. That gives me mental energy. What can also give me a boost is a good telephone conversation with my parents or friends. I am convinced that you can only achieve peak performance if you tap into energy from different sources.'*

If you use a lot of energy, it is crucial to recharge your batteries regularly and sufficiently. As already mentioned, drawing more heavily on one of your energy sources can help to compensate for a shortage in another source for short periods, but this is not sustainable in the long run.

In sport, top performers take account of the phenomenon of supercompensation. When an elite athlete makes a serious and sustained physical effort during training, their body is put under such strain that their performance falls below the level prior to training. When this happens, the body needs a period of recovery, which gradually takes it back to a new level of performance that is higher than its original level. This 'bonus' in performance is the so-called supercompensation and it is the ideal moment to start with a new training stimulus to repeat the process. Some physical trainers try to calculate the period when supercompensation will occur, so that it will coincide with important competitions.

It is therefore important for top performers to understand that high standards of performance are not possible without the necessary periods of rest and recuperation. It has even been proven scientifically that training at the wrong moment can do more harm than good.

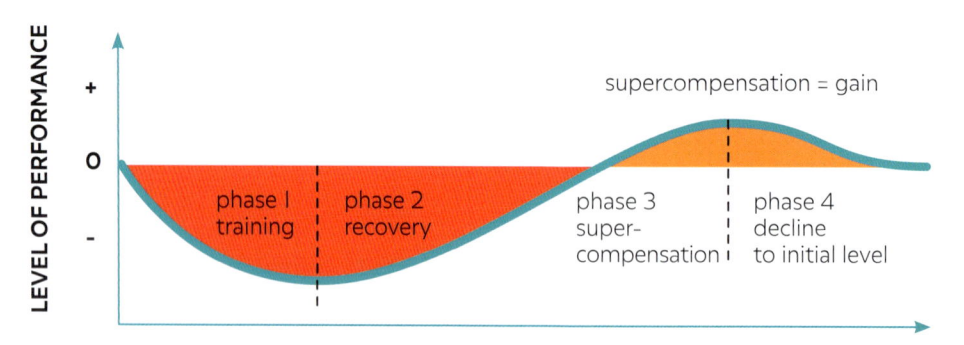

Elite athletes spend much more time preparing for competition than performing in competition. They train for hours and hours each week, followed by regular sessions on the physiotherapist's table to help them recover from their efforts. However, my experience as an HR manager taught me that many people in the business world are in an almost non-stop competition mode. This makes it all the stranger that the supercompensation phenomenon is only really known and exploited in the sporting domain. What separates high performers from the rest is the amount of time they dare to spend in recovering from intense activity. After meeting a difficult deadline, you are almost certain to be physically, mentally and emotionally tired. We would all be much more productive if we sometimes took an afternoon nap at work or went on a few days leave after completing a tough assignment. Our body tells us when it needs to rest, so that it can recover, but all too often we ignore these signals. If we start too soon trying to meet a new deadline, because this is what others expect of us or we expect it of ourselves, we inevitably tap into energy reserves that have not yet been fully topped up, so that they risk being knocked out of balance. And if your energy sources are out of balance for too long or are used too deeply, there is a risk that they will become completely exhausted. As an employee, you have then reached the point of burn-out; as an athlete, you are overtrained. You no longer recognise yourself, doubt all your certainties and are no longer capable of functioning normally. As a result, you are now forced to rest, because you have hit rock bottom. Your brain and your will power are no longer in charge; in desperation, your body has taken control of your actions.

Make sure that you always gain more energy than you use. **Your levels of effort and recovery must always be in balance**.

Improve your awareness: what gives you energy and what costs you energy?

133

Top performers are well aware of the things that give them energy and cost them energy. This awareness allows them to regulate their energy levels optimally. This will mean different things for different people. For one person, attending a business function where you are expected to socialise can be a huge source of energy, whereas for someone else the superficial nature of these events costs them energy and sends them home feeling tired out! Knowing yourself, as we discussed in the chapter on the 'Lead and Make Others Better' attitude, is one of the key building blocks for finding balance.

 Heleen Jaques found optimal energy management one of the biggest challenges during her international career as a professional footballer, but gradually found ways to develop the necessary balance: *'During my sporting career, I sometimes had energy dips. Thanks in part to the guidance I received from Ellen, I eventually learnt to understand myself better. By searching for the causes of these dips, daring to give them a name and taking proper account of them in the future, I was able to better regulate my energy levels. I think that one of my most important characteristics is that I am highly sensitive. I have a tendency to perceive things in great detail and am oversensitive to my environment. For example, I take other people's reactions too personally. Similarly, I can feel when there are undercurrents at play in a team, but I don't always know what I should do about it. In the past, things like this used to worry me and cost me a lot of mental energy. But now I know that I am sensitive to the atmosphere in a team, so that after each intense team moment I now build in more time for rest. I try consciously to relax in a way that allows me to temporarily forget about football.'*

Put simply, Heleen has learned to identify her energy-eaters. This has made it possible for her to deal with her environment in a positive manner and has increased her mental resilience. **Reflecting on your experiences in this way heightens your awareness and increases your ability to spot both your energy-eaters and your energy-givers.** And the more you reflect, the more it becomes clear that you are constantly exposed to different energy systems that influence each other. If you want to avoid your batteries unintentionally running dry, it is best to map out your energy-eaters and energy-givers in the different energy domains.

	ENERGY-GIVERS	**ENERGY-EATERS**
PHYSICAL ENERGY	A healthy diet	Going to bed too late
MENTAL ENERGY	Following a course to sharpen up my competencies	Worrying too much about things I can't control
RELATIONAL ENERGY	Spending time with friends	Conflicts with colleagues
EXISTENTIAL ENERGY	Having a job that matches my values	Doing things that fail to contribute to the bigger picture

This table contains just a few possible examples. Search for your own energy-eaters and energy-givers and make sure that you take account of them in the future!

—— Increase your control over your energy-givers and energy-eaters

Would you like to have a decent dose of energy left at the end of each day, so you can finish off the evening in style? If so, you will need to have a good level of control over your **energy-givers** and **energy-eaters**. Once you have made a list of all the things that influence your daily energy levels, we recommend that you check to see how many of these things you have under control and how you can influence them positively. You may have noted, for example, that starting your day with an early morning run gives you an energy boost or that eating a heavy lunch causes an energy dip in the afternoon. These are things that you can control and can build into your daily routine in a positive manner.

In his book *Seven Habits of Highly Effective People*, Stephen Covey describes the seven attributes that successful people have in common. He also explains how focusing on the things that you can control allows you to save precious energy.

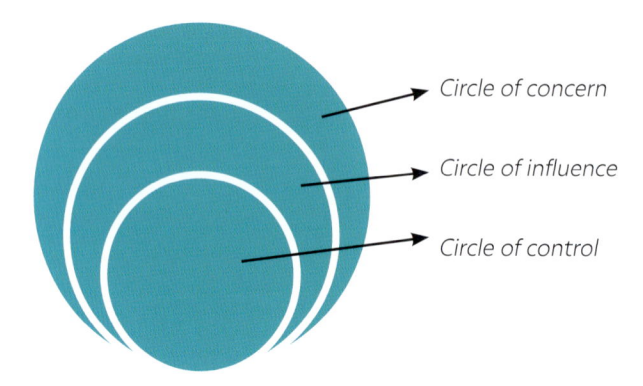

Circle of concern

Circle of influence

Circle of control

This simple model is useful for gaining insight into the best way to use your energy. In essence, Covey argues that we should only expend energy in situations that we can control. Conversely, we should not expend energy on situations over which we have no influence, even though they may be a cause for concern.

With this in mind, Covey describes three circles:
— The circle of concern contains a wide variety of subjects that you feel involved with and perhaps even worry about, but which are ultimately beyond your range of influence. These subjects might be as diverse as the COVID pandemic, the war in Ukraine or the rules and regulations in your sport. These are all interesting and important matters about which you have an opinion, but over which you have no leverage.
— The circle of influence is much smaller. It contains subjects over which you do indeed have a degree of leverage, but without having full control. For example, the result of a particular match will depend to a significant extent on your personal performance, but the performance of the rest of your team and your opponents will also influence the outcome. The size of your circle of influence is dependent on the role and responsibilities you have. If you are the president of the United States, you will have a much larger circle of influence than you and I!

— The circle of control is the smallest circle, but also the most important one. It contains all the elements, situations and challenges over which you have full control: your attitude, the time you go to bed, what you eat, and so on.

Top performers understand the needs of their body

If we talk about energy in general terms, we usually mean **physical energy**. This form of energy is heavily influenced by your habits and lifestyle, as well as being closely related to your general condition of health.

If you wish to be productive all day at work or want to run a top time out on the athletics track, it helps to have had a good night's sleep and to have eaten and drunk the right things. In addition, routines and consistency are crucial. An elite athlete knows that going to bed early just once a week is not enough to start each new day full of beans. You need to do it (almost) every night.

—— The importance of exercise and relaxation

In our western society, people take too little exercise. Most of us do not reach the recommended minimum of ten thousands steps per day. Our sedentary lifestyle is the silent killer of our generation, according to the celebrated author Tom Rath in his book *Eat, Move, Sleep*. Too much sitting forms a threat to your energy levels, because the less you move, the less energy you have. For this reason, we applaud the initiatives that are now taking place in most companies to get their employees moving and/or exercising more often.

Although these conclusions are relevant for the large majority of people, they do not apply to elite athletes. Some of them, however, face a very different kind of problem: their level of performance falls through overtraining.

 Imbalances in her physical energy were an issue for sprinter **Elodie Ouédraogo** throughout her career: *'Because I had a high pain threshold during training, I was a classic example of someone who constantly tried to box above her weight. If the training plan said "six times 150" but I was already exhausted after four times, this meant that I would have to do the final two times almost on my hands and knees. In other words, pushing myself too far. But that is what I did. I didn't train with a 'work smart' attitude and I didn't have enough confidence in my own judgement to know when I was no longer doing quality training. I should have said more often: "This is all I can do today; tomorrow I will try again". That was my weakness.'*

Elodie now thinks that she could have avoided some of her injuries if she had trained 'more sensibly'. Many of these injuries happened towards the end of training sessions, when she was tired and her level of concentration was falling.

Although employees and athletes sometimes are at opposite ends of the scale in terms of their physical energy use, there is one thing that they both have in common: the need for sufficient rest and relaxation. Again, this varies from person to person. Some people find a brisk walk in the fresh air relaxing. For others, it is yoga, chatting with friends or just doing nothing. After these recovery moments we feel fitter, can concentrate more easily and are generally in a better mood. In this way, we boost our productivity.

—— The importance of sleep

Our busy lives mean that it is often late in the evening before we are able to relax. This is why we systematically push the time when we go to bed later and later, unintentionally creating a habit that is not good for us.

Most experts agree that to function optimally people need between seven and nine hours of sleep. If we do not get enough sleep, we have less energy, make poorer decisions and have less fruitful interactions with others. Our interviews with elite athletes revealed that all of them deal consciously with their sleep and sleeping patterns.

Her sleep is very important for athlete **Cynthia Bolingo**: *'I need a certain number of hours of sleep to be able to function optimally and productively throughout the day. Sleep is vital for both my muscles and my brain. The most important change I made in comparison with the past is that I am now difficult for others to reach after ten o'clock in the evening. It needs to be something very urgent before I answer my phone or reply to a text message. I try to keep to a regular sleep cycle, with the same hours of sleep each night, because I know that this will help me in the long term. This means that I get up at the same time each morning, regardless of what is scheduled in my daily planning.'*

A research study (Lastella, Lovell & Sargent, 2014) into the relationship between pre-competitive sleep behaviour, the resulting pre-competitive mood and the actual performance of athletes concluded that their sleep the night before the competition is often more disturbed than normal and that this can have a negative effect on their pre-competitive mood. Another study demonstrated that young gymnasts who sleep well experience less pre-competitive stress and perform better (Silva & Paiva, 2013).

It is not only the quantity of sleep but also its quality that is important. Many books have been written about the factors that influence sleep quality and there is no need for us to look at this in detail here, but we do need to emphasise just how crucial sleep can be for achieving a great performance. It not only has an impact on your physical energy levels, but also on your mental energy and resilience.

Author Tom Rath believes that consciously eating a healthy diet will help you to live longer. In view of the fact that roughly half of the Belgian population is overweight, it would seem that healthy eating is more important than ever. Rath recommends avoiding the latest 'hype' diets, but suggests that instead you should simply ask yourself whether what you are eating is doing you good. In his opinion, the quality of the food we eat is more important than the quantity. Eating three hundred calories of junk food is not the same as eating three hundred calories of spinach. If you eat wisely, you will have enough energy to meet the challenges of each new day and your performance will improve. A healthy diet with few added sugars will prevent unwanted increases in your blood sugar level and will help you to remain focused on your tasks.

 This is another area where top performers know themselves through and through. Athlete **Cynthia Bolingo** is a good example: *'I know that for me it is better not to eat too much in the evening, because then I usually sleep less well. The next morning I feel less rested, which poses both physical and mental challenges for the day ahead. For this reason, I have changed my eating habits. Breakfast and lunch are now my larger meals, but still healthy. In the evening I adopt the principle that I still need certain nutrients but not too much, because my body will soon be sleeping.'*

Nowadays, everyone knows and understands that alcohol has a negative impact on performance. That being said, most people like a beer or a glass of wine every now and then, perhaps especially after an intense physical effort. Top performers know when this is possible for them and when it is not.

When I was giving guidance to the women's national hockey team, the **Red Panthers** made a pact with each other that none of them would drink a drop of alcohol in the last hundred days leading up to a major tournament. This important statement elevated self-discipline to the team level, which increased the likelihood that they would all stick to the agreement.

────── Physical well-being and sickness absence

The level of sickness absence in Belgium has increased systematically during the past decade. More and more Belgians are off work for longer periods as a result of illnesses and injuries of one kind or another. This is estimated to cost society an average of one thousand euros per fulltime employee. Fortunately, growing awareness about the importance of the physical well-being of employees has led to an increasing number of health initiatives at company level. Physical activity and movement during working hours are now encouraged. Think, for example, of group fitness sessions during the lunch break or cycle lease plans that stimulate employees to use pedal power to get to and from their place of work. Some companies even issue smartwatches to their personnel and organise sporting challenges between colleagues who work in different departments. We also attach importance to this at Smart Mind. Online programmes dealing with themes like energy, the stimulation of a growth mindset and the development of healthy habits can now be found on the Move to Happiness platform. Move To Happiness helps companies to translate their ESG strategy into employee practice via a single central platform. Through a series of webinars, online applications devised by Move To Happiness experts (including Ellen and Tara), challenges, communication feeds and events, important subjects like sustainability, well-being, diversity and inclusion are made tangible for employees.

Top performers regard mental energy as a decisive factor

While there are still huge gains to be made in the business world in terms of physical energy and energy recovery, the same cannot be said of the sporting world. This is something at which top performers already excel. Their ability to effectively recharge and efficiently use their energy is what makes it possible for them to perform so well. But that is not the only crucial factor. As briefly mentioned in the introduction, investing sufficiently in **mental energy** also makes all the difference at the highest levels in sport.

—— Observing mental energy

When our mental energy batteries are fully charged, everything seems easy and we are ready to take on the world! If you feel good in your head, your body can also do much more. But the opposite is also true: maintaining and recharging your physical energy levels also gives a huge boost to your reserves of mental energy. A good night's sleep, a healthy diet, sufficient movement and proper hydration are all crucial for your focus.

Like our muscles, our brain also needs energy before it can function at its best. In fact, no less than 20 percent of our available energy is used up by brain activity, which is remarkable for an organ that only represents 2 percent of our total body mass. This makes the brain the body's biggest energy-eater of all! What's more, our brain is never at rest. Even when we are sleeping at night, the brain uses up roughly the same amount of energy as during the day. This is the price we pay for the brain's constant vigilance.

How can we best describe mental energy? Mental energy is something that is difficult to measure, but when I talk to top performers about it there are always two words that crop up in the conversation: **willpower** and **purpose**. The extent to which both these elements are present indicate the level of mental energy in the person concerned. This helps to make mental energy more observable!

—— Focus, motivation and flow

People with willpower are characterised by the way in which they distribute and manage their mental energy. They set themselves various goals and allocate their mental energy accordingly. They then work towards these goals in an organised and focused manner, using positive self-talk to motivate themselves to take countless conscious decisions each day. It is **willpower that allows top performers to do what they have to do** in order to stimulate their further growth and self-development, even though they don't always feel like it.

We make optimal use of our mental energy when we are in a state of flow. Flow is a concept first developed by the Hungarian-American psychologist Mihali Csikszentmihalyi (1990; 1999). When we are in flow, we are absorbed completely in our task and are no longer aware of time. We even forget to eat and drink. Achieving flow is only possible if the following three conditions are met:

1. The task is sufficiently challenging and you have the necessary abilities to complete it successfully.
2. You set clear goals and know exactly what you need to do in order to achieve them.
3. You get immediate feedback from others to indicate whether or not you are on the right track or need to make minor adjustments.

Mihály Csíkszentmihályi's flow model
as related to challenge and ability

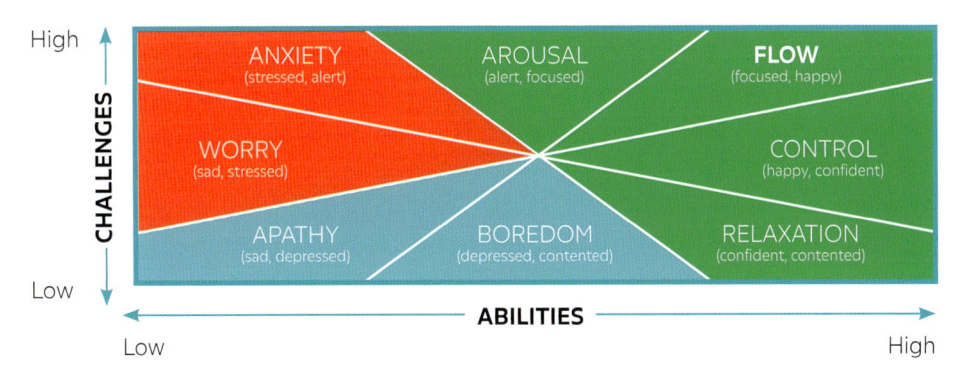

When people are in flow, they experience a high degree of focus. They are so immersed in their task that awareness of the surrounding environment fades away. They are immune to distraction and time seems to pass more quickly.

Elite athletes have a strong focus on their tasks and goals, both during training and in competition. At such moments, you will seldom see them reach for their smartphone or stop for a quick coffee. Instead, they concentrate fully on themselves and what they are doing. For them, the world has been reduced to the sports ground and the other people in it. They are experts at blocking out all peripheral matters, so that they can direct all their attention to their preparation and performance. It is only afterwards that they again find space to let other things into their consciousness.

Nowadays, our smartphones make it very difficult for most of us to achieve flow. There is hardly a moment during the working day when we are left undisturbed for long enough to find the necessary serenity and focus. The constant stream of text messages and e-mails makes it impossible to forget time and our surroundings, so that we cannot immerse ourselves completely in our tasks.
Temporarily blocking your incoming calls, messages and mails is the only way to prevent constant interruption, so that you can focus your full attention on what you are doing.

You can also charge your mental energy batteries by making sufficient time for self-development. The fact that you are reading this book shows that this is something that you are actively and consciously pursuing. **Learning new things gives you energy and helps to stimulate your desire to take action.**

 Ambre Ballenghien, hockey player: *'For me, mental energy is a feeling of balance. That gives me the strength, purpose and motivation that I need to train hard and take further steps towards the goals that I have set for myself. It ensures that I have sufficient energy to do what I need to do, while still remaining true to myself. Having the feeling that you have sufficient reserves of mental energy helps to get you through the difficult moments.'*

As far as mental energy is concerned, it is the interaction between the attitudes 'Be Highly Motivated & Work Smart', 'Be Coachable' and 'Innovate' that has the most positive effect. If you display these attitudes optimally, you will also be able to use your mental energy optimally.

Top performers surround themselves with people who have a positive impact

Within the environment in which you live and work, you maintain a series of relationships with others. Some of these relationships help you to recharge your batteries, whereas others cost you energy. For example, conflicts with colleagues or relational problems at home can be a huge energy drain.

To reinforce their **relational energy**, many organisations now invest in teambuilding and the development of interpersonal skills: how to give feedback, how to lead a team, how to deal with conflicts, and so on. On the one hand, these skills make it easier to relate to and connect with others or to raise difficult subjects for discussion. On the other hand, they also make it possible to be creative with others and to have fun with each other. When you are able to build up and maintain good relations with those around you, you help to generate a high level of relational energy in your environment.

 Hockey player **Aisling D'Hooghe** is well aware of the importance of relational energy for herself as a person and for her performance: *'I get my energy from others. That is why I attach great importance to what my team mates are feeling. When we enjoy ourselves together as a team or when our confidence levels are high, this gives me a huge boost. The more people around me who feel good, the better I also feel and perform. In that sense, you could say that my desire to motivate and help others is selfish: when I help my team mates, this also has an indirect positive impact on myself and my performance. The energy around me is infectious, both in positive and negative terms. In a team, it is important to be aware of this. If you start moaning and complaining as a team or if you start to focus your attention on one specific team member who irritates you, you need to get the problem out in the open as quickly as*

possible. This kind of vicious circle must be broken immediately, because the things on which you focus your attention inevitably grow. Both in a good way and in a bad way.'

—— The power of team cohesion

The Belgian Cats and the Belgian Cheetahs are two teams in which relational energy serves as the motor that drives their performance. On some occasions, it has even made the difference between winning and losing.

In my experience, the results in close games – games that are either narrowly won or narrowly lost – are often dependent on the level of team cohesion. The extent to which the team members feel connected to the team as a whole and its goals is the decisive factor.

Research has confirmed that team cohesion has a positive influence on team performance (Dion, 2000; Hoegl & Gemuenden 2001, Mullen & Copper, 1994). In particular, the members of a close-knit team make greater efforts to achieve the team's goals.

The athletes in the **Belgian Cheetahs** often run faster in their relay races than in their individual events. In the Belgian Cats, this same spirit finds expression in an unselfish willingness to pass the ball to a team mate in a better position to score. In both cases, it is clear that there is no place for a negative form of competition within the team, so that the team's interests always take precedence over self-interest. Fantastic things can be achieved when team members share a common goal and are prepared to do everything for each other. **They form a compact, coherent and close-knit unit.** Top performers attach great importance to the way they interact with others. They surround themselves with people who radiate positive energy and share the same values and goals, creating mutually beneficial relationships.

Organisational success in the business world is also often attributed to the ability of teams to work together and perform at a high level. There is also plenty of evidence that in general employees prefer to work in teams with colleagues who have the same opinions, beliefs and attitudes. This does not mean that you must always be in agreement with your fellow team members. Thinking differently is not a problem and can sometimes actually be productive. The important thing is that differences must be aired and discussed. This is the only way for conflict to be constructive. In his book *The 5 Dysfunctions of a Team*, Patrick Lencioni argues that 'artificial harmony' can be damaging for team performance. He points out that there is often disagreement in even the best teams, which is only logical: each team member has a responsibility to the team to express their opinions.

Team cohesion is a dynamic process and changes over time as a result of the interaction between team members, team processes, team results and variations in the context. Because team cohesion is not directly visible, it is necessary to take steps to promote this cohesion proactively. Research has shown that there are four factors that have an influence on team cohesion: a clear role for each of the team members, a willingness to make personal sacrifices for the team, the quality of communication between the team members, and the common goals of the team (Martin, Carron & Burke, 2009).

—— In a team there is room for personality but not for egos!

The **Belgian Cats** make a conscious choice to select the best team, and not necessarily the twelve best Belgian players. In team sport, it is crucial that the team is central and takes priority. Individual performance must be subordinated to team performance. If there are super-talented players who place too much emphasis on themselves, this will inevitably be harmful to the team's wider interests.

Originally, every member of the **Belgian Cheetahs** relay team was an individual athlete and for many years they focused primarily on their individual performance. When they decided a few years ago to form a national team, their common starting point was the dream of taking part in the Olympic Games.

In the teams that I assist, we attach great importance to setting team goals that are supported by every team member. If there are any doubts about the team's goals and their feasibility, these are discussed with the entire team. Without a consensus, it is not possible for the players or athletes as individuals to identify with the team, so that it costs them huge amounts of energy to support a project in which they do not fully believe.

Like the individual team members, teams are also in constant evolution. This makes it imperative to work actively to build up the team's interpersonal relationships and to strengthen identification with the team as a whole. For this reason, the team workshops of the Belgian Cheetahs often revolve around team values, in which we discuss (amongst other things) how we relate to each other. To further enhance our team identity, we have developed our own team logo and we are mightily proud of our team yell: 'Cheetahs on fire!'

—— The bow can't always stand bent

What I have observed as a sport psychologist with both the Belgian Cats and the Belgian Cheetahs is a team spirit that is characterised by mutual connectedness and a certain gratitude for being allowed to form part of such a special team. When we come together, it is usually to prepare for an important match or competition. At such moments, the team needs to train hard and with the necessary discipline. But in spite of this pressure to perform, we still have plenty of fun, allowing the players' batteries to be fully recharged with lots of relational energy.

The feeling of being loved and valued has a positive influence on performance. Even so, there is a constant theme running through the story of almost every athlete: the lack of time for family and friends.

 This is something that athlete **Cynthia Bolingo** experiences every day: *'One of the things that I still find difficult is putting my sporting needs ahead of my relational needs. At certain moments in my career, I have needed to sacrifice relational energy. I still try to maintain good relationships, because that is important for my performance, but there are times when I have to put people on hold, so that I can focus 100 percent on my running. When that happens, I think: "If I can't see them now, I will make up for it later".'*

In the interests of their career, it is not always possible for top performers to be present at family celebrations or for the birthdays of their friends. This means that they do not always have the possibility to recharge their batteries with relational energy. This requires careful attention. Exhausting the energy supply in one energy domain will inevitably have an impact on the other three domains. This can lead to a lack of motivation and focus or even result in a drop-out or burn-out.

A recent study by Burns, Weissensteiner & Cohen (2019) questioned Olympic athletes about their interpersonal relationships and the impact on their performance and careers. It became clear that these athletes owe their success in part to the strength of their social network. This network helps them to deal with stress, resulting in better performance.

This information is important for coaches. On the one hand, it is their responsibility to build up and maintain meaningful relationships with their athletes. On the other hand, they must encourage their athletes to still find ways to invest time in their family and friends.

 Thomas Pieters is looking forward to his upcoming fatherhood: *'I used to think: I train a lot more than my opponent, because he has children, but yet he plays better. That athlete is probably perfectly balanced mentally, while I expect too much or feel too much stress. I'm also looking forward to taking on that role as a father. That's another new challenge.'*

Top performers give meaning to different life domains

The fourth energy domain in the Kopman Wheel is **existential energy**. This relates to the meaning that life gives and has in your eyes. Nowadays, their work is an important source of meaning for many people. We want to be of service, to do something of value, to make a contribution towards the world. If you feel that your work serves no purpose and contributes little, this will be a heavy drain on your available existential energy. At the other extreme, there are some people who think that they have been put on this earth for a specific **purpose**. If they experience that their work is in keeping with that purpose, this gives them a huge energy boost. Inner disquiet and conflict arise when it is not possible for you to serve a meaningful goal. Again, this leads to a massive loss of energy.

Top performers succeed in combining different roles

Top performers succeed in combining a number of different roles. Many Belgian athletes are not only busy building a professional sporting career, but are also fulltime or parttime students or employees in one capacity or another. What's more, they wish to be successful in all these different aspects of their life. Not just now, but also in the future. After their sporting career, they want to do something meaningful that corresponds with their life goals.

Switching between the roles of athlete and student or athlete and employee uses up much more physical and mental energy than if you are active in just a single domain, all the more so because top performers wish to grow and excel at everything they do. The players in the Belgian national hockey teams are living proof of this. They train at the highest level and take part in world championships and Olympic Games, but at the same time many of them are also following demanding university courses to qualify as engineers, doctors, lawyers or physiotherapists.

 Based on her experiences as a career guidance adviser for Flanders Sport, **Kristel Taelman** knows just how difficult this balancing act can be: '*Making the switch between the two different worlds is tiring and demands both energy and motivation. The sporting students arrive home exhausted from training, make themselves something to eat and then have to settle down to their books. After a hard day, most of us can relax in front of the television during the evening. This is a luxury that sporting students do not have. There is an important potential pitfall in the combination of sport and academic studies. Namely, the risk of overdoing things and drawing too heavily on your energy reserves. Elite athletes are so motivated and so ambitious that they will try to do too much, so that they eventually hit a brick wall. They are used to the pain and suffering that is necessary to push their boundaries in their sport and they want to do the same in their private sphere. This is possible up to a certain point, but you must be very careful not to take things too far. Otherwise, you overstretch your energy reserves and knock them out of balance. This can lead to both physical and mental difficulties, from which it is not easy to recover.*'

In other words, the combination of sport and academic studies is far from simple. Consequently, you need to prepare yourself for the fact that it will be difficult. A great deal will be expected of you in all the different parts of your life. You will need to be at your best in your lessons, group work and exams, but also in your training and competition for your sport, whilst at the same time making sure that you eat healthily and get enough sleep, as well as maintaining your relationships with family and friends! Life for a young elite athlete is complex. Highly complex.

When we look at the combination of sport with higher education and/or a(nother) professional activity, the most difficult thing for many athletes is to manage the time pressure. This, again, is something you need to prepare for. Making the right choices at the start of your course of studies is equally important. If problems arise once you have started, this can have a negative effect on your concentration and your sporting performance. Getting the correct guidance for both these matters is essential.

 Fencer **Stef De Greef** has succeeded in achieving the right balance between his sport and his studies: *'I devote a lot of attention to finding a good balance. Sport, studies and family and friends are the three most important blocks in this balance. I have goals relating to all three blocks and it is important to me that I perform well in each of them. This might mean that I see my friends less during my exam periods and also reduce the emphasis on fencing. But when an important competition is coming up, my focus switches back to fencing, training, travel arrangements and mental preparation. This does not mean that I neglect the other two blocks. If I am going through a bad patch with my fencing, I can boost my energy and resilience by spending a bit of time with my friends. I simply ask my coach to cancel a training session or I postpone a group work meeting at college, explaining that at the moment it is more important to me to see my friends.'*

Different professional lives

In the context of modern day society, the term 'slasher' takes on a new and dynamic meaning, reflecting a growing trend whereby individuals embrace multiple professional roles or occupational identities. First coined by Marci Alboher in his book *One Person/Multiple Careers* (2007), the term primarily refers to the slash sign, '/', symbolising the diverse slashes that separate different professional roles within an individual's life.

 Aisling D'Hooghe has a natural talent when it comes to combining different roles and responsibilities: *'I have three professional lives: one at my club, one in the national team and one as a councillor for the municipality of Waterloo. To make possible my desire to have children, I had to set one of these three careers temporarily on hold. To combine three professional lives, you need to be very clear in your communication with your three teams. Sometimes, I leave home at seven o'clock in the morning with three different sets of clothes on the back seat. I start my day by pulling on my kit for training with the national team. Next, I change into my day clothes to receive people in my role as a local councillor. In the evening, I switch into a different kit for my club training. It is often ten-thirty in the evening before I get home, but I have at least managed to combine my three lives and my three teams in a single day! During the temporary break that I have now decided to take my full focus will be on my partner and our wish for children. There was no point in lying to myself. Trying to combine my three roles with a pregnancy and starting a family was simply not possible. It would have pushed me beyond my limits and led to a burn-out. That would be no good for anyone. I prefer to take difficult decisions before it is too late.'*

The essence of being a slasher lies in the ability to seamlessly transition between different roles, leveraging a diverse skill set to excel in various fields. This concept extends beyond the corporate world and finds resonance in the lives of elite athletes who, in addition to their rigorous sports careers, balance the demands of academic or other professional pursuits.

One compelling aspect of the slasher lifestyle is the enrichment it brings to an individual's skill repertoire. By engaging in different domains, a slasher cultivates a broad range of expertise and experiences, fostering a unique perspective that can be applied across various disciplines. This cross-pollination of skills often results in innovative problem-solving and a holistic approach to challenges.

Furthermore, the slasher lifestyle challenges traditional notions of a linear career path. Instead of pursuing a single-track profession, slashers navigate a dynamic and interconnected web of roles. This non-linear trajectory not only allows for continuous learning but also promotes resilience in the face of career uncertainties.

The slasher lifestyle also has implications for the broader work culture. It challenges the traditional 9-to-5 paradigm and encourages a more flexible and fluid approach to work. As individuals increasingly seek fulfilment from diverse sources, employers are prompted to embrace and accommodate these multifaceted professional identities.

However, it is essential to recognize the potential challenges associated with the slasher lifestyle, such as burn-out and the need for effective self-care strategies. Juggling multiple roles can be demanding, requiring a delicate balance and a keen awareness of personal limits. That being said, embracing the slashes in our lives can lead to a more enriching and fulfilling career experience, where the intersections of diverse roles create a tapestry of resilience, innovation and continuous growth.

—— Connectedness

In the chapter about daring, we have already mentioned how important it is to know yourself and on that basis to then find a group in which you fit and where you feel comfortable. Feeling connected with your family, friends and colleagues is a crucial factor in generating the existential energy that you need.

In the business world, this is translated into the 'fit' that exists between the company and its organisational culture and the employee and his personal values. It is becoming increasingly apparent that recruiting people simply on the basis of the competencies listed in their CV is no longer sufficient to assess whether or not the person in question is a good match for the function and, in the longer term, the company. Nowadays, the values of the employee and the company must be on the same wavelength. Once again, this can vary from person to person. A highly competitive environment might be an excellent fit for one person but could be exhausting and energy-sapping for someone else. It is only in instances where a good fit is possible that the employee will internalise the values and goals of the company and her colleagues. In this case, she will feel part of a group in which she can be herself and which makes her feel contented. This will result in high levels of energy, motivation, pleasure and performance.

Scientific research (Moynigan & Pandey, 2008) has shown that employees who have a strong social network within the organisation and who also feel that their values are in line with those of the company are more likely to stay with that company in the long term.

Elite athletes have this same feeling of connectedness when they are selected for the national team and can represent their country in major international tournaments. In all sports, the players of national teams feel closely connected with each and every one of their fellow-countrymen who are present in the stadium. They have worked hard for many years to have the opportunity to make a difference for their nation and to give the best of themselves in competition with the world's other great teams to the loud applause of their fellow-citizens.

This desire for a convergence of values also applies during the transition of elite athletes to their post-sport career. They must be able to find themselves in the values of the organisation for which they will work and must be able to accept the manner in which they will have an impact on other people. They know better than anyone else what it is like to work towards an important moment that can change the rest of your life.

 Hockey player **Emmanuel Stockbroekx** knows exactly where to find the energy he needs: '*For me, inspiring people is hugely important. I get great satisfaction if I can motivate people through my story or by the way I train. I'm a real beast in training! I also live like a monk and give 200 percent for my sport: no alcohol, no night life, a good diet, total commitment during practice, and so on. If there is a game, I leave absolutely everything out on the pitch. Of course, there are moments when I ask myself what on earth I am doing. Then I say to myself: "If you one day become an Olympic champion, you will have achieved everything an athlete can achieve. You will not only inspire your country, but also crown decades of hard work to create a great national team". This feeling of doing something that has never been done before in Belgium is an extra driving force for me and the rest of the team. We are pioneers. That is what we train for every day. That is what makes it all worthwhile.*'

In the business world, the nature of an organisation's key overarching goal is not always clear; nor is the manner in which an individual employee can contribute towards this goal. If you spend all day filling in figures on an Excel spreadsheet, it is not easy to see how this is helping to make society a better place! For this reason, we advise all companies and their managers to make crystal clear to all their people precisely how their specific tasks help the organisation to achieve its goal and how reaching that goal can have a positive impact for others. If there is a good fit between the individual and the organisation, this will have a stimulating and motivating effect.

Out of balance

In our way of thinking about the development of high performance attitudes, there is an important basic principle that we wish to clarify. If you want to display and use these attitudes in the best possible way, it is important to realise that:

— you need to find a balance between showing either too much or too little of a particular attitude.

— the context in which you wish to perform will determine to a significant degree the opportunity and suitability of displaying particular attitudes.

On the page 'Coach yourself', you can use the dashboards to indicate whether or not you display the different aspects of the relevant chapter's attitude 'too little', 'optimally' or 'too much'. In this way, we hope to stimulate your self-insight.

Experience shows that before you can consistently display an attitude in an optimal manner, you will sometimes get things out of balance. This is not a problem, as long as you recognise the imbalance and adjust it to reflect the situation you are in. So that you are able to recognise your imbalanced behaviour, we will provide you with a list of the most common characteristics that indicate the display of too much or too little of the attitude.

Kevin Borlée – atletics

Stef De Greef – fencing

Antonia Delaere – basketball

Too little *energy use, too much energy refuel*

Too much *energy use, too little energy refuel*

You go from one physical challenge to the next, constantly challenging the limits of your body.

———

You exercise too little, so that you use too little physical energy.

———

You work long days, overworking yourself and exhausting your reserves of mental energy.

———

Your eating and sleeping patterns are unhealthy or irregular.

———

You find it difficult to relax or to allow periods of recovery after mental and physical effort.

———

You find it difficult to work in a concentrated manner and are easily distracted.

———

You take too much care of others and too little of yourself.

———

You lose more energy than you gain from your relationships with others.

———

Your brain is never at rest, but is constantly thinking about possibilities and difficulties.

———

You seldom or never feel motivated to learn new things.

———

You have committed yourself to take part in so many projects that you feel that others are too dependent on you.

———

You experience too little meaning in your professional life and feel no real connection with your organisation.

Your willpower is so strong that you never give up, even when you are exhausted.

Coach yourself!

—— Describe your next ultimate victory!

....

....

STEP 1 Give yourself a score for the following aspects of this attitude.

- I make conscious choices to keep my life in balance.
- I manage my energy levels in a sustainable way.
- I know my energy-givers and energy-eaters, and I keep them in balance.
- I take sufficient exercise, eat healthily and feel refreshed after sleep.
- I make time for myself and my personal development.
- I spend enough time with the people who are dear to me.
- I feel that I am living a meaningful life.

STEP 2 Indicate how important it is for you to further develop this attitude as a means to achieving your goal.

0   10
(unimportant)   (very important)

STEP 3 Identify your challenges and your levers. (See part 2.)

—— My challenges: ....

—— My levers: ....

STEP 4 Identify your mental skills that will help you to deal positively with challenges. (See part 3.)

—— How will these mental skills help you?

....

STEP 5 Name the concrete actions you will take on the road towards your ultimate victory.

....

....

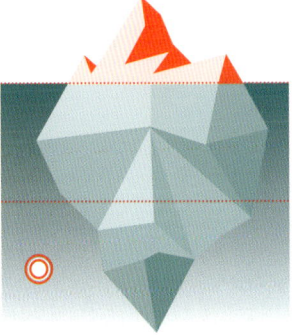

ATTITUDE 7

ENJOY AND CELEBRATE

'I enjoy the rush of adrenalin as soon as I enter the stadium, before the competition starts. But also during the competition, when the public shouts for me before an event starts or when they cheer if I clear the high jump bar. That feeling is wonderful, truly indescribable…'

—— **Noor Vidts**, heptathlete

Definition

'Enjoy & celebrate'

We describe this as an attitude typified by the passion and enthusiasm with which someone goes through life. People who display this attitude are consciously grateful for the life that they lead and experience pleasure in sharing important and personal milestone moments in that life.

This attitude reflects their enjoyment and their appreciation of every step – whether great or small – that leads them towards their ultimate victory and they consciously organise celebrations to mark each of those steps and any other occasion that is worth celebrating.

Characteristics of top performers with this attitude

— They enjoy their journey to the top.
— They derive pleasure from their life.
— They consciously pause to reflect on their life and show gratitude.
— They are passionate about what they do, almost to the point of being obsessive.
— They like being in the spotlight.
— They celebrate exuberantly but soon get back to business.

Top performers enjoy their journey to the top

Although this is the final attitude in our book, it is also one of the most important. Its presence is essential if you want to secure your **ultimate victory**. Most of the athletes that we have interviewed value all parts of the process that is necessary for them to achieve personal excellence. They are passionate about their sport and are motivated by growth and development. Athletes who are driven by the process rather than by results perform more consistently at a higher standard.

As already mentioned, the **ultimate victory** is a very dynamic concept. Throughout your life and career, you will achieve many **ultimate victories**. The journey towards self-realisation is long and never really ends. Moreover, it is a journey full of ups and downs. And precisely because you will be confronted by dips and disappointments along the way, it is crucial that you never lose sight of the importance of enjoying. Even if it seems like you are making no progress, try to enjoy such moments as well. Always search for the positive things around you – because you will always find some.

 Bart Swings: *'If I could speak to my younger self, I would now recommend setting realistic intermediary goals, trying to improve myself step by step. Progression is also a kind of victory. This is something that I now pursue actively and consciously. Patience is important. I want to continue making progress, because I know that this will allow me to continue competing at the top, and that makes me happy.'*

To remain **intrinsically motivated** during the peaks and troughs of your journey, finding pleasure in what you do, in the process that you are going through and in the intermediary successes you achieve as you move forward, is vital. There is a powerful link between enjoyment and motivation, with both attitudes influencing each other constantly.

Putting together the right team around you is equally important, if you want your journey to be as carefree as possible. Making things harder by surrounding yourself with the wrong people creates nothing but additional stress and avoidable difficulties. Of course, it is always possible that not everyone will stay with you throughout the entire length of your journey. During the different stages of the journey, different people might make contributions at different times. Once you have jumped a particular hurdle, you may have outgrown what they are able to teach you.

Getting joy from feedback is another of the characteristics characteristic. Actively searching for points for improvement and enjoying the process of learning something new and making progress **each day is part of their identity**. No one is ever too old or too wise to learn, and regarding such lessons as fun is essential for discovering more joy in your life.

Linked to this is the seemingly endless **repetition** of certain exercises and movements to which top performers subject themselves. They may not always enjoy this repetition at the moment it takes place, but their wider enjoyment of the process persuades them to keep going. It is all about **finding pleasure in trying new things and leaving your comfort zone**.

And when you occasionally step too far out of that comfort zone, so that you sometimes run into a brick wall, your passion for what you do will ensure that you do not simply throw in the towel, but instead **will give you the strength to carry on and bounce back stronger than ever before.**

Last but not least, **consciously pausing to monitor your energy levels and striving to keep them in balance** will provide you with inner calm and long-term dedication for your sport. So the message is clear: when the six other attitudes all come together, they combine to ensure that as an outstanding performer you will be able to **enjoy your journey to the top**.

Top performers enjoy life

—— Ikigai

Getting pleasure from what you do, jumping out of bed each morning with energy, full of enthusiasm to start the new day: these are characteristics of the Japanese concept of **ikigai**. The word means 'reason for existence' and is therefore closely related to your dream goal. *Ikigai* combines four important elements, which together contribute to enjoyment and happiness. The four elements are:

— what you love;
— what you are good at;
— what the world needs;
— what you can/want to be rewarded for.

You will get huge pleasure from your job or profession if you can find a way to position yourself at the intersection where the four *ikigai* circles meet. Pausing to assess your current position in relation to these circles is a good way to estimate whether or not you have already found your *ikigai*.

—— What you love

Top performers often have a dream goal from an early age. They take the first concrete steps towards this goal while they are still young. For example, by the time they are sixteen years old many elite athletes already dream of being among the best in the world. They can almost hear the spectators in the stadium cheering! By the time they are eighteen, they have probably already had their first experience of the professional sporting environment at the highest level. And just a few years later the whole country is watching them perform remarkable feats of sporting excellence. For top performers of this kind, the origin and basis for their performance – the idea or dream from which everything flows – is constantly and clearly present.

What was your dream as a child. Did you want to be a professional footballer? A fireman? A doctor? It is possible that this is exactly what you are doing now. But it is also possible that you followed a totally different path. Whichever choices you eventually made, reflecting on your childhood dream is a good way to give you insight into the **values** and **motives** that are important to you. Discovering these values and motives in your current profession is crucial if you want to find your ikigai. If, for example, helping others is one of your important values, you will do your job with passion when this value finds expression in what you do. This will give you extra energy, even at the end of a long day, as well as giving you the feeling that you are on the right track.

 Judoka **Jorre Verstraeten** has already been on the podium a number of times at European championships. The pleasure he derives from his sport is one of the keys to his success: *'In judo I feel constantly challenged. And the challenge gets bigger as time passes. That is what gives me so much pleasure in this sport. There are still so many things, both great and small, that I need to improve. The idea that you can never be the "perfect" judoka stimulates me. It is fun trying to achieve that perfection, as long as you realise that it will never be possible. Learning new things each day and correcting my weak points gives me huge satisfaction. Finding the techniques that match my style of judo and repeating them day after day, so that I can use them to score in competition – for me, that is still a wonderful challenge.'*

For Jorre, self-development is an important value, something he works at every day. His testimony shows clearly that he gets great pleasure from constantly challenging himself and raising the bar higher and higher. He seeks to achieve perfection, but understands that it is an impossible goal. But that doesn't stop him from trying.

—— What you are good at

As we get older, our ideas about what we like to do and what we do well (and what not) become increasingly clear. That being said, even young children have preferences in these matters. Some will reach for a colouring book, while others prefer to play football.

If you want to develop your potential fully, this implies that you must actively make use of it. When you do things that you are good at, you create success experiences for yourself. These experiences give you pleasure. That is why we so often say that the things **we do well are the things we love doing.**

Snowboarder **Jules De Sloover** explains: '*During a competition I always try to play to my strengths, so that I can give full expression to my potential. By doing the tricks that I know I can do well, I experience more pleasure and have less of a feeling that I need to prove myself. In this way I can be who I really am and who I want to be on my board.*'

When Jules is on his snowboard and does the tricks that he likes and can master, his performance looks almost effortless, because he is being who he truly is. At such moments, he enjoys his sport intensely and gets great energy from his actions.

—— What the world needs

This aspect of *ikigai* (and the experiencing of fulfilment as a result) is something that we have already examined in the chapter on energy. The feeling that what you are doing in some way contributes to a **more important whole** and that you are having a positive impact on the lives of the people around you gives **great satisfaction and a sense of purpose**. It shows that you can make a difference.

Of course, **offering the world what it needs is also very important** in the world of business. In the labour market, it is vital to find a connection between your competencies and the needs of the company. You must be able to add value to the company's current range of activities. Each year, employment agencies draw up lists of so-called 'bottleneck' professions, jobs for which there is a shortage of personnel. The aim is to channel people into making choices that will lead them to take on one of these jobs, which will benefit society as a whole.

As an entrepreneur, it is also important to respond to what the market needs. The best product in the world will never sell if there is no demand for it. Any product or service that you bring to market must provide a solution to a problem or create added value for the people who will use it.

—— What you can/want to be rewarded for

We are not going to deny that extrinsic motives also play a significant role. Being able to pay the bills at the end of the month is important for everyone. If this is not possible, it will not contribute to your general happiness. Quite the reverse. In other words, **doing something for which you can be paid enough** to meet your needs is crucial in our present-day society. In short, you really need a job.

If you are someone's employee, it is self-evident that you get paid for what you do. Legally agreed pay scales mean that this payment is usually fair. This is not always the case for entrepreneurs and athletes. We have already heard from **Jorre Verstraeten**. Although judo is his passion and although he excels at it and serves as an ambassador both for his sport and his country, his salary as a judoka is modest. Like many other elite athletes, he will not be able to retire on what he earned from his sport once his career is over.

Entrepreneurs also often work many hours without proper compensation. Experience shows that it is not always easy as a self-employed person or an entrepreneur to receive fair remuneration for what you do. For example, there is always someone else who also does what you do, only cheaper. Even so, maintaining your own prices and standards of quality is crucial, since this will eventually lead you to your ideal customers.

All athletes who are at the top of their sport are doing something that they love doing, heart and soul. If you give them a choice, there is nothing they would rather do than train and perform in their chosen sport. They find their greatest pleasure on the training ground or in the competitive arena.

Scientific research (Cambre, De Bosscher & Depelchin, 2015) involving young volleyball players has revealed that the expectation of fun is the most important reason for joining a volleyball club. And a lack of enjoyment once they have joined is the most important reason for leaving again.

A lack of enjoyment will inevitably have a negative effect on the display of all the other key attitudes we have discussed. It is difficult to be resilient when you do not enjoy what you are doing. In these circumstances, giving up will seem increasingly attractive. By contrast, if you enjoy your sport or your job it will be easier to keep on going, even during the moments that are far from enjoyable. Doing something that you like gives you intrinsic motivation to keep on pushing and working even harder. In spite of the difficulty, you are enjoying the process and you require little to no help from extrinsic factors. In the rest of this chapter, the strong link between enjoyment and motivation will become increasingly clear.

Top performers reflect on their career and are grateful for it

—— Gratitude for the extraordinary life they lead

One of the common denominators in all our interviews with elite athletes was their **gratitude** for the kind of life that they can lead because of their sport. They have all been able to successfully turn their hobby into their profession, although in most cases they still actually regard it as a hobby that just kept on going further and further.

The hard training sessions, the pressure, the difficult choices: they accept all these things with pleasure, because every day they are doing what they dreamed of doing since they were a child. They travel the world and are admired by their fans. They are, quite literally, living their dream, so that all the sacrifices and hardships seem worthwhile.

Of course, it is not always easy for them to be consciously aware every day of the pleasure they derive from their sport. They know there will be setbacks and disappointments, but their mental flexibility allows them to move on quickly to the next phase of their career. Likewise, the euphoria created by achieving significant milestones in their career also quickly evaporates. For example, qualifying for the Olympic Games is great, but it is no more than a stepping stone to performing in those Games – and so they celebrate briefly and then move on. Top performers enjoy their performances, but they do not dwell in the past. They immediately look forward to the future – and the next challenge.

This constant focus on the next step means that elite athletes also start to think relatively early about their career after professional sport. Again, this is something we have discussed in an earlier chapter, but here will look a little more deeply into the specific aspects associated with the approaching end of a sporting career. **As this end approaches, some athletes become increasingly aware of their need to express gratitude**. After so much hard work and with the end now in sight, they begin to appreciate the special moments and even the not-so-special moments more and more.

In one of my coaching sessions with sprinter **Hanne Claes**, I asked her when she would regard her sporting career as a success. At first, she found this a difficult question to answer and so I asked her instead about the mindset with which she would later approach her final season. Hanne then realised that it would not be a single race or top time that would define the way she would look back on her career. Even today, while she is still active as an athlete, she is already proud of the way in which she has dealt with the ups and downs of sporting life and is grateful for the many fine meetings with people that have enriched her career, as well as so much more besides.'

—— Consciously reflecting on victory and growth

It is important for top performers to look back regularly on the milestones in their career and to relive the enjoyment of those moments. Constantly setting the bar higher and higher can sometimes give athletes the feeling that they still have a long way to go. Occasionally pausing to reflect on how far they have already come strengthens their belief in their own ability. Such moments of reflection give athletes new drive, enhancing their feeling of competence and giving a boost to their self-confidence.

Elite athletes are often privileged to enjoy 'once-in-a-lifetime' experiences, although they do not always appreciate the special significance of these moments at the time. For example, qualifying for the Olympic Games for the first time is a moment that exceeds your wildest dreams!

 Basketball player **Emma Meesseman** explains how she felt after the final whistle in the Olympic qualifying tournament in Ostend: *'Of course, I felt euphoric, but I don't think any of us truly realised what we had done and that we would really be going to the Olympic Games. It had been a childhood dream for all of us.'*

Likewise in the business world, there is not always time to enjoy your successes and personal victories. In this respect, young employees and entrepreneurs can often benefit from having a mentor; someone who will help them to consciously reflect on their successes with the necessary gratitude and enjoyment.

Scientific research (Chen & Chang, 2016; Chan, 2011) has demonstrated that gratitude is linked to a higher level of well-being and a lower level of burn-out, both for athletes and for employees.

Showing gratitude helps you to look at the world in a positive manner. As a result, even hard lessons can help you to take huge steps forward. In turn, this also has a further positive impact on your well-being. In the chapter on energy, we saw that positive energy leads to more positive thinking. And in our opinion, **gratitude also has this same chain-reaction effect!**

Regularly pausing to look back on the highpoints of your career can therefore increase the sense of enjoyment you experience. The moments themselves often pass too quickly, but looking at photographs taken at the time or sharing memories with others can often call up the same feelings and help you to relate more consciously with pleasure and gratitude. If you prefer, you can start small, by thinking every day about one thing that you are grateful for.

Top performers feel passion, bordering on obsession

—— Harmonious or obsessive passion

Every interview that we had with elite athletes was an experience for Tara and myself. We were given the opportunity to talk with forty passionate people about what they most like doing in all the world. One of the nicest things about talking with people about their **personal passion** is that you can quite literally see their eyes shine. After each interview, we both felt an energy boost: such was the infectious **enthusiasm** of the athletes concerned.

What characterises **Vincent Kompany** and all the other elite athletes we spoke to is the fact that they live for their sport: *'I think that my passion almost borders the obsessive. But it is not obsession, because I know when and how to let go. It makes me very happy when I feel that during the week I have worked with great passion. But if I feel that I am taking things too far and risk going over the edge, I stop. I can decide to take half a day off to relax or spend time with my children. In that way, my passion doesn't get the better of me. Passion only becomes obsession when you can't sleep at night or you don't get any enjoyment out of it.'*

Once again, this testimony shows how important it is to keep a balance. When passion becomes obsession, this balance is disturbed. Being passionate about your sport, job or company is good. It means that it will usually give you pleasure and satisfaction. Even so, you need to be careful that this does not upset the other important balances in your life.

The healthy passion that athletes have for their sport means that they have no real difficulty in coming to terms with the unusual rhythms of their sporting life. Their 'job' is not nine-to-five. In theory, it is 24/7! In fact, being a top performer is more a lifestyle than a job and there are often peak moments during the weekend – while the rest of us are relaxing – when they have to perform at their best. At such moments, it is their passion for their sport and the progress they are making that helps them to rise to the occasion.

Athlete **Camille Laus** tells us how she lives for her sport: *'While I am falling asleep, I think about my races and what I was feeling during training. If I know that another heavy training session is scheduled for the next day, I think: "Yes, that is exactly what I want!" These things keep going through my head. Thinking about my races and my results gives me a boost. Of course, I can think and talk about other things as well, but it is my sport that occupies most of my thoughts and energy. I am truly passionate about it. I live to run fast.'*

Recent research studies (Verner-Filion & Vallerand, 2018; Schiphof-Godart & Hettinga, 2017) have made a distinction between harmonious passion and obsessive passion. Harmonious passion strengthens an athlete's sense of well-being, while obsessive passion detracts from that well-being. Although both kinds of passion can lead to short-term success, obsessive passion can negatively influence an athlete's welfare – and therefore their performance – over the long term. Obsessive passion pushes the athlete to overtrain, increasing the risk of injuries or even burn-out (Gustafsson, Hassmen & Hassmen, 2011).

If we extrapolate this to the business world, it seems reasonable to assume that employees with a higher level of harmonious passion will feel a greater sense of well-being, will display greater engagement and will perform to a higher standard in the long run. For this reason, it is essential to be aware of the four quadrants of the Kopman Wheel and to understand the importance of **optimal energy management** (attitude 6).

In addition to being passionate about their work and getting satisfaction from it, it is also necessary to monitor employees, to ensure that they do not take things too far. Working hard for long periods can be fantastic, both for the individual and for the organisation, but it needs to be done in a healthy manner. If that is not the case, the passion and the pleasure will soon disappear, resulting in overwork rather than optimum work, which is not a good recipe for a happy personal life.

—— A passion for entrepreneurship

Entrepreneurship is also often associated with passion. Self-employed people clock up long hours, seldom take holidays and have little time for anything other than work. Sometimes it can be difficult for entrepreneurs – both young and old alike – to properly channel this passion and enthusiasm. Working for yourself can give you an unbelievable rush of adrenalin and doing what you most like doing is everyone's dream. What's more, as an entrepreneur you are often responsible for everything, which brings a lot of extra work with it. However, because you are so passionate about your project, you can sometimes find it difficult to delegate part of it to others. Your company is like your child and you are not prepared to entrust it to just anyone!

Passion can be compared with a fire burning inside a person. With enough oxygen and combustible material, the fire can be kept going forever and not even the best fireman in the world will be able to put it out. But if the flame is not fed with sufficient oxygen, it will eventually extinguish itself. This again emphasises the importance of balance. Make sure you build enough rest periods into your busy programme, so that you can keep your inner flame well supplied with that crucial oxygen. At the same time, a good supply of combustible material is also necessary. Be aware that you may not be able to provide this material alone and have the courage to involve others in your project. For an entrepreneur who wishes to pass on his flame to the next generation, this is vital.

Finally, it is important to keep your flame well regulated. Putting too much wood on your fire may cause it to flare up out of control or, alternatively, might smother it completely. As so often, balance is the key.

In other words, **the channelling and sometimes even the restraining of your passion is important for continuing to perform optimally over time**. Trying to do too much, too often and for too long is seldom a good idea. Give your passion and creativity enough oxygen by regularly taking a step away from your work and simply enjoying the moment.

Top performers like being in the limelight

Top performers are often the focus of attention. Some of them like it; others prefer to remain under the radar. But one thing is certain: when they are actually performing, they are fully in the spotlight – and they love it! Public participation and even adulation adds something extra to the performance experience and the pleasure it gives.

In this sense, elite athletes can be compared with the world's best stage artists. These artists also love to show off the talent they possess.

—— Sharing enjoyment

Michael Jackson once said: *'Being on stage is magic. There is nothing like it. You feel the energy of everybody who's out there. You feel it all over your body, I swear.'*

The ability to share enjoyment gives an extra dimension to the performance and how the performer experiences it. When they see the audience taking their seats in the auditorium or arena, they can already feel the pleasure of what is to come. And seeing the excitement of the fans during the actual performance heightens their own experience even further. Giving people powerful emotions and making them happy, while you are doing what you most like doing in the world: what could be better than that?

 Basketball player **Emma Meesseman** vividly remembers the historic night when the Belgian Cats qualified for the Olympic Games in Ostend: *'It doesn't happen very often that you get the chance to make your dreams come true. And we were able to do it in front of our home public! Our friends and family were all in Ostend. For me, that is what made the moment extra-special. Playing the game you love and achieving your dream in the presence of all the people who are important to you. It is moments like that which make you realise why you do it, why you work so hard and why you are away from your loved-ones so often.'*

—— Social facilitation and social inhibition

It is the personality and experience of the athlete in question that determine whether or not the presence of spectators gives a boost to their performance. Top performers who have a strong connection with their fans clearly missed them during the corona pandemic, whereas young and more nervous athletes at the start of their career were probably glad that they were not there. In this context, we speak of two concepts: social facilitation and social inhibition. **Social facilitation** refers to the better performance of simple tasks when other people are watching. However, an audience watching can also have an opposite effect, when the person performing the task has not yet fully mastered it. This increases the pressure on the person concerned, making them less confident or less inclined to make the necessary effort, resulting in a decline in performance.

When the presence of others prevents you from doing your best, we refer to this as **social inhibition**. This occurs when you are doing things that you have not yet fully learned, so that you are more afraid of making mistakes when everyone's eyes are on you. There are also other related factors in play: nobody likes to disappoint people who are expecting a lot of them and nobody likes to feel a failure. For this reason, there is a simple comparison that I make when I am giving guidance to elite athletes: I call it 'You are not a jar of chocolate spread'. This is a metaphor that I have carried over from my family life. Once a week, on a Sunday morning, I put a jar of chocolate spread on our breakfast table, which instantly makes my husband and children happy. The jar doesn't have to do anything special. All it has to do is to appear: it will automatically be welcomed and cheered. But an athlete is not a jar of choco. You cannot expect people to automatically be happy every time you appear or perform. Having such an expectation simply sets the bar too high for yourself, so that the pressure you feel increases and your pleasure diminishes.

Top performers have learned to channel their thoughts, narrow their focus and manage their adrenalin levels, so that they are no longer bothered by the presence of the public or by other people's opinions of their performance. This actually allows them to enjoy their interaction with the crowd in a manner that gives them an extra push in the back, an added advantage that often leads to better results.

——— Home support and home advantage

Social facilitation also helps to explain why playing at home is usually an advantage in most competitive sports. Elite athletes generally feel better and perform better in a familiar environment, where they can see, hear and 'feel' their own home supporters.

The majority of the top performers we interviewed said that they like to know where their family are sitting during a race or match. This gives them extra **mental calm** and a **feeling of added control**. If they need it, they know exactly where to look to get an encouraging smile or wave. In particular, parents and partners tend to know best what athletes require at these moments of extreme pressure or self-doubt and can respond accordingly. This is also a tip that I give quite often to other people, not only to my own children when they have to give a book presentation in class, but also to businessmen who need to make a speech at their company's new year's reception: first make a connection with the people in the room and then search the room for the looks that seem receptive to your message and are responding enthusiastically. This will make your own performance all the more fascinating for everyone concerned.

I also always try to arrive in good time whenever I am giving a keynote to companies. I like to soak up the atmosphere, walk through the auditorium and see the place where I will be standing to talk. I like to watch the personnel, the way they enter the room and the way they interact with each other. These few moments give me time to **acclimatise** to the surroundings, before it is my turn to perform. Professional footballers do exactly the same, when they come out onto the pitch half an hour before the kick-off for a brief warm-up.

The truth of the claim that your own supporters are vitally important, not only for the level of your performance but also for the joy and pleasure that you gain from that performance, is something that we were fortunate enough to experience with the Belgian Cats when we won against the host nation Spain at the world championships in Tenerife. After the game, all of the Belgian supporters who had made the trip were waiting for us outside the arena. We had played a fantastic game and the fans gave each of us a tremendous round of applause as we boarded the team bus.

Antonia Delaere describes what it felt like: *'Throughout the game, you could hear our supporters cheering us. And God knows how hard they had to try to make that possible. Three hundred Belgians against four thousand five hundred Spaniards! When we were being led out to the bus after the game, a sea of people was waiting to greet us. They chanted our names and sang songs. Just thinking about it gives me goosebumps, even now. Whether you know the supporters or not, your home public always gives you an extra boost. They are strangers, but you feel a connection with the Belgian people. They increase your confidence and give you energy. It's wonderful.'*

This is why I like working so much with national teams. It is an indescribable feeling to be part of something that is bigger than yourself and gives you the opportunity to put Belgian sport on the map. And the fact that I am the daughter of a French-speaking mother and a Dutch-speaking father makes it all the more enjoyable. That is also part of my joy.

—— Enthusiasm is contagious

We have already said it several times: top performers are passionate about their profession. As a rule, they are enthusiastic about what they do and how they do it. **This enthusiasm is contagious and helps to connect people.**

Snowboarder **Seppe Smits** explains how the world's best competitors in his sport get along with each other: *'Although we are rivals, we can sometimes discuss different tricks for hours. Why? I don't really have an explanation, but we do it anyway. I think that it is probably because we have plenty of mutual respect for each other. In our sport, you take a lot of physical risks. We love snowboarding because it allows you to push your boundaries. But if one of us pushes his boundaries that little bit further, we all love to see the result. And it immediately gives you a new personal challenge to work towards. At the same time, you also know how happy that person must be to have done that new trick, which also makes you feel happy as well. There is one moment I will never forget: the moment when someone successfully landed a back-to-back triple 16 for the first time. The rest of us were all at the bottom of the run, watching and waiting. We all had the same idea, but would he actually do it? We knew that he could do the two tricks separately, but no one had ever done them consecutively without falling. But that is precisely what he now did. It was a world performance that left us all speechless. All we could say was "Wow!". We all ran to meet him off the run and threw him shoulder-high in celebration. It was a very special feeling for all of us, because it meant that our sport had progressed. All the riders were super-happy, including me, even though I didn't have a run that day.'*

When I read this, it instantly makes me happy as well. It shows just how fantastic sport can sometimes be. Am I happy if a rival performs better than me? Of course I am – for them. Am I annoyed if the team of another sport psychologist is more successful than mine? Never. That is what true sportsmanship is all about.

——— Sharing in the success and inspiration of others

Human beings are social creatures. By nature, they seek attention. Social contact fulfils our need to be seen, to be heard, to belong. As a result of the attention we receive, we feel both valued and happy.

This desire for popularity is characteristic of our generation and will perhaps be even more dominant in the next, which has grown up with social media. Having lots of friends, both in the real world and the digital one, is often seen as both important and admirable. The short-term kick of a like stimulates people of all ages to be active on their social media accounts for hours each day. These accounts and the internet have made our lives more visible than ever before. Whether on work-related platforms like LinkedIn or social platforms like Facebook and Instagram, we love to share our successes, achievements and happiness. Being seen as much as possible is what counts.

Thanks to their skilful use of social media, top performers succeed in building up a positive image around themselves and their activities. They usually do this by remaining as close as possible to who they really are and by communicating this in an **authentic manner**. As a result, elite athletes not only post their successes, but also their disappointments. When they talk about a lost game, elimination from a championship or even an injury, they always try to include a positive message somewhere along the line.

 Snowboarder **Jules De Sloover** has experienced how the smart use of social media has helped his career, but also sometimes created added pressure: '*Social media play a big role in snowboarding. It is a role that is often underestimated, but it is crucial for your competitions and for your career as a whole. A lot of snowboard competitions are by invitation only. And you only get an invite when the organiser thinks you are a good snowboarder or likes the tricks that you do. Performing well in a competition can suddenly bring you instant fame, but you need to maintain it on social media. At the same time, this brings extra pressure, because you have to post things regularly and you need to make sure that people still like you. Having lots of followers also helps to attract sponsors and sponsors can sometimes get you into some of the big competitions. It is a kind of unconscious pressure, but it's always there.*'

Fans are not necessarily looking for superheroes against whom they can measure themselves – which can often end up with them feeling disappointed. More often than not, they are looking for the real person behind the superhero and this is a connection that can be made more easily when the hero's story is authentic, in both good times and bad. For this reason, it is also important as a top performer to sometimes communicate about less positive experiences that you have managed to turn around. This helps to explain, for example, why Jules recently posted a video that showed him landing badly from a ten-metre high jump that put him in hospital – and not for the first time.

In the chapter on leadership we discussed the importance of a team and many top performers are now expert at building up a team around them in the virtual environment, with whom they can share their triumphs and disasters.

We all know that messages on social media are not always pleasant or positive. Top performers know this as well. In sport, your performances are constantly evaluated by hundreds if not thousands of different people worldwide. Once again, it is worth remembering that you are not a jar of chococolate spread! The important thing is to realise that there are only a handful of people – who you yourself have selected – whose **opinions you need to take seriously**. All the rest you can take with a pinch of salt.

 Britt Herbots, volleyball player: '*When I was younger, I wanted everyone to think that I was good and fun. That creates a lot of pressure, because it simply isn't possible. You can't please everyone.*'

The key thing to remember is that you decide how you want to use social media. If you find that it is having a negative effect on you, change your habits. Deal with your online presence with greater awareness. For example, only go online at fixed moments during the day. In this way, you can limit its impact on the rest of your daily programme.

Top performers celebrate exuberantly but then get straight back to business!

After a game they had won, **Daniel Goethals**, – an ex-basketball player and now a coach at international level – told his team: 'Enjoy this moment, but remember: you are only heroes for one day!' In this way, he emphasised the importance of celebrating victories, but also underlined that tomorrow is another day – and back to work! As a result, he prevented his players from getting carried away on the euphoria of their triumph and made clear that from the next morning more hard training would be necessary if they wished to repeat their success.

When I worked in the business world, my finest experience was as part of a recruitment team for an international player in the energy market. Together with my colleagues, it was our job to hire new people at all organisational levels, in a labour market which at that time was characterised by the so-called 'war for talent'. In this tight labour situation, we needed to find and attract the best candidates, if we wanted to stay ahead of our competitors. The team's goals for the number of recruitments were clear. And each time someone brought us a bit closer to one of those goals, we celebrated! First came the congratulations, followed by a dance through the corridor and a lunch or a drink after work. **Work hard, play hard**: that was our motto. We were all highly motivated and very ambitious, but we didn't begrudge each other our individual successes. Instead, we enjoyed them and embraced them. This further improved or team's cohesion and drive. We really were the business!

Research (Moll, Jordet & Pepping, 2010) has revealed that team performance in sport is positively influenced when players celebrate a goal together, rather than with the public or alone. Their report concluded: '*If you cheer with the fans after you have scored a penalty, they will be wildly enthusiastic. That is fine, but they are not the people with whom you have to perform for the rest of the game after the match is restarted. You need to play further with your team mates, so celebrate with them: this makes scoring infectious.*'

In other high performance contexts, such as the world of stage and screen, many actors and artists organise a party to mark the opening night of a new film, play or series of concerts. The months before the premiere are demanding and the evening itself is usually tense, while the public's reaction remains uncertain. Turning that evening into a celebration helps to have a positive effect on the entire team, providing them with an opportunity to recognise and express gratitude for each other's contributions.

The message is clear: if you want to continue performing to a high standard, you need to regularly reflect on what you have achieved and celebrate your successes, both as an individual and as a team. For this reason, I like to compare top performers with formula 1 racing cars: they can speed around the race track with amazing speed, but still need to be refuelled every once in a while. So enjoy the life that you lead and be grateful for it. Celebration is the petrol that will keep the engine of your supercar running and running.

 When cyclist **Victor Campenaerts** analyses the season in which he broke the world hour record, he now concludes that he failed to celebrate this magnificent performance sufficiently: *'During that season, breaking the hour record was the ultimate goal. But if I look back at that season now, I realise that we made a mistake as a team: after we had broken the record, we neglected to take a long enough rest and never really had a moment when we could celebrate what we had achieved. Later on in the season, that missed opportunity had a negative effect on my performance.'*

It is precisely for this reason that it is important to think carefully about **how you celebrate your successes**. Something improvised is one possibility and this can often be the most fun option. But whatever your preference, just make sure that you celebrate, one way or another. And learn from the feedback you get, so that you can do it even better next time. Do not exaggerate your defeats. And never undervalue your victories.

Out of balance

In our way of thinking about the development of high performance attitudes, there is an important basic principle that we wish to clarify. If you want to display and use these attitudes in the best possible way, it is important to realise that:

— you need to find a balance between showing either too much or too little of a particular attitude;

— the context in which you wish to perform will determine to a significant degree the opportunity and suitability of displaying particular attitudes.

On the page 'Coach yourself', you can use the dashboards to indicate whether or not you display the different aspects of the relevant chapter's attitude 'too little', 'optimally' or 'too much'. In this way, we hope to stimulate your self-insight.

Experience shows that before you can consistently display an attitude in an optimal manner, you will sometimes get things out of balance. This is not a problem, as long as you recognise the imbalance and adjust it to reflect the situation you are in. So that you are able to recognise your imbalanced behaviour, we will provide you with a list of the most common characteristics that indicate the display of too much or too little of the attitude.

Thibaut Vervoort – 3x3 basketball

Tiesj Benoot – cycling

Grégory Wathelet – show jumping

Too little
enjoy
& celebrate

Too much
enjoy
& celebrate

You place too much emphasis on result goals,
so that you cannot enjoy the path that leads to them.

———

You find it difficult to relax or to enjoy other activities that are
not related to your performance in the short term.

———

You think the glass is half empty, not half full.
You are overcritical and focus too much on shortcomings
and not enough on growth opportunities.

———

You work from necessity, not passion.

———

You are so focused on your performance that the manner of
your performing does not interest you.

———

You act too much on 'automatic pilot',
so that you do not realise sufficiently
how you can get pleasure from what you do.

———

You do things because you have to, not because you want to.

You attach too little importance to result goals
and are more interested in having fun.

———

Your lack of efficiency makes you a distraction
for your team mates.

———

Your lack of a sense of reality and your carefree attitude make
you over enthusiastic, so that you overestimate your abilities
and begin tasks without proper preparation.

———

Your passion means that you do not pause to reflect sufficiently
on what you do and why you do it.

———

Your passion means that you commit to too many projects,
so that you lose your way in too many activities.

———

You only do what you want to do, not what you should do.

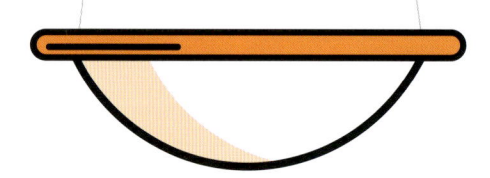

Coach yourself!

—— Describe your next ultimate victory!

....

....

STEP 1 Give yourself a score for the following aspects of this attitude.

- I get as much pleasure from the little things in life as from important achievements.
- I know my *ikigai* and derive sufficient pleasure and meaning from it.
- I follow my passion without it becoming an obsession.
- I like to share my passion, dreams, pleasure and successes with others.
- I see that my enthusiasm is infectious for others.
- I like to celebrate my successes and take the necessary time to do it.

STEP 2 Indicate how important it is for you to further develop this attitude as a means to achieving your goal.

0 .... **10**

(unimportant)   (very important)

STEP 3 Identify your challenges and your levers. (See part 2.)

—— My challenges: ....

—— My levers: ....

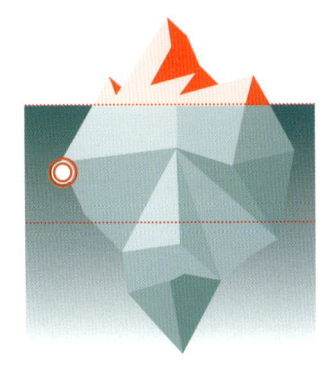

STEP 4 Identify your mental skills that will help you to deal positively with challenges. (See part 3.)

—— How will these mental skills help you?

....

....

STEP 5 Name the concrete actions you will take on the road towards your ultimate victory.

....

....

PART 2

CHALLENGES AND LEVERS

At Smart Mind, we hold the following firm belief: *'Your* **ultimate victories** *will only follow each other in succession if you optimally develop and use your talent. By putting the emphasis on growth and the cultivation of high performance attitudes, top performance can be achieved consistently and repeatedly.'* The testimonies of the top performers in this book are living proof of this claim.

However, we know from experience that it is not always simple to display these high performance attitudes in the best possible way. Sometimes we are not coachable enough, sometimes we lack the necessary courage, and so on.

To understand why we display certain types of behaviour, it is important for us to consciously investigate what elements disturb the balance that we need to perform well, as a result of which we display one or more attitudes too much or too little in particular situations.

One thing of which we can be certain is that our behaviour will be assessed and judged, whether we like it or not. Our coach, manager, parents, colleagues: they will all have an opinion about why you are not coachable or courageous enough. Even so, you are the only one who will be able to provide the right answers to these key questions.

For this reason, it is vital that all these other people who genuinely want to help us stop making assumptions and start learning how to ask questions! In other words, these people need to adopt a coaching attitude – and it can work wonders! Seeking in an objective manner – and not through guess work – to find the reasons for our observable behaviour is the key to achieving excellent performance time after time.

Under the waterline: challenges and levers

To discover these important insights, we recommend that you – alone or accompanied – dive below the waterline to find out which challenges either make possible or hinder the optimal display of a crucial attitude at a crucial moment.
In the first part of the book, we identified in detail the behavioural traits that top performers have in common. In other words: **'what'** they do. In this part of the book, the **'why'** question will be central.

—— Challenges

We are now going to leave the top of the iceberg and look more closely at the underlying challenges that will confront us on the path that leads towards our **ultimate victory**. These challenges may help to explain why we sometimes lose our all-important balance.

Our Smart Mind model is based on the belief that the more competent a person feels to deal with their challenges, the greater the likelihood that they will be able to make optimal use of the high performance attitudes to achieve excellent results. If a person feels insufficiently competent, it becomes more likely that these attitudes will not be developed and displayed enough, or conversely, will be developed and displayed too much.

Self-knowledge, they say, is the start of all wisdom. This is something that we agree with wholeheartedly. It is only when you have clearly identified the challenges that you need to deal with more effectively that you can start to search for appropriate solutions.

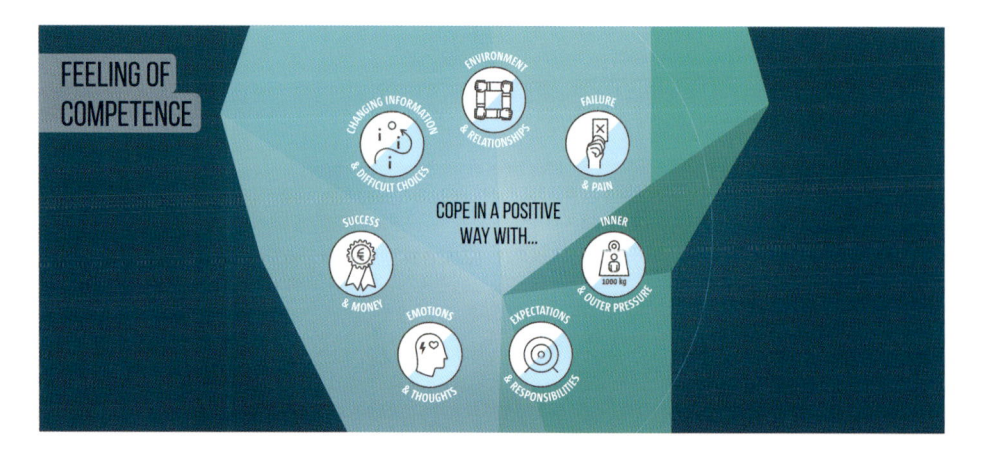

—— Levers

At the same time, it is important to remember that each of these challenges can have a positive impact on your feeling of competence to deal with the situation. If that is the case, we refer to levers.

Here is a summary with some concrete examples of challenges and levers:

	Challenge	Lever
ENVIRONMENT & RELATIONSHIPS	**Environment – relationships with others**	
	— You are working/living for the first time abroad and know no one locally. — You find it difficult to connect with people in your (new) team. — Your significant others are insufficiently supportive, over-critical and demanding. — ...	— Your manager or coach believes in your potential and shows it. — Your parents provide a safe and stimulating domestic environment. — Your positive relations with your team members give you confidence. — ...
FAILURE & PAIN	**Fear of failure – physical/mental pain**	
	— You are afraid that you will fail. — You experience physical or mental pain that distracts you or holds you back. — ...	— Your fear of failure stimulates you to prepare well. — The emotional pain you experience gives you a kind of strength that helps you to carry on. — ...

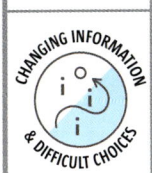

Internal pressure – external pressure

— The pressure that you put on yourself paralyses you. — The pressure that you experience from the outside world has a negative effect on you. — ...	— The pressure that you put on yourself helps you to leave your comfort zone. — The pressure that you experience from your coach or manager stimulates you to learn. — ...

Expectations – responsibilities

— The limited expectations of your coach or manager do not encourage you to take responsibility. — Your too high expectations of yourself limit your creativity. — Your sense of responsibility prevents you from being daring. — ...	— The expectations of your team members give you the courage to lead. — Your sense of responsibility stimulates you to greater self-leadership. — Extra responsibilities generate increased motivation. — The captain's armband gives you legitimacy and encourages you to speak more freely. — ...

Emotions – thoughts

— The emotions of others influence your mood negatively. — Your own thoughts are counterproductive and reduce your focus. — ...	— The emotions of others give you strength to carry on. — Positive thoughts make you more coachable. — ...

Presence or absence of success and/or money

— You are successful but do not earn enough to live from it, so you need to take on extra work and cannot rest properly. — You have not yet achieved anything significant, but already have a good contract and sponsoring at an early age, so you lose your sense of reality and motivation. — ...	— Your performance is recognised and suitably rewarded, so you can focus on what you do, allowing you to improve even more. — ...

Difficult choices – dealing with (too much) information that changes quickly

— Your coach or manager gives you too much new information, so that you can no longer see the wood for the trees. — In your eyes, choosing is losing, so you postpone decisions and find it hard to set priorities. — ...	— Information that changes rapidly stimulates your creativity, curiosity and growth. — You know that it is necessary to make choices if you want to work efficiently and effectively, so you make whatever decisions are needed. — ...

When can we talk about challenges and when can we talk about levers? This depends entirely on the interpretation of the individual. It might be that their lack of 'motivation' is the result of an environment that does not support them completely or perhaps not at all. On the other hand, the optimal display of the 'enjoy' attitude might indicate that they are surrounded by an encouraging environment that offers them a warm safety net.

Consequently, at this level, under the waterline, it is not only important to identify the challenges that will make you feel more competent, but you must also establish whether or not there are levers present that can help you to display the associated attitudes optimally. By identifying these levers, you will give yourself additional resources, allowing you to focus on things that work well and therefore have a facilitating effect.

These levers and resources can also be used to strengthen your feeling of competence. If, for example, someone finds it difficult to deal with injuries, being surrounded by a good and competent environment is essential. This support team can ensure that injuries are avoided as far as possible and, if they do occur, that they are treated correctly.

The importance of context

The challenges that will confront you during your journey to your **ultimate victory** are probably not known to you today. They depend entirely on the context in which you find yourself at the different moments of your journey. The only certainty is that you will face challenges at one time or another. The extent to which you feel competent to deal with them will determine whether or not you can turn these challenges to your advantage.

Let's look at an example from professional sport. Athletes prepare for months in advance to take part in European championships, world championships and Olympic Games. These events are often the defining moment of their season and their performance can be important for future qualifications, their position in the rankings and the possible breaking of records. At the same time, the eyes of tens of thousands of people are focused on their performance. This context creates pressure for even the most cold-blooded of athletes, because they know that these moments are crucial 'all-or-nothing' moments. This pressure is the challenge that the athlete meets on the road to their **ultimate victory**. The extent to which they feel competent to deal with this challenge will determine their ability to display the attitudes they need to be successful. Elite athletes who feel competent to deal with the challenges they face will perform consistently well. Those who feel less competent will struggle.

Moving to the workplace, the need to give a presentation can also be experienced by some people as a serious challenge, whereas other people feel competent enough to deal with this challenge without too much difficulty. In other words, different people in the same context can feel either more or less competent to deal with the challenges that the context presents. As a result, these different people will experience the same challenges differently. Let's return briefly to the example that we gave in the introduction: a talented volleyball player can deal with external pressure in their own local team, so that their 'daring' attitude allows them to smash the ball decisively over the net time after time. When they play for the national team, however, they now feel less competent to deal with this same pressure, so that in this new situation they are less willing to take the initiative. Conclusion? Sometimes people find it hard to display a particular attitude in a specific context.

Learning the necessary mental skills and training yourself to use them will make you feel more competent over time to deal with the challenges you face. That being said, every journey to your next **ultimate victory** will throw up new challenges, so it is vital to continue training and improving your mental skills. The road to success is not finite, but ever-changing.

Hendrik Tuerlinckx – volleyball

PART 3

MENTAL SKILLS

TOOLS FOR THE MIND

Taking your mental skills to the next level through constant training and use will help you to deal more effectively with the challenges that will you meet on your journey. This will result in an increased feeling of competence, which in turn will allow you to display the necessary attitudes optimally and consistently.

If you do not yet regard yourself as a top performer, the development of the right mental skills will bring you one step closer towards achieving your **ultimate victory**.

In the following section, you can find a summary of the mental skills that most top performers learn, train and apply.

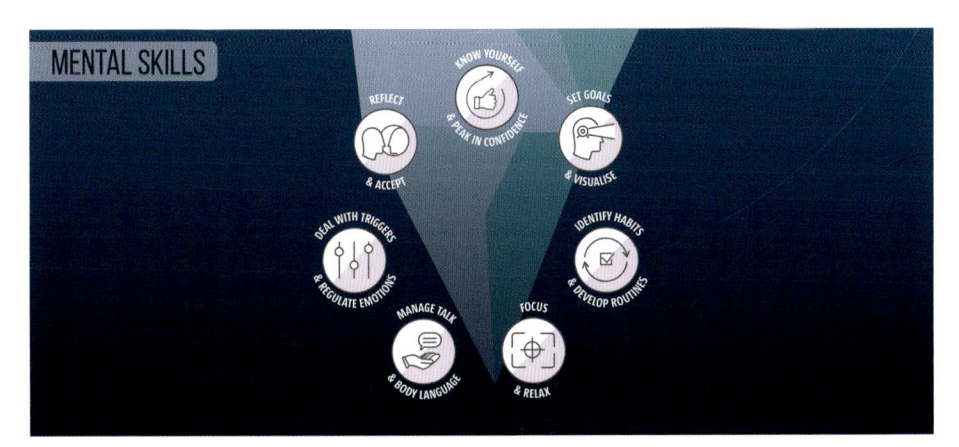

It is not our intention to discuss these mental skills in depth, but rather to give a clear overview of the skills involved. In each case, we will give an example of how one of our sports personalities or teams trains and applies that specific mental skill in their own sport. On our website www.smart-mind.be you can find the titles of books that describe the relevant techniques more fully. Everyone is welcome at Smart Mind for team and individual coaching sessions, trainings and workshops that will help you to discover and improve your own skills.

Set goals and visualise

——— Set goals for yourself

What is it and how does it work?
We set goals from an early age, often without knowing it: today, I am going to eat more healthily; from tomorrow, I am going to exercise more; during the weekend, I am going to spend more time with the kids; and so on. However, sometimes goals are the result of a conscious process of thought. If you have never played sport, there is not much chance that you will wake up one morning with the idea of taking part in the Olympic Games. Your process will have to start much earlier than that. First, you take up a sport. If you like it and are good at it, you next develop your talent. It is only once you excel at it and achieve outstanding results that your goal really starts to come alive. Only then can you say: 'My goal is to qualify for the Olympic Games.'

'As a professional sportsman, it is important to have clear goals. Then I know why and what I am training for. This helps me to focus and train more efficiently.'
—— Laurens Devos, table tennis player

In professional sport, I compare the conscious setting of goals with mental warming-up. Whether physically or mentally, a good warm-up is essential if you want to achieve top performance. I recommend this to everyone who wants to perform at the highest level: define what you want to achieve, why it is so important to you, and detail the steps that ideally will allow you to reach your goal.

It is possible to distinguish three different kinds of goal:

— **Result goals.** Here the emphasis is placed on clearly defined results: earning 10 percent more next year; selling ten thousand books; becoming European champion in a record time; and so on. These goals are aimed at a **specific target** and provide you with a strong focus. However, they also have an important disadvantage: in order to reach them, you are theoretically dependent on others and on the context.

— **Performance goals.** Here the emphasis is placed on improving your level of performance: losing five kilos in weight; increasing the number of press-ups you can do in sixty seconds; knocking two minutes off your best time for the London Marathon; and so on. Because performance goals are focused primarily on personal growth, they are more controllable than result goals.

— **Process goals.** Here the emphasis is not on your **ultimate victory**, but on the manner in which you will reach it. In other words, it is not about the **'what'** (results and performance); it is about the **'how'**. These are the goals over which you have maximum control.

 Fernando Oliva, athletics coach: *'Athletes must be well prepared. As a coach, you need to do good pre-briefings throughout the year and not just immediately prior to competition. Afterwards, you need to do a debriefing, because debriefing is crucial. From a structured debriefing, it emerges that thoughts are linked to the outcome. Sometimes, I also do an evaluation just before a competition. This is purely about the process goal. Then I say: "Here is a thought and you can choose to think about it this way or you can choose to think about it some other way." You provide a stimulus, challenging them to think in a specific way.'*

Goals related to high performance attitudes are goals focused on the **'how'** and are therefore largely under your own control. To achieve your **ultimate victory**, we recommend that you should have a mix of goals. This mean that you not only focus on your opponents, but also (and primarily) on yourself and on what you can do to reach your goal.

 Elodie Ouédraogo, ex-athlete: *'If you achieve your goal, you can raise the bar a little higher. But if you set the bar too high, so that you can never get over it, you risk becoming frustrated. You need to be on your guard against this. At the start of a new season, I think that there are many athletes who say: "Last year my record was X, and so this year I must do at least as well". But if they don't, they start to panic. They can no longer see all the good things, the things that they are still doing right. As a result, they no longer get anything positive out of their training. If equalling or beating their record is the only thing on their mind, they will soon be*

in trouble. For this reason, it is much better to think in steps and set realistic goals. If you set intermediary goals, you will have much more chance of reaching your end goal. You can certainly have "breaking the Belgian record" as your goal, but it shouldn't be your ambition to do it at the start of the season. You must first make sure that you stay fit, train well and that your times are improving. Only then should you start to think about the record as as goal.'

We recommend that you adopt a SMART approach:

| Specific | Measurable | Attainable | Relevant | Time Based |

— Your goals must be described as clearly as possible and always in positive terms.
— Your goals must be realistic and challenging.
— Your goals must be focused on both results and the process. You can do this by also setting goals that relate to high performance attitudes.
— Your goals must be as measurable as possible, but must also leave room to take account of your gut feeling: not everything is quantifiable.
— Your goals must be monitored and your progress towards them evaluated regularly, both by yourself and through the feedback of others.

This is a good way to set goals, but never forget the importance of trying to stay as close as possible to who you really are. To do this, it is crucial to know yourself through and through. Only then will you be able to set strong and feasible goals. Dare to look at yourself in the mirror and question yourself and your assumptions regularly. Are you stimulated during training or at work by challenges and the breaking of records? Or are you a competition animal, only at your best in the heat of battle? Do you get a kick from rolling out a perfect plan? Or are your goals so strongly value-driven that their achievement will give you the feeling of having helped mankind? Some top performers write down their goals. Others hang them in a visible place, like a mirror in their changing room. Yet others lock them in a drawer and only look at them every once in a while.

Whatever your preferred approach, make sure that your goals set you in motion and keep you moving forward. The ideal recipe? A healthy mix of result and process goals, with a good helping of authenticity!

—— Mental imagery: visualisation

What is it and how does it work?

Whenever you make a movement, your brain makes a pattern of it, a kind of blueprint. The more often you repeat the movement, the stronger and more accurate the pattern in your brain becomes and the better you can perform the movement in question the next time. This is why repetition is so important, not only in sport but also in business and at school. What's more, you can do this either actively, by actually performing the movement, or passively, by imagining or visualising it.

Scientific research, supported by the evidence of brain scans and electromyograms, has proven that visualisation of a movement activates the same areas of the brain as the actual performance of that movement. For example, when snowboarders visualise a particular run, the brain sends the same signals to the relevant muscles as it would during a real competition. The same neural paths are activated and used. This means that the connections in these neural paths become systematically stronger with repetition.

But what is visualisation, exactly? It is defined as a mental process in which you use all your senses to (re)create an experience in thoughts. It is almost as if you are able to bring real situations to life inside your head.

'I have very strong powers of imagination. I use visualisation almost daily. When I go to a competition, I have the feeling that I have been there already.'
—— Jaouad Achab, taekwondoka

Visualisation means that you do not have to be on a field, in a bobsleigh or on a snowboard to train and improve your performance. You can maintain and enhance both your technical skills – for example, taking a free shot or a penalty – and your mental resilience by simply imagining how you will do it and how you will react if, say, you miss. Visualisation therefore helps you to focus attention on things that can positively contribute to your performance.

Sadly, visualisation does not work equally well for everyone. Some people are able to benefit from it more than others. As always, however, the golden rule applies: the more consciously you practise, the better you will become. In this way, you strengthen your muscle memory. What's more, our brain understands images better than thoughts. As a result, image material and visualisation are now used widely in elite sport. Almost all the athletes who we interviewed for this book said that they use images as part of their training regimes.

An example from practice

 Hanne Claes, hurdler: *'Visualisation has helped me a lot. It gives you a feeling of calm and control. You know what to do at every moment of every race, so that your focus is kept away from the result. This helps to relieve a lot of the pressure. You are not thinking about the finish or the time you will run or your position in the race. You are focused on what you have to do within your process. You are completely wrapped up in your own thing, so that you are less easily distracted by your opponents. I know that if I do what I am supposed to do, I will get a good result. This gives me a huge amount of confidence. It sounds crazy, but it's true. In recent years I have been doing it a lot during the competition season. I visualise the race at the location where I know it will be run. This year, which is normally an Olympic year, I had that one race, the Olympic final, in my head during every training session, day after day. This meant that I could visualise that race at any moment during training, especially when things were difficult. That gave me such a boost. My preparation has never been as good as it is this year. That's great for my motivation.'*

We recommend:
— Before you start with your visualisation, define a clear goal and formulate it positively; for example, 'improving your technique' or 'remaining calm in tense match situations'.

— Find a quiet place where you can relax and will not be disturbed while you are performing your visualisations.
— Make your visualisations as realistic as possible. Do this by making use of all your senses. Let's say that you are a swimmer. Visualise yourself entering the pool and walking up to your starting block. Stand on the block, as though you are waiting for the start signal. Smell the chlorine in the water. Imagine the temperature when you dive in. Listen to the sounds around you, including the sploshing of the water. Feel how your body moves through that water once the race has started. Taste the water's chemical tang in your mouth.
— Anticipate certain events that might happen (as discussed in the chapter on mental resilience); for example, that you make a mistake. More importantly, imagine how you will react.

The Smart Mind model: the link between 'set goals and visualise' and high performance attitudes

Mental training based on 'set goals and visualise' has a positive impact on the following attitudes.

	Clearly defined goals that are realistic, measurable and stimulating have a positive impact on your motivation. A good mix of process and result goals ensure that you not only work hard but also cleverly and efficiently. By visualising your goals as often as you can, you come closer each day to your **ultimate victory**.
	Setting and pursuing challenging goals enhances your self-leadership and gives you a feeling of control and autonomy. Because you know where you want to go and how you want to get there, you help to make others enthusiastic for your project, allowing you to build a strong team around you.
	When you set goals, you get more out of your training and competitive events. You know why you are present and what you want to get out of the moment. By setting goals that are focused on the process, you are more coachable and more open to learning new things. Visualisation makes it possible for you to train your skills constantly, whenever and wherever you want.
	Visualisations have a positive impact on your creativity and daring. Because you have set goals and because you have already experienced the challenge or situation mentally, you increase your willingness to leave your comfort zone and display a bit more boldness. After a failure, you also dare to repeat the situation until you can master it or else you dare to change the path that leads to your goal.
	Because you know what your (ultimate) goal is – where you want to go and why you want to get there – you will have greater perseverance and will be able to recover more quickly from setbacks. By taking account in your visualisations of what might go wrong and how you will react, you increase your mental resilience.

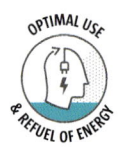	Setting yourself goals gives you a strong focus and increases your mental energy. The use of visualisations allows you to conserve both your physical and mental energy, as well as reducing the risk of injury or illness.
	By achieving victories both great and small every day on your path towards your goal, you experience satisfaction and pleasure. The setting and realisation of intermediary goals means that you will not wait to celebrate and enjoy your success until after your **ultimate victory** has been achieved. These intermediary triumphs are ideal moments for being proud of yourself and having some fun.

Identify habits & Develop routines

—— Identify habits

What is it and how does it work?

If you want to improve an attitude or a mode of behaviour, you first need to know the difference between a habit and a routine.

A habit is an action about which you no longer need to think. A good example is tying your shoelaces. You do this without looking or thinking, perhaps even while your coach is still giving you a few last-minute instructions before stepping out onto the training field. The action no longer requires your attention (or mental energy), so that this gives you the chance to focus on other things. In contrast, a routine is a behaviour that requires awareness, concentration or effort.

Before an attitude or a mode of behaviour can become a habit, it first needs to be 'practised' as a regularly performed routine. The precondition for this is that you must be able to devote the necessary time to it. Living healthily, for example, is a habit based in part on taking enough exercise. If you want to make a routine of exercise by cycling to work each day instead of using the car, you will need to plan this into your daily programme and will probably have to get up earlier in the morning and go to bed earlier in the evening.

The learning of new behaviour and the development of routines that create the right habits demand a great deal of effort. Be prepared for the discomfort and inconvenience that this will involve. You will need plenty of perseverance!

During our lifetime we occasionally develop habits that do not contribute in a positive way to our general well-being or our performance. Many of us will watch a series on television at the end of the day, but sometimes it is difficult to turn off the TV after just one episode. We want to see a second and maybe even a third. As a result, we get less sleep than is good for us. Watching a series is not a bad habit per se, because it allows us to relax at the end of a hard day. But cutting down on our number of hours of sleep as a result is a bad habit.

Habits that have a positive impact should be kept. Habits that have a negative impact should be changed or even eliminated.

'In the past, I always watched the draw on the day of the competition. Now I don't do that anymore. I also turn off my telephone. I want to avoid all distractions.'
—— Jorre Verstraeten, judoka

Stopping some habits completely can be difficult. Fortunately, a small adjustment can often turn a negative habit into a positive one. If we return to our example of healthy living, a sensible diet is also needed in addition to enough exercise. If you like nibbling something while you are watching your series on TV, try fruit instead of a bag of crisps. In this way, you keep your habit of enjoying a late-night snack, but avoid the unhealthiness caused by eating crisps each evening.

Research (Lally, van Jaarsveld, Potts & Wardle, 2009) has shown that on average it takes 66 days to create a new habit. However, there were wide variations among the test subjects. Variables such as personality, context and degree of difficulty meant that one test subject had established a habit after just 18 days, while at the opposite extreme it took another test subject 254 days.

The time needed to create a habit

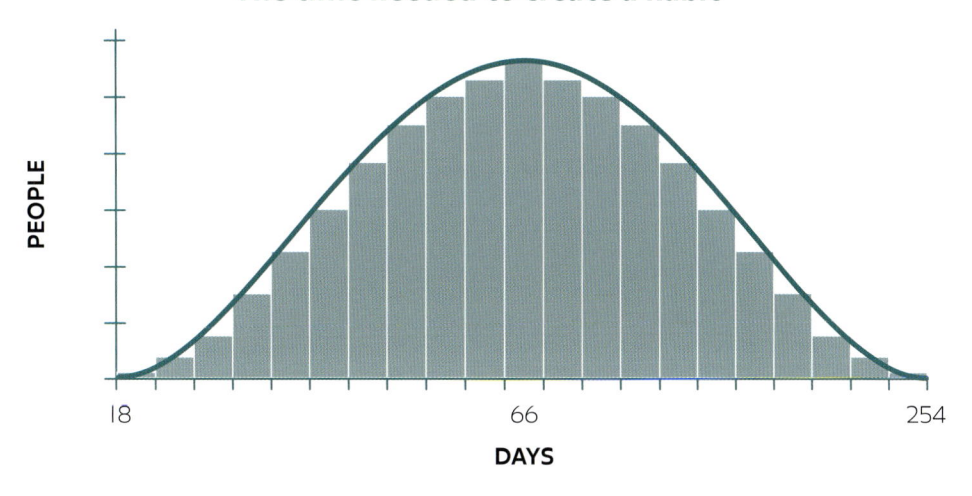

An example from practice

Joachim Gérard, wheelchair tennis player: '*The most dangerous enemy I have had throughout my career has not been my opponents, but myself! I say this because I have a habit of making less effort once I have achieved a particular victory or level of performance. As soon as everything is going well, I put myself under less pressure and become less disciplined, because I like staying in my comfort zone. As a result, I am not consistent enough in the way that I display certain attitudes. And that is really stupid. It is only when I step out of my comfort zone and start questioning myself that I achieve my best performance! And the same is true of my mental training. As long as everything is going well, I hardly spend any time on it. I am too quick to trust the improvements I make, but those improvements soon disappear if you rest on your laurels. That's when the problems start again. As a result, I need to train every day, just to make sure I can beat myself!*'

We recommend:

— Identify your habits and increase your awareness as a result.
— Identify the impact of your habits on your well-being and performance.
— Draw up a plan to develop new habits and to change or eliminate negative ones.
— Be prepared to have the necessary discipline, patience and determination. Remember that it takes an average of 66 days to turn a routine into a habit!

—— Develop routines

What is it and how does it work?

As soon as you know what habits you have and what new behaviour or habits you want to develop, we recommend that you create your own new routines that will increase your well-being and allow you to achieve better performances. As already mentioned, creating a routine requires plenty of extra attention and effort. You cannot carry out routines on automatic pilot, because they are not yet habits.

Research (Cotterill, 2010) has demonstrated that routines are most effective when they consist of a combination of mental components and physical actions. For example, before a game you can make it a routine to say five positive things in your head, following which you then do your physical warm-up. You then repeat this routine before every game. As you carry out the routine, you are preparing both physically and mentally for the peak moment that follows.

In addition to creating new habits, routines also have the added advantage of giving you an increased feeling of control, so that your fear of failure (if any) is diminished.

'I prepare for every race in a specific way, but without being too rigid about it. In that way, I can control what is controllable. This helps me to deal with the pressure.'
—— Kevin Borlée, athlete

Situations where a lot is at stake are often uncontrollable. For example, other people might be involved, so that your performance is to some extent dependent on theirs. This can mean that you have to surrender part of your feeling of control, accepting that the outcome of the important moment that follows will not be determined entirely by your own efforts. Performing a routine that maximises your chances of success can offer a solution.

An example from practice

 Victor Campenaerts, cyclist: *'I know what works for me and I write it all down. Nowadays, you can keep all that on your smartphone and store it in the Cloud. On the day of a time trail and also the day before, everything is timed down to the last minute. You can also simulate time trail days exactly during training days, because with experience you are familiar with all the variable parameters in races. I run through everything and use the same routine that led to good performances in the past. I think that if I do it again, I will perform well again. And usually it works, because it means that you have thought carefully about when you should do your warming-up, when you should take your caffeine shot and when you should start your activation through your stabilisation exercises. We have also investigated scientifically how this activation can best be done. If it is done well, I don't think it makes much difference if you come off the rollers*

five minutes earlier or later. I always try to repeat my most successful routines and copy the same day programme before each new race. Of course, there are sometimes moments when I can't follow that programme ideally. Because I have already ridden in so many races, I know that unexpected things can often happen. As a result, you have to be flexible about your programme, so that over time you actually start to develop a number of programmes.'

We recommend:

— Use routines that involve a combination of mental and physical components.
— Do not overestimate the importance of your routines; belief in your own ability is still the most important thing.
— Make regular small adjustments to your routines, to prevent them from becoming stale.

——— The Smart Mind model: the link between 'identify habits and develop routines' and high performance attitudes

Mental training based on 'identify habits and develop routines' has a positive impact on the following attitudes.

BE HIGHLY MOTIVATED & WORK SMART	As a top performer, you will be able to work more efficiently, because you know exactly what you need to do and when. This gives you focus and certainty. The implementation of routines also increases your self-discipline.
LEAD & MAKE OTHERS BETTER	Routines reduce the pressure and anxiety that you can feel at important moments. When you feel calm, this also has a positive effect on your team members and the surrounding environment. As a result, you will perform well and they will do the same.
BE COACHABLE & FOLLOW	Identifying habits strengthens your ability to think critically about yourself and makes it easier to accept the feedback of others.
INNOVATE DARE & REPEAT	Creating a habit across different contexts will increase your willingness to be bold. Daring to speak up for yourself at the family breakfast table will also have a positive impact on your willingness to speak up for yourself in your team.
BE RESILIENT & BOUNCE BACK	Make a habit of speaking positively to yourself after a mistake. This will increase your resilience, allowing you to come back stronger, rather than weaker.

	Creating good habits with regard to your sleep, diet and use of alcohol will help you to start your next performance challenge with the best possible levels of energy.
	Making a habit of coming together with your team after a goal, a victory or the completion of a project strengthens your feeling of pleasure and stimulates the celebration of successes.

Focus & Relax

—— Focus

What is it and how does it work?

Being able to focus on a particular task is a mental technique that we use often in our daily life. Focus helps us to carry out even the most mundane of tasks. By employing our focus optimally, we can eliminate distractions and devote attention to the things that are important for the correct implementation of the task or for the realisation of a particular goal.

'In basketball, it is often the third quarter of the game that is decisive. For that reason, we give ourselves a concrete goal for that quarter and focus as a team on making, say, three stops in a row at the start of the second half. This helps us to focus as a team on the same short-term goal.'
—— Antonia Delaere, basketball player

Our brains receive thousands of stimuli each second, all of which need to be processed. It is impossible for all this processing to be carried out consciously. For example, you are not consciously aware every second that you are wearing a watch or a pair of socks. Likewise, you are not constantly occupied with everything that is happening around you. And just as well! You receive so many external stimuli per second that you would soon be exhausted. The smart use of focus allows us to channel our attention on specific things and tasks. You can compare it with a torch that only lights up part of the surrounding darkness. Everything beyond the range of its beam is not processed.

This also explains the difference between focus and concentration. When you focus, you consciously direct your attention on something – like when you point a torch at something specific in the dark. **Concentration** is the mental state in which you find yourself if you succeed in focusing on that something correctly.

We often hear coaches and parents shouting at players, both young and old, that they have to concentrate. This is not much help to the players concerned. In all probability they are already concentrating, but they are focusing on the wrong things. This means that the coaches and parents would do better to shout out the specific things on which they must focus. "Watch out for that overlapping full back!"

In **Eberspächer's circles of attention** distracting thoughts or perceptions that can disturb your focus on your specific task are depicted as circles. The greater the distance between the task and the distracting element, the harder it is to reestablish your focus.

When a football player fails to score a simple chance following a great cross from the wing, it is unlikely that he will immediately be able to put this miss out of his thoughts. In the following minutes, he will replay the chance over and over in his head, so that his attention is directed to the past. As a result, he will no longer be sufficiently aware of what is happening around him in the present, because part of his focus is being channelled elsewhere.

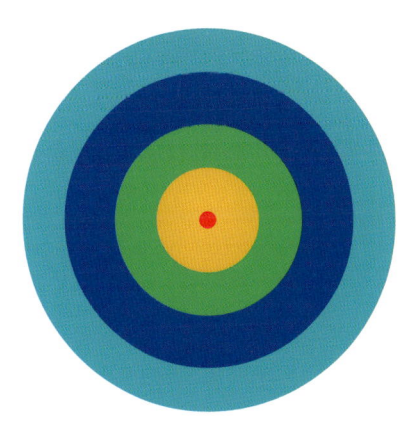

1. Me and my task

2. Direct distraction (referee, weather conditions, opponents, public)

3. What it is versus what it should be (missed chances, wrong choices)

4. Winning versus losing + consequences (top-three place, selection)

5. Purpose: what am I doing here?

Targeted focus therefore makes it possible for us to complete tasks with our full attention. At important moments, focusing on the right things is crucial. In the middle of an important meeting you don't want to be wondering what might happen if things go wrong or, worse still, be thinking about your evening meal. At that moment, you need to focus fully on the words that are being spoken, the body language of the other participants, and the slides that are being shown. In other words, you want to focus exclusively on the task in front of you in the here and now.

An adult person can maintain an unbroken state of focus for a maximum of 45 minutes. After that, some attention is inevitably devoted to distractions, so that you move into one of the other Eberspächer circles. This is not a problem, but it is important to refocus on your task as quickly as you can.

An example from practice

 Noor Vidts, heptathlete: '*I make a deliberate choice not to look at the intermediate scores. I don't want to focus on the end result, only on the next event. Of course, you can feel if you are doing really well, but that's when you need to stay inside your bubble. Don't think about what has already happened, focus on what is still to come. And if things are not going well, try to pep yourself up. After all, there are still other events where you can catch up.*'

We recommend:
- Be conscious of the things on which you are focusing.
- Focus above all on things that you can control and are relevant to your task.
- Carefully choose the moments when you want to be fully focused.
- Accept that you will occasionally give in to distractions.
- Avoid multitasking: this will only result in you doing each of the tasks with less attention.
- Build moments into your daily programme when you consciously eliminate as many stimuli as possible; turn off your phone and go and relax somewhere.
- Make use of other mental techniques to reset your focus once it has slipped: repeating your goals, controlled breathing, positive self-talk and running through your routines can all help.

—— Relax

What is it and how does it work?

If you want to perform at top level, you need to find the right balance between anxiety and relaxation. A degree of anxiety is necessary for good performance. Research has proven that we all have an individual zone of optimal functioning or IZOF (Hanin, 1997; 2000). In this zone, an optimal balance between anxiety and relaxation is reached and the pressure you feel is optimally regulated. It is this balance that makes record-breaking performances possible.

'My whole life revolves around my horses and my sport. Until recently, there wasn't a moment in the day when I wasn't occupied with one or the other. But now I only do things after eight o'clock in the evening that have no connection with my profession. For example, I play football with people who know nothing about show jumping. This helps me to relax.'
—— Grégory Wathelet, show jumper

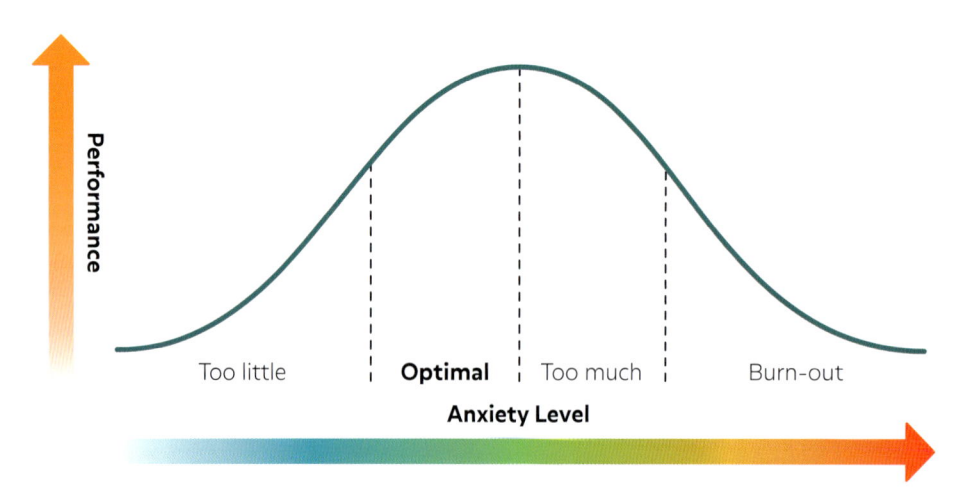

Adapted from Hanin (1997; 2000)

9

Too little anxiety and too much anxiety can both lead to reduced performance. For this, reason, the correct regulating of the anxiety level is crucial. Fortunately, there are techniques that we can use control the level of stress we feel.

In practice, the importance of this stress regulation should not be underestimated. It is an essential component if you want to achieve your **ultimate victory**. What's more, it is a very personal process. Some top performers need to turn up the pressure they feel to arrive in their IZOF; others need to turn it down.

A classic way of reducing the stress you feel at a particular moment is to focus on your breathing. When you have your breathing under your control, your hands will sweat less, your throat will feel less dry and you will be able to think more clearly. Biofeedback also allows you to monitor the effect of your breathing exercises. For example, you will notice that your heart rate immediately begins to fall.

Another such technique is progressive muscle relaxation. By tensing and then relaxing certain muscle groups, you can teach yourself how to regulate your level of tension. By becoming better aware of how your muscles feel when they are tense and relaxed, after a time you will be able to maintain the relaxed state more frequently during the day.

A third technique is autogene training. This involves improving your perception of different sensations in your body, such as warmth and heaviness in your limbs.

An example from practice

 Jill Boon, hockey player: '*Breathe in, breathe out and think of what lies ahead of you. That is how I try to find inner calm. During the past two years I have been training with pilates and yoga. From a certain age, every athlete should include these disciplines in her daily training and reduce the amount of work with weights. If you are always pushing your body hard, you eventually cause it to break down. If you can train in a more focused way that is more appropriate for your age, you can carry on with your sport for longer.*'

We recommend:
- — Identify the moments when your performance is at its best: do you perform best when the pressure is high or low?
- — Experiment with different relaxation techniques and find out which of them works best for you.

The Smart Mind model: the link between 'focus and relax' and high performance attitudes

Mental training based on 'focus and relax' has a positive impact on the following attitudes.

BE HIGHLY MOTIVATED & WORK SMART	Relaxing regularly has a positive impact on your motivation. Moments of optimal focus will maximise your output.
LEAD & MAKE OTHERS BETTER	Regulating your own anxiety will have a positive effect, not only on you but also on your contact with team members. By finding and staying in your zone of optimal functioning, you will increase the likelihood that you focus on the right things, which will help you to manage both yourself and others.
BE COACHABLE & FOLLOW	A relaxed state and the right focus ensure that you are more receptive for the feedback of the important people around you, which has a positive effect on your development.
INNOVATE DARE & REPEAT	The ability to regulate the anxiety you feel in your body allows you to remain calm under pressure. This will make it easier for you to be daring and to repeat your actions after you have made mistakes.
BE RESILIENT & BOUNCE BACK	After a setback, it helps to regulate your anxiety level and to immediately set a new focus on a positive goal that you can achieve in the short term. In this way, you avoid getting caught up in too much negative thinking.
OPTIMAL USE & REFUEL OF ENERGY	Finding the right balance between anxiety and relaxation will give you an energy boost and allow you to make use of it in the most efficient way.
ENJOY & CELEBRATE	Relaxing regularly helps you to enjoy yourself and to look forward to the next challenge.

Manage your communication and body language

—— Manage your communication

There are two aspects to this: how you communicate with yourself and how you communicate with others.

'Before a penalty, short corner or shoot-out, I always say to myself: "To score, they will have to get past me and to do that they will need to be bloody good." In this way, I create a mental advantage for myself over my opponent.'
—— Vincent Vanasch, hockey goalkeeper

Learning how to manage your self-talk, so that it helps you to perform better, is a key form of mental training.

What is it and how does it work?

Self-talk

Your thoughts can manifest themselves in different ways. Usually, they take the form of words and sentences inside your head, so that you have an almost constant inner dialogue with yourself. Sometimes mental images can also intrude into this conversation. These thoughts 'programme' your behaviour. They can be beneficial for your self-confidence and performance, but they can also generate doubt, anxiety and stress. In other words, the way you talk to yourself can be both positive and negative.

Not all negative self-talk has an immediate negative effect on your performance in the short-term. For example, the effect of being angry with yourself can sometimes give you a wake-up call that leads to better performance. But if you want your self-talk to have a consistently positive effect on your performance, it is important to recognise which voice you allow most frequently into your thoughts. Is it the angel who motivates you and gives you hope? Or is it the devil who always reminds you how bad you are? Having control over these voices – and therefore over your thoughts – is vital. Why? Because thoughts determine our feelings and these feelings have an influence on our attitude (behaviour) and, ultimately, our performance.

Positive self-talk can be both motivating and directive. It can pep you up or calm you down. Elite athletes often use key words to give themselves positive self-talk instructions or else call up specific mental images that trigger them to relax.

Communicating with others

There are hundreds of courses and thousands of books devoted to the theme of 'efficient communication'. As we have already mentioned, we do not intend to go into too much detail here. We do, however, wish to look at some of the more important mental communication skills and explore which of these you can develop to help you deal with challenges in a positive manner.

The words that you use in your communication with others is just as important as your self-talk. They have an impact on the team dynamic and, therefore, indirectly on yourself. In this context, do not underestimate the importance of humour. Although humour can sometimes be interpreted the wrong way, it can be a powerful tool to reduce tension and/or increase motivation in difficult situations. A little bit of humour is enough. Too much at the wrong moment can be a distraction.

As a coach or manager, it is important to give the team member who has a talent for this kind of thing the freedom to use that talent, but with the necessary guidance and support.

Examples from practice

 Tiesj Benoot, cyclist: '*During the race I try to talk to myself and think about how I would like to see myself cycling, if I was sitting at home and watching me on the television. I then try to adopt that attitude. In the race, you are locked in your own cocoon. It is from there that you experience the race. When things are hard, it is sometimes tempting to choose the easier option.*'

 Laurens Devos, table tennis player: '*When I am playing an important match, I try to turn my thoughts to my advantage. An example: there is a big crowd, I lose a point and everyone claps. Even though that applause is for my opponent, I listen to it as though it was for me. If there are a lot of spectators, that really helps me. Since I have been doing that, I find it more pleasant to play in front of big crowds.*'

We recommend:
— Recognise negative thoughts for what they are and do not fight against them. Accept that they will occur from time to time.
— When this happens, try to park the negative thoughts somewhere in your head.
— Having done that, immediately replace the negative thoughts with a thought that will have a positive effect on your mood and performance.
— Next, focus your attention without delay on your Next Best Action (NBA).

In other words, the positive use of self-talk requires you to know yourself thoroughly. What are the right words for you and in which situations? It is important to have an arsenal of self-affirming and motivating words and sentences that you can call and use at all times.

—— Body language

What is it and how does it work?

Body language is fascinating: even when we are not talking, our non-verbal behaviour is constantly sending out signals. Body language is universal and often instinctive, although cultural influences can result in variations. Many aspects of body language are innate. For example, research (Tracy & Matsumoto, 2008) has demonstrated that people who are born blind also put their hands in the air to celebrate when they win. As it is impossible for them to have seen this from others, the research concluded that it must be inborn.

It is not only the brain that has an impact on the body; the body can also have an impact on the brain. Our deportment, posture and facial expressions all have an influence on our thoughts, our feelings and the way we perceive ourselves.

'During games I pep myself up and show this through my body language. This gets me into the right flow more quickly. By paying attention to this, I really do play better. It also helps my team mates, because it creates a vibe between us. At the same time, body language that is full of confidence and aggression can help to intimidate your opponents.'
—— Hendrik Tuerlinckx, volleyball player

This form of communication sometimes takes place consciously, but more often than not it is unconscious.

Dr Amy Cuddy, an expert In body language at the Harvard Business School, has conducted experiments which show that positive body language and adopting a power pose have the ability to improve performance. Your posture affects your hormone balance and therefore your thoughts in such a way that you are able to deal more positively with pressure. If you do not know what a power pose looks like, search the internet for pictures of Usain Bolt after he has won a race!

An athlete not only wants to feel self-confident but also wants to radiate that confidence. Why? So that the crowd and their opponents can see through their body language just how confident they are. In other words, body language can have an indirect effect on how others estimate their own chances of victory. A brilliant example of this is the haka that the All Blacks, the national rugby team of New -Zealand, perform before the start of every game. It is one of the most well-known sporting rituals in the world and symbolises the team's spirit, passion and power. This ancient tribal dance offers them a number of advantages: it makes them feel united, it gives them an energy boost, it intimidates the opposing team and it drives the crowd wild with excitement. This underlines the importance of being aware of your body language and adjusting it to reflect the situation.

An example from practice

 Toma Nikiforov, judoka: *'My biggest challenge is controlling my own excitement. I do this by focusing more on my breathing, but above all through smiling. By smiling, my brain gets an indirect stimulus, which it passes on to the rest of my body, so that I immediately relax physically. I also know that my body language is highly expressive. And if you know how to use this body language, it can be a big advantage. Judo is a combat sport, a macho sport in which the strongest man wins. Looking angry and using provocative language is all part of the game. But I turn all that on its head, by laughing and giving my opponents a clap on the shoulder. They aren't expecting that and it knocks them off balance.'*

You can learn how to use your body language optimally by broadening your awareness. How? Observe yourself in front of a mirror, watch yourself in video recordings, or ask for the advice and feedback of others. In particular, video feedback and analysis has become increasingly important in the sporting world in recent years. More and more coaches now understand the impact of body language on the performance of their athletes and film their behaviour (body language and verbal communication) to monitor and maximise its effectiveness.

Watch out for the following things:

- — Stand, walk and sit as upright as possible.
- — Keep your shoulders and chest pushed forwards.
- — Hold your chin up and your head high.
- — Laugh, smile and maintain eye contact.
- — Encourage team members, both verbally and non-verbally.
- — Celebrate successes by coming together (form a huddle).

We recommend:

- — Adopt a positive and self-confident posture, using a role model if that helps.
- — Try to smile and laugh as much as possible, since this will affect your mood and those around you positively.
- — Fake it till you make it: even if you don't feel self-confident, strike a self-confident pose. If you do it often enough and long enough, your confidence and assertiveness will grow.

—— The Smart Mind model: the link between 'manage your communication and body language' and high performance attitudes

Mental training based on 'manage your communication and body language' has a positive impact on the following attitudes.

BE HIGHLY MOTIVATED & WORK SMART	Positive self-talk and body language have a self-evident positive effect on your motivation. Think in terms of solutions rather than problems and focus on things that will help you to perform.
LEAD & MAKE OTHERS BETTER	Positive communication and body language will influence the people around you positively and help them to grow. Choose your words carefully and adopt a positive attitude and pose. In this way, your feedback to others will have a more positive impact.
BE COACHABLE & FOLLOW	By being positive in your thoughts, attitudes and body language, you consciously and unconsciously increase your coachability. Important people around you (your coach or your colleagues) will give you more honest feedback more readily, so that you will learn and make progress more quickly.
INNOVATE DARE & REPEAT	By talking to yourself positively in a motivating and directive manner, you increase the chance that you will be able to display more daring and creativity in situations that require it.
BE RESILIENT & BOUNCE BACK	By going through life with a positive approach, you will have an indirect effect on the way you deal with setbacks. Positive thinking eliminates negativity and increases your perseverance.

	Positive thoughts give you more energy than negative thoughts. By switching your focus to opportunities and chances, you boost both your physical and mental energy and attract other positive people.
	By converting negative thoughts into positive ones and focusing on the things that motivate you and make you happy, you increase the likelihood that you will derive enjoyment from your journey to your **ultimate victory**.

Deal with triggers and regulate emotions

—— Deal with triggers

What is it and how does it work?

A trigger can be a smell, a sound, an image or a thought that sets a process in motion. Every person reacts differently, also to triggers. You can compare a trigger with a button that is pushed and leads to an almost immediate reaction.

Parents, coaches, managers and colleagues can all serve as triggers, either consciously or unconsciously, or can activate, strengthen or mitigate triggers by the way they (re)act.

A trigger can generate either a positive or negative reaction or sensation. For example, the mistakes that we make can make us feel uncomfortable: a missed shot, an error in an Excel spreadsheet, stumbling over your words in a presentation. Everyone makes mistakes of this kind, and yet these triggers almost instantly give us a feeling of guilt, shame, frustration, anger and/or anxiety. On the other side of the coin, comfortable or familiar situations – a ground where you have scored, a track where you have run well – gives you a positive feeling and boosts your self-confidence. But be careful: this might also make you unconsciously relax, so that you lack the necessary tension and focus to perform well.

'I can play in a game in front of 15,000 people without hearing what they are shouting. That helps me at moments when the atmosphere is hostile, which it often is. By repeating our agreed tactics in my head, I can close myself off fully from the surroundings. I am in the game – and nothing else.'
—— Hendrik Tuerlinckx, volleyball player

Identifying these triggers and developing a strategy to deal with them positively is an important part of the work of sport psychologists. The aim is to use the reaction time between the trigger and the response in the best possible way, so that athletes can gain control over how they react at key moments.

An example from practice

Jorre Verstraeten, judoka: *'For me, there is almost no difference between a fight I win and a fight I lose. If you win, you want to talk about it and that stays in your head. And it is the same if you lose, but with the opposite emotions. To make sure that my emotions do not have too strong an influence on my next fight, I empty my head each time I leave the mat. I evacuate all my emotions by putting all my thoughts about the last fight in my judo bag and putting it away somewhere.'*

We recommend:
— Identify your triggers and their effect on your performance.
— If possible, eliminate triggers that have a negative impact.
— Develop a new routine that you can use every time the trigger is activated.
— Replace the negative thoughts caused by the trigger with positive thoughts that call up positive emotions.

——— Regulate emotions

What is it and how does it work?
Sport is emotion and emotion is sport. And not just during the game or event. Emotions also make their presence felt before and afterwards, in both the participants and the spectators. Emotions influence our mood, our energy levels, our behaviour and our performance.

In the chapter on 'Be resilient and bounce back' attitude, we said that top performers are aware of the emotions they experience and their impact on themselves and others. As a result, they know how to manage these emotions to obtain the best possible level of performance.

'You are in the final of the Davis Cup. You are playing for your country. Your family, friends and coach are all there for you. You feel that everyone is behind you; that they all believe in you. At such a moment, that gives you huge energy and courage. For me, emotion creates extra motivation, so that I can give more of myself than normal.'
——— Steve Darcis, ex-tennis player

Emotions can be either positive or negative and they can have either a positive or a negative effect on performance. In this way, for example, an 'unpleasant' emotion like anger does not always have a negative impact on how you perform. It can also give you power and spur you on to greater effort, which in some situations can be a huge advantage.

Britt Herbots, volleyball player: *'If someone pats you on the back and says "Good passes today", that may seem like something trivial but if it comes from a person who at that moment is important to you, it has a thousand times more impact than if it comes from someone else.'*

An example from practice

Stef De Greef, fencer: *'Competitions in fencing can sometimes last all day. There are some fencers who like to wander around and talk to others, but I prefer to stay in our Belgian corner. Sometimes I close my eyes. In the first instance,*

I don't want to be confronted with the energy of others, because that can lead to "emotional contagon". For example, I don't want to hear from someone else that he had a really bad match in the first round. I try to avoid that kind of thing. Of course, I talk to the other Belgians and our coach, but no one else. I usually like to listen to music between matches or read the text messages from my father, if he cannot be present.'

We recommend:
— Increase your self-knowledge by identifying which situations lead to which emotions.
- Compile an emotional matrix like the one below, in which you make clear which emotions have what effect on your performance.
— Make as much use as possible of emotions with a positive impact in your mental training (visualisations and relaxation exercises). This will make it possible to call up these emotions more quickly in situations where they can improve your performance.
— Learn how to become aware as quickly as possible of the emergence of emotions that can have a negative impact on your performance, so that you can convert these emotions into something positive. You can do this by using the following mental techniques:
  — Controlling your breathing.
  — Redirecting your thoughts through positive self-talk or the use of a trigger word.
  — Calling up an image, sound or smell in your mind (via visualisation) that helps to calm you, so that you get new energy and/or inspiration to carry.
— Make emotions discussable! This can relieve a lot of tension and anxiety, as well as leading to greater understanding within your entourage.

Denying your emotions and pushing them away never works. This simply increases the likelihood that they will emerge again, sooner or later, and usually at a crucial moment when you are under pressure. And it is precisely at such moments that the possibility of their having a negative effect on your performance is at its greatest.

———— The Smart Mind model: the link between 'deal with triggers and regulate emotions' and high performance attitudes

Mental training based on 'deal with triggers and regulate emotions' has a positive impact on the following attitudes.

	Your efficiency and motivation will be positively influenced when you can convert potentially distracting triggers and emotions in a manner that allows you to use them positively to deal with the challenges you face.
	Emotions are contagious. If you can succeed in displaying largely positive emotions and behaviour, this will have a positive snowball effect on the atmosphere and the people around you.

BE COACHABLE & FOLLOW	Accepting and implementing feedback is easier if you have more control over the emotions that feedback can generate. This will make you more open to advice from others and will give a boost to your development.
INNOVATE DARE & REPEAT	When you learn to recognise your triggers and emotions, so that you can convert them into positive thoughts, you will be able to react more quickly and more appropriately in situations that require a daring approach.
BE RESILIENT & BOUNCE BACK	When you better understand why certain things trigger you or how certain setbacks lead to certain emotions, there is a greater likelihood that you will respond more appropriately. In other words, you will show more mental resilience.
OPTIMAL USE & REFUEL OF ENERGY	Triggers and emotions have a strong influence on our energy levels. For instance, worrying unnecessarily as a reaction to a feeling of shame can cost you a huge amount of mental energy. Recognising, rationalising and accepting emotions can help you to save energy.
ENJOY & CELEBRATE	It goes without saying that the ability to deal effectively with triggers and emotions will have a positive effect on the levels of pleasure you experience.

Reflect and accept

—— Reflect

What is it and how does it work?

Reflecting is a mental technique in which you look at yourself, as it were, under a magnifying glass, zooming in on a number of aspects of your behaviour and personality that have an effect on how you function.

'After the 2012 Olympic Games, I went through a difficult period for two years. It is not that you suddenly feel better the next day. It is a real process. The important thing is to take a step back, put enough distance between you and the situation, and analyse it rationally.'
—— Kevin Borlée, athlete

You can reflect on your personal performance, but also on the performance of the team to which you belong.

As a concrete example, let's look at the role of a coach or a sport psychologist in a national team. In the course of a year, this team comes together only for a few weeks, usually in the run-up to qualification matches or a major competition. These weeks can be viewed as a kind of

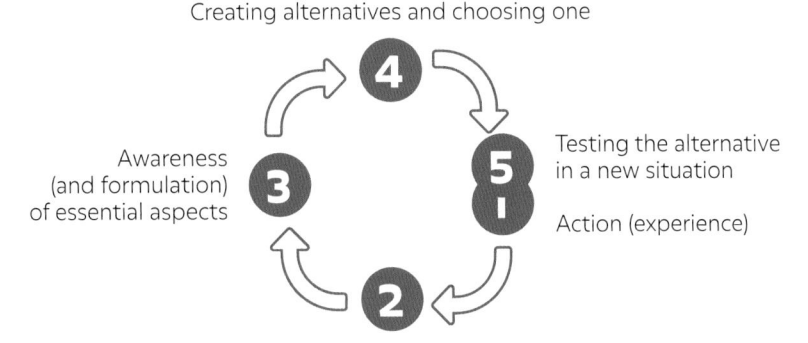

project. If, at the end of those weeks, you only stop to ask if the goals have been reached or not, you miss huge learning opportunities, both for yourself and the team.

Reflection is an easy technique that you can use daily. But you need to make the necessary time for it. During the weeks when the national team is together, various workshops are held and individual conversations take place with the players, coaches and other staff. These are all moments from which you can learn. You do not need to wait until something goes wrong before you start your reflective process. Identifying what has contributed to past success and therefore needs to be repeated in the future is just as important as identifying the errors that you want to eliminate.

You can reflect in a highly structured manner. For example, Korthagen and Vasalos (2002) developed a method that you can implement to make you more aware of your feelings and to check how your choices contribute to reaching your goal (or not). You simply ask yourself a number fixed questions each day or week.

Creating alternatives and choosing one

Testing the alternative
in a new situation

Action (experience)

Awareness
(and formulation)
of essential aspects

Looking back on action (experience)

Reflection was of huge importance for the **Belgian Cheetahs** on their Road to Tokyo and their qualification for the Olympic Games. After a disappointing performance at the European indoor championships in 2019, they discussed with each other openly and honestly in a number of reflective sessions why they had not achieved their goal, why they had missed out on a medal and why they only came in fourth. After looking back at the experience, they became aware that too much energy had been wasted supporting the individual races of the team members. This meant that they had not had enough rest moments to perform well in the relay race. As a result, they decided that at the next competition the other team members would not support each individual as she raced, but would use this time to relax and rest. A few months later, this choice had an immediate impact on the team's result and they were able to qualify for the world championship in Doha.

Another less structured way to reflect is simply to note down your daily thoughts in a diary. You put down everything that comes into your head while you are writing. In this way, you can reflect on the events of a particular moment, consider how these events made you feel and decide how you will approach similar situations in the future.
Both these methods or a mixture of the two will help you to increase your self-knowledge and self-awareness. By better learning from your own failures and successes, you will be able to make faster progress. Consciously pausing to reflect on your emotions in certain situations will ensure that you soon recognise the situations in which you feel good and will try to find them again. Conversely, you will be quicker to avoid less positive situations.

An example from practice

Vincent Kompany, ex-footballer and coach: '*I try to question myself every day. I first assess whether things went well or badly. In both cases I question myself about the "what" and the "why". This has helped me to develop all kinds of positive attitudes. In the beginning, I didn't have this kind of knowledge about myself. I simply learned from my mistakes. I would never have had the career I have had if I hadn't been able to get back up every time I was knocked down.*'

We recommend:
— Do not only self-reflect after negative experiences, but also after positive ones. For example, write down each day one thing that you were grateful for that day. Or note down after each important moment two things that made you proud.
— Record the results of your reflection in a diary or on your laptop or smartphone. Regularly look back at what you have written; this will help you to put things in perspective. The things that frustrated you a few weeks ago might now have been corrected or eliminated, so that they are no longer important.
— Plan a fixed moment for daily or weekly reflection.
— Be careful that your reflection does not lead to doubt. After each reflective moment, it is important to identify clear points for action that you can apply in the future.

 Accept

What is it and how does it work?
Acceptance is a powerful but often underestimated mental technique that can bring mental calm.

When people approach us with coaching questions, we will always encourage them and assist them to implement certain positive changes: setting good goals, visualisation, relaxation, focusing on the right moments, regulating emotions and thoughts, controlling body language, improving communication techniques, and so on.

Even so, there are some things that cannot be controlled or influenced. Moreover, these things can still have an impact on you and your performance, whether you like it or not. Consciously or unconsciously, you can lose a great amount of energy when you worry about these uncontrollable elements, such as traffic, other people's choices, corona regulations or bad weather (to name but a few).

These are just things that we simply have to accept – so don't waste any energy on them. Instead, focus on your own progression and on the things that you can control. If you consciously decide to accept the things that you cannot change, you will go through life more freely and more positively

'During difficult periods, you need to put things in perspective and stay positive. You never know what might happen. In the end, everything will work out for the best. That is something that I have always told myself.'
—— Steve Darcis, ex-tennis player

In these uncontrollable situations, humour is an easy and light-hearted way to play down what has happened and to increase your willingness to accept the inevitable. If you can see the humour in a situation or use humour to break the tension, this immediately reduces negative thoughts and feelings.

An example from practice

 Laurens Devos, table tennis player: '*I don't know if my physical limitations have driven me forward. That is difficult to say, because I accepted my limitation from the moment of my birth. I have never known differently. I simply accepted my limitation completely. I am how I am. I have a bad right side, but I have never known what it is like to have two good sides, and so for me that is normal.*'

We recommend:
— Do not waste energy on things that you cannot change or influence.
— Put your challenges in their proper perspective – for example, through the use of humour – but do not minimise them.
— Always continue to think carefully about how you can change a situation but accept it gracefully when it becomes clear that you can't.

The Smart Mind model: the link between 'reflect and accept' and high performance attitudes

Mental training based on 'reflect and accept' has a positive impact on the following attitudes.

BE HIGHLY MOTIVATED & WORK SMART	Reflecting on your functioning and actions will increase the efficiency of your training and performance.
LEAD & MAKE OTHERS BETTER	Reflecting on how you function within a team benefits everyone. If you are able to identify the things that have contributed to the team's success in the past, you can repeat these things in the future.
BE COACHABLE & FOLLOW	Reflecting means looking at yourself in the mirror and being coachable about what you see. You dare to think critically about yourself and are willing to accept mistakes, because you believe that you can make unlimited progress.
INNOVATE DARE & REPEAT	Reflection requires plenty of daring, because you leave yourself open to the possible negative feedback of others. This teaches you to think critically and improves your ability to deal with new methods and insights.

 BE RESILIENT & BOUNCE BACK	Acceptance and the use of humour can help you to deal better with setbacks. Accepting what has happened is the first step.
 OPTIMAL USE & REFUEL OF ENERGY	The acceptance of certain things that you cannot change will save you energy, which you can then invest in the things that you can control and change.
 ENJOY & CELEBRATE	The way you reflect and the things on which you reflect will have a major impact of your feelings of satisfaction, pleasure and gratitude. It is all about choice.

Know yourself and peak in confidence

What is it and how does it work?

In this chapter we have looked at the most important skills necessary for top performance. We are aware that this summary is not fully comprehensive, but the most important techniques have been covered. Training in these mental skills will allow you to master them over time, making you stronger and stronger. Our brain works like all the other muscles in the body: the more you train it, the better it gets.

By regularly practising your mental skills you will feel more competent to deal with the challenges you face. For example, the more you train yourself in relaxation, the easier you will find it to cope with anxiety and pressure.

This brings us to the matter of self-efficacy, a concept that relates to our belief in our own ability in certain situations. The more competent you feel to deal with anxiety and pressure in a particular situation, the greater your level of self-efficacy will be in that situation.

Ultimately, this belief in your own ability across different situations leads to (more) self-confidence.

'Telling myself that I will play well makes me calm and gives me confidence. Next, I visualise that playing well in my head. I don't always do this with images, but even so it gives me a feeling that I will play a good game.'
— Antonia Delaere, basketball player

When you know that you feel competent to deal with anxiety and pressure – whether at home, at work or with strangers – this will result in a more general feeling of self-confidence, depending on the situation in which you find yourself. In this way, you develop growing self-confidence through your experiences. In contrast to self-efficacy, self-confidence is relatively stable in all situations.

Thibaut Vervoort: *'I think that if I had known earlier that you actually have two main aspects to prepare for, the physical and the mental, that I would have found a way to mentally prepare better for competitions, that I would have dared more or done more faster.'*

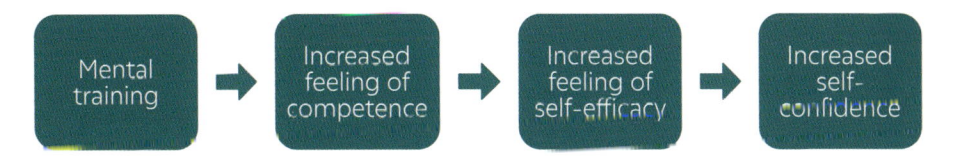

As with our seven attitudes, there is also an optimal level of self-confidence. Too little self-confidence is not good, because it leads to doubts about your own ability. Too much self-confidence leads to arrogance. And as the old proverb says: 'Pride [or arrogance] comes before a fall'. Arrogance will always prevent you from achieving your **ultimate victory**.

Examples from practice

 Heleen Jaques, footballer: *'Over the years, I got to know myself better and learned how to work not only on my weaknesses, but also on my strengths. You have to base your game on your strengths. People often tell you what you need to improve, so that you sometimes lose sight of these strengths. This is what happened to me. You are strong precisely because of your strengths. You must never lose sight of this as a player. Always focus on your strengths and, if you can, minimise your weaknesses. That is what I learned over time. Building periods of rest into my programme also helped me to know myself better and I now do this regularly. As a result, I have learned more about myself both in daily life and on the football pitch.'*

 Fanny Lecluyse, swimmer: *'For my best performances, I knew in advance that I would win. Like when I became European champion. My preparation started in September, after two weeks of rest in August. I never stated my goal openly, but I knew in my head that I wanted to be European champion. I swam in the Belgian championships in November and broke one record after another. That gave me plenty of self-confidence, even though I hadn't really prepared 100 percent to take part. A week later, with the European championship approaching, my coach sent me a message with the tune of the Belgian national anthem and the words: "Start training. You never know..." I have always remembered that. I was bursting with confidence, which was a daring move on my part, because it could have easily backfired. But on the starting blocks I was certain I was going to win. I felt good and technically everything was perfect. I swam the race exactly how I had visualised it in my head. I knew how many stokes I had to do in every part of every length. After the heats, I had the second fastest time, which put me in lane 5 for the final. But that was also exactly what I wanted, because the fastest qualifier in lane 4 always feels extra pressure. In the last 25 metres, I just swam away from everyone else. If you can do that in the way that you had visualised, at first you don't believe it. You just hope that you are not dreaming. I was lucky enough to experience that on many occasions. Everything that I had prepared so well in my head actually happened the way I had planned it. Of course, that wasn't the case in every race...'*

We recommend:

— Think often about your points for growth and your strengths.
— Identify the challenges for which you need to feel more competent.
— Identify the mental skills that you need to develop.
— Build up your self-confidence step by step.
— Take a look at www.smart-mind.be and learn more about our training courses and how you can develop your own mental skills.

The Smart Mind model: the link between 'know yourself and peak in confidence' and high performance attitude

Mental training based on 'know yourself and peak in confidence' has a positive impact on the following attitudes.

BE HIGHLY MOTIVATED & WORK SMART	Self-confidence will boost your intrinsic motivation and ensure that you are not dependent on extrinsic motivation. You will also be less troubled by limiting beliefs and have more belief in your own ability.
LEAD & MAKE OTHERS BETTER	Knowing yourself thoroughly and radiating self-confidence will increase your impact as a leader. You will give others confidence and help them to believe in their ability. Your self-confidence also means that you do not feel threatened by others.
BE COACHABLE & FOLLOW	Your self-knowledge and self-confidence allow you to be open to the feedback of others. You do not regard this feedback as a threat and know that it is the key to your further growth. Your constant desire is to become the best possible version of yourself.
INNOVATE DARE & REPEAT	Self-confidence leads to boldness and a willingness to dare. Trying out new things does not worry you. You understand that this is part of the learning process that will make you stronger.
BE RESILIENT & BOUNCE BACK	It is easier to be mentally resilient when you believe in yourself. Because you are self-confident, you know that you will be able to deal with difficult moments. You also know that these moments will make you stronger.
OPTIMAL USE & REFUEL OF ENERGY	Your excellent self-knowledge allows you to allocate and use your energy wisely. You respect your own boundaries and recharge your batteries in good time.
ENJOY & CELEBRATE	Your self-confidence allows you to approach new phases in your development without fear. In fact, you look forward to these new phases, because they bring you closer and closer to your **ultimate victory**.

Word of thanks

'If you want to go fast, go alone, if you want to go far, go together.'

This wonderful book has been written together with (and thanks to the help and support of) the following top performers:

Lars — Robbe — Gunter — Linda — Jens — Anouk — Julie — Louise — Jaouad Cynthia — Jill — Kevin — Kimberly — Victor — Hanne — Bruno — Aisling — Steve — Stef — Jules — Margo — Antonia — Laurens — Frauke — Joachim — Sofie — Justine — Heleen — Pascal — Vincent — Camille — Fanny — Emma — Philip — Dominique — Toma — Elodie — Thomas — Heidi — Jean-Michel — Seppe — Emmanuel — Hendrik — Steven — Jorre — Grégory — Daniel — Olaf — Jef — Jean — Kristel — Peter — Olivier — Kristien — Sylvie — Jean-François — Ruben — Ambre — Britt — Thibaut — Jeremy — Noor — Fernando — the Belgian Cats — the Belgian Cheetahs

Reference list

— Cotterill, S. (2010). Pre-performance routines in sport: Current understanding and future directions. *International Review of Sport and Exercise Psychology*, 3, 2, 132-153.

— Tracy, J.L., & Matsumoto, D. (2008). The spontaneous expression of pride and shame: Evidence for biologically innate nonverbal displays. *Proceedings of the National Academy of Sciences*, 105, 33, 1655-1660.

— Staufenbiel, K., Lobinger, B., & Strauss, B. (2015). Home advantage in soccer: A matter of expectations, goal setting and tactical decisions of coaches? *Journal of Sports Sciences*, 33, 18, 1932-1941.

— Hanin, Y.L. (2000). Individual Zones of Optimal Functioning (IZOF) Model: Emotion-performance relationship in sport. In Y. L. Hanin (Ed.), *Emotions in sport* (p. 65–89). Human Kinetics.

— Fransen, K., Boen, F., Vansteenkiste, M., Mertens, N., & Vande Broek, G. (2018). The power of competence support: The impact of coaches and athlete leaders on intrinsic motivation and performance. *Scandinavian Journal of Medicine & Science in Sports*, 28, 2, 725-745.

— Fransen, K., Vansteenkiste, M., Vande Broek, G., & Boen, F. (2018). The competence-supportive and competence-thwarting role of athlete leaders: An experimental test in a soccer context. *PLoS One*, 13, 7. doi: 10.1371/journal.pone.0200480

— Park, S., Lavallee, D., & Tod, D. (2013). Athletes' career transition out of sport: a systematic review, *International Review of Sport and Exercise Psychology*, 6, 1, 22-53.

— Ofman, D. (2011). *Hé ik daar?!*

— Cowden, R. G., & Meyer-Weitz, A. (2016). Self-reflection and self-insight predict resilience and stress in competitive tennis. *Social Behavior and Personality*, 44, 7, 1133-1149.

— Neck, C.P., & Houghton, J.D. (2006). Two decades of self-leadership theory and research: Past developments, present trends, and future possibilities. *Journal of Managerial Psychology*, 21, 4, 270-295.

— Murphy, S.E., & Ensher, E.A. (2001). The Role of Mentoring Support and Self-Management Strategies on Reported Career Outcomes. *Journal of Career Development*, 27, F, 229-246.

— Raabe, B., Frese, M., & Beehr, T.A., (2007). Action regulation theory and career self-management. *Journal of Vocational Behavior*, 70, 2, 297-311.

— Goleman, D. (2013). *Emotionele intelligentie*. Business Contact

— Fransen, K., Steffens, N. K., Haslam, S. A., Vanbeselaere, N., Vande Broek, G., & Boen, F. (2015). We will be champions: Leaders' confidence in "us" inspires team members' team confidence and performance. *Scandinavian Journal of Medicine and Science in Sports*, 26, 12, 1455-1469.

— Fransen, K., Haslam, S. A., Steffens, N. K., & Boens, F. (2020). Standing out from the crowd: Identifying the traits and behaviors that characterize high-quality athlete leaders. *Scandinavian Journal of Medicine and Science in Sports*, 30, 766-786.

— Fransen, K., Vanbeselaere, N., De Cuyper, B., Vande Broek, G., & Boen, F. (2014). The myth of the team captain as principal leader: extending the athlete leadership classification within sport teams. *Journal of Sport Sciences*, 32, 14, 1389-1397.

— Konings, M. J., & Hettinga, F. J. (2018). Pacing decision making in sport and the effects of interpersonal competition: A critical review. *Sports Medicine*, 48, 1829-1843.

— Parton, B. J., & Neumann, D. L. (2019). The effects of competitiveness and challenge level on virtual reality rowing performance. *Psychology of Sport and Exercise*, 41, 191-199.
— Passos, P., Araujo, D., & Davids, K. (2016). Competitiveness and the Process of Co-adaptation in Team Sport Performance. *Frontiers in Psychology*, 7, 1562.
— Dweck, C.S. (2016). *Mindset*. Random House USA Inc
— Kramaley, D. T., & Wishart, J. (2020). Can fixed versus growth mindset theories in intelligence and chess ability, together with deliberate practice, improve our understanding of expert performance? *Gifted Education International*, 36, 1, 3-16.
— Cutumisu, M. (2019). The association between feedback-seeking and performance is moderated by growth mindset in a digital assessment game. *Computers in Human Behavior*, 93, 267-278.
— Barker-Ruchti, N., Rynne, S. R., Lee, J., & Barker, D. M. (2014). Athlete learning in Olympic sport. *Sports Coaching Review*, 3, 2, 162-178.
— Ericsson, K.A. (2008). Deliberate Practice and Acquisition of Expert Performance: A General Overview. *Academic Emergency Medicine*, 15, 11, 988-994.
— Lencioni, P.M. (2002). *The five dysfunctions of a team*. John Wiley & Sons Inc
— Hendry, D. T., Williams, A. M., & Hodges, N. J. (2018). Coach ratings of skills and their relations to practice, play and successful transitions from youth-elite to adult-professional status in soccer. *Journal of Sports Sciences*, 36, 17, 2009-2017.
— Phillips, E., Davids, K. Renshaw, I. & Portus, M. (2010). Expert performance in sport and the dynamics of talent development. *Sports Medicine*, 40, 4, 271-283.
— Vaughan, J., Mallett, C. J., Davids, K., Potrac, P., & Lopez-Felip, M. A. (2019). Developing creativity to enhance human potential in sport: A wicked transdisciplinary challenge. *Frontiers in Psychology*, 10. doi: 10.3389/fpsyg.2019.02090
— Hill, N. (2016). *Think and grow rich*. Skyhorse Publishing
— Cavallerio, F., Wadey, R., & Wagstaff, C.R.D. (2016). Understanding overuse injuries in rhythmic gymnastics: A 12-month ethnographic study. *Psychology of Sport and Exercise*, 100-109.
— Seligman, M. (2018). *Learned Optimism*. John Murray Press
— Turner, M., & Barker, J. (2014). *What business can learn from sport psychology*. Bennion Kearny Ltd
— Li, C., Chi, L., Yeh, S., Guo, K., Ou, C., & Kao, C. (2011). Prediction of intrinsic motivation and sports performance using 2x2 achievement goal framework. *Psychological Reports*, 108, 2, 625-637.
— Dispenza, J. (2019). *Becoming supernatural*. Hay House Uk Ltd
— Beschuyt, P. (2019). *Het Kopmanwiel*. Kessels & Smit, the learning company
— Covey, S.R. (2020). *The 7 habits of highly effective people*. Simon & Schuster
— Lastella, M., Lovell, G. P., & Sargent, C. (2014). Athletes' precompetitive sleep behavior and its relationship with subsequent precompetitive mood and performance. *European Journal of Sport Science*, 14, 1, 123-130. Opgehaald van https://doi-org.kuleuven.ezproxy.kuleuven.be/10.1080/17461391.2012.660505
— Silva, M., & Paiva, T. (2013). Sleep, precompetition stress and achievements in young performance athletes. *Sleep Medicine*, 14, 1, 269. Opgehaald van https://doi.org/10.1016/j.sleep.2013.11.656
— Csikszentmihalyi, M. (1990). *Flow: the psychology of optimal experience*. Harper Perennial
— Longman, D., Stock, J.T., & Wells, J.C.K. (2017). A trade-off between cognitive and physical performance, with relative preservation of brain function. *Scientific Reports*, 7, 1-6.
— https://nieuws.kuleuven.be/nl/2019/een-op-de-zes-werkende-vlamingen-kampt-met-burn-outklachten-of-loopt-er-risico-op
— Dion, K. (2000). Group cohesion: From "field of forces" to multidimensional construct. *Group Dynamics: Theory, Research and Practice*, 4, 1, 7-26.
— Hoegl, M., & Gemuenden, H.G. (2001). Teamwork Quality and the Success of Innovative Projects: A Theoretical Concept and Empirical Evidence. *Organization Science*, 12, 4, 435-449.
— Mullen, B., & Copper, C. (1994). The relation between group cohesiveness and performance: An integration. *Psychological Bulletin*, 115(2), 210–227.
— Martin, L.C., Carron, A., & Burke, S. (2009). Team building interventions in sport: A meta-analysis. *International Review of Sport and Exercise Psychology*, 5, 3-18.
— Burns, L., Weissensteiner, J. R., & Cohen, M. (2019). Supportive interpersonal relationships: a key component to high-performance sport. *British Journal of Sports Medicine*, 53, 22, 1387-1390
— Moynihan, D.P., & Pandey, S.K. (2008). The Ties That Bind: Social Networks, Person-Organization Value Fit, and Turnover Intention. *Journal of Public Administration Research and Theory*, 18, 2, 205-227.
— Cambre, R., De Bosscher, V., & Depelchin, S. (2015). *Redenen van drop-out in de sport. Volleybal als case study*. Opgehaald via https://www.sport.vlaanderen/media/1226/151001_vub27_redenen-van-drop-out-in-de-sport_volleybal.pdf
— Chan, D.W. (2011). Burnout and life satisfaction: Does gratitude intervention make a difference among Chinese school teachers in Hong Kong? *Educational Psychology*, 31, 7, 809-823.
— Chen, L.H., Wu, C., & Chang, J. (2016). Gratitude and athletes' life satisfaction: the moderating role of mindfulness. *Journal of Happiness Studies*. ISSN 1389-4978 DOI: 10.1007/s10902-016-9764-7
— Verner-Filion, J., & Vallerand, R. J. (2018). A longitudinal examination of elite youth soccer players: The role of passion and basic need satisfaction in athletes' optimal functioning. *Psychology of Sport and Exercise*, 39, 20-28.
— Schiphof-Godart, L., & Hettinga, F. J. (2017). Passion and pacing in endurance performance. *Frontiers in Physiology*, 8, 83. doi: 10.3389/fphys.2017.00083
— Gustafsson, H., Hassmen, P., & Hassmen, N. (2011). Are athletes burning out with passion? *European Journal of Sport Science*, 11, 6, 387-395.
— Moll, T., Jordet, G., & Pepping, G. (2010). Emotional contagion in soccer penalty shootouts: Celebration of individual success is associated with ultimate team success. *Journal of Sports Sciences*, 28, 9, 983-992.
— Lally, P., van Jaarsveld, C.H.M., Potts, H.W.W. and Wardle, J. (2010). How are habits formed: Modelling habit formation in the real world. *Eur. J. Soc. Psychol.*, 40, 998-1009. https://doi.org/10.1002/ejsp.674
— Korthagen, F., & Vasalos, A. (2002). Niveaus in reflectie: naar maatwerk in begeleiding. *VELON Tijdschrift voor lerarenopleiders*, 23, 1, 29-38.